Vir Willie
van Pa en Ma.
20 Jan. 1999

AFRICA
The Time Has Come

SELECTED SPEECHES
Thabo Mbeki

TAFELBERG ● MAFUBE

Editorial board:
Frank Chikane, Willie Esterhuyse,
Mandla Langa, Vusi Mavimbela, Essop Pahad.
Photograph – courtesy of *Leadership* magazine – David Goldblatt.
Extracts from 'Sailing to Byzantium' by W.B. Yeats
reprinted with permission of A.P. Watt Ltd
on behalf of Michael B. Yeats

First published in 1998 jointly by
Tafelberg Publishers Ltd, 28 Wale Street, Cape Town
Mafube Publishing (Pty) Ltd, 91 Central Street, Houghton, Johannesburg

Cover design by Simon Ford
Typography by Etienne van Duyker
Set in 11 pt on 13 pt Times New Roman
Printed and bound by National Book Printers, Drukkery Street,
Goodwood, Western Cape
First edition, first impression 1998
Second impression 1999

ISBN 0 624 03733 9

The publication of this book was made possible
by a generous grant from the Billiton group of companies.
The editorial board and the publishers
wish to express their gratitude towards the group.

Contents

Biographical Sketch of Thabo Mbeki

THIS BOOK CONTAINS A SELECTION of speeches by the president of the African National Congress and deputy president of the Republic of South Africa, Thabo Mbeki, most of them made in the period since the country's first democratic elections in 1994.

These speeches cover a relatively wide range of subjects. They are important, because they raise many of the strategic and tactical questions which our new democracy must answer with regard to both its domestic and its international policies.

Their significance also derives from the fact that they are the first corpus of important public statements which can be attributed publicly to the author.

This is because until the birth of the new government in 1994, Thabo Mbeki served a considerable amount of time as a speech-writer. Almost all the speeches and documents he prepared were therefore published under the names of the leaders and organs of the ANC which presented them publicly.

For instance, the item which appears in this book under the title 'An Historical Injustice' was drafted for the then president of the ANC, the late Oliver Tambo, who found it impossible to deliver the speech himself. Mbeki was asked by Tambo to stand in for him and was able to deliver the speech as his own – which, of course, it was.

It cannot and does not happen that anybody, out of nowhere, is entrusted with the responsibility to commit to paper the views and perspectives of the ANC. The question must therefore arise as to who this Thabo Mbeki is and what helped to form and prepare him for his role as one of the theoreticians and strategists of the ANC.

Thabo Mbeki was born at the Mbewuleni Village in Idutywa in the Transkei on 18 June 1942. His parents, Epainette and Govan Mbeki, had four children, Linda, Thabo, Moeletsi and Jama. Epainette is a wonderful, strong-willed person with considerable courage. Her warm personality and patience are deeply appreciated in that part of the Transkei. Linda is in private employment and Moeletsi is a media consultant. Jama, a lawyer by profession, disappeared in Lesotho in 1982. Jama's fate and that of a cousin, Phindile Mfeti, who disappeared in Durban in 1987 while still a student, inflicted immeasurable pain and anguish on the Mbeki family.

Though teachers by profession, Epainette and Govan Mbeki ran a general dealer's store in the part of the village whose population consisted of what the Xhosa called *amaqaba* – the people who decorated themselves with red, yellow and white ochre and dressed in traditional clothes – these being the peasants who remained steeped in the traditional ways which remained after more than a century of colonisation of this part of South Africa.

As opposed to their neighbours across the valley, described as *amakholwa* – the Christian believers who went to school and dressed in European clothes – these uneducated residents of eMbewuleni formed a visible and direct link to South Africa's precolonial past.

These were the customers of the family general dealer, and the milieu in which the Mbeki children grew up. These children should themselves have been described as *amakholwa*, but because of the shop and its location, they grew more attached to the 'primitives' than to the 'sophisticated' across the valley. Thus the Mbeki children were exposed to the lifestyle, the beliefs, the mores, and the troubles and tribulations of the traditional rural African society of the day.

In this milieu, Thabo Mbeki picked up the elements which ensured the cohesion of this small African community. These included the devotion of the adults to children and the disciplined indulgence extended to the very young. But it also entailed the detailed manner in which the young were taught to respect those older than themselves.

The youth also had their prescribed jobs which taught them that they had their own responsibilities to themselves, their families and the community without whose discharge they could never be acceptable members of society.

The message among this community, including the illiterate, was that education was important and that those who managed to go through school, to whatever level, had an obligation to use their knowledge to help the village to solve its problems. At the same time, even these who would be educated in modern schools had to fulfil the requirement of absorbing all the important lessons of the traditional system of education about culture, beliefs, the work ethic, male and female responsibilities, traditional systems of government and so on.

The intrusion of the Mbeki children into this world was further strengthened by the fact that their parents owned the general dealer's shop and that this shop also served as the village post office.

In this society, the shop was 'the market'. Those who had maize or wool to sell sold it to the shop. Sometimes this was done to generate cash which would be used to buy stock, such as cattle, sheep or horses. Or the money might be used to pay part of the lobola demanded for a bride. In other instances, the money might be used in the same shop to buy mealie-meal, sugar, salt, tea, coffee, a blanket, cloth, paraffin, sweets, bread, ochre, beads, medicaments or any of the other products sold by a general dealer in an African village.

Living in such circumstances, the Mbeki children gained intimate knowledge of 'how the masses live'. This would sensitise them to be conscious of the need to respond to human situations of suffering, as would happen with the extension of credit to families that needed to acquire consumer products for which they could pay only after they had harvested their small fields of maize.

This was enhanced by the fact that they also had to handle the mail which came through the shop – letters and money exchanged between the families in the village and their fathers and sons who had left as migrant workers to work in the coal, gold and diamond mines.

As young Thabo became literate, he had to participate in reading to the recipients the letters, which especially the illiterate wives received from their husbands working in the mines. Later on he would also have to write down the responses dictated by these wives, in which they would give an account of the health of the children, which relatives were ill or had died, the material needs of the family left behind in the village as well as occasional titbits of juicy gossip.

This work of letter-reader and writer carried with it an unwritten rule binding young Thabo to confidentiality. It was prohibited that he should say anything at all, except to his mother, as to what the migrant husband might have written and what the response of his wife might have been.

Like the rest of the village, the Mbeki family also had to receive those migrant husbands back in their rural world – but as people on the eve of death. These were miners who had been broken by the mines, which then spewed them out to die in the superficially idyllic surroundings of the undulating hills of this part of the Eastern Cape.

Enslaved by ignorance, the village knew nothing of phthisis, the lung disease brought on by mine dust, which sent the miners back to the village to die. What Mbeki remembers of these victims of the absence of adequate or sometimes any health safeguards for the black mineworkers who built modern South Africa are emaciated returnees with bloodshot eyes, who coughed incessantly, coughed blood and died.

And what he knew from what the villagers said was that these corpses of profit at all costs died because they had been kicked on the chest by the killer-bird used by witches – *impundulu* – with the witches themselves having been hired by a jealous or vengeful villager or somebody else determined to kill.

At the same time as he was exposed to these traditional beliefs and explanations of nature, young Thabo was also surrounded by the books which his parents, especially his father, had accumulated over the years, as well as the contemporary magazines to which his mother subscribed.

The eldest two of the children, Linda and Thabo, were able to start their formal education a year earlier than the prescribed school-going age because their mother taught them at home.

Though located within a traditional rural African setting of unschooled peasants, much intellectual discussion took place within the Mbeki family. From an early age, the Mbeki children were exposed to the challenge to defend their views in debate, during which they grew to understand that what they considered to be their store of knowledge was not necessarily correct knowledge.

They had to know that mere familiarity with A.C. Jordan's *Ingqumbo yemiNyanya* was not sufficient. They had to make a judgement also as to what lessons, if any, could be drawn from this Xhosa novel. In the end, they quickly learnt that the appeal to traditional belief would not help to persuade the parents to meet those material needs of the children they could not afford.

Young Thabo, who demonstrated an ability to spend time away from other children even in his pre-teens, content to be by himself, was drawn to the books around him to find out what knowledge they contained. In his early teens, he tried to plough through a text by Plato, Dostoyevsky's *Crime and Punishment*, biographical material on Aggrey umAfrika, John Bunyan's *Pilgrim's Progress* and so forth. He developed an attachment and devotion to books which still remains.

But this was also a political family. Young Thabo grew up in conditions in which politics presented itself to a mind in the process of formation as a natural and inevitable pursuit. Politics was discussed and practised at the Mbeki home, and during their visits, his parents' political colleagues, both local and national, treated the children as people who obviously had to be interested in politics.

The conditions of life in his village, what he knew from the migrant workers' letters, the destruction of his parents' shop by a tornado in 1954 – which plunged them into debt and poverty and drove the father back to teaching to make ends meet – all these and much else said to the child that there was obviously something wrong.

Thabo Mbeki's first consciously political act occurred in 1952 in the Eastern Cape town of Queenstown, where he attended primary school. He and his younger cousin, Kabeli Moerane, stole out of their home to attend a rally at which one of the ANC leaders of the time, Dr J.L.Z. Njongwe, was organising volunteers to participate in that year's Campaign of Defiance of Unjust Laws.

Inspired by the call to go to jail in defiance of unjust laws to end the apartheid system, Thabo and his cousin joined others older than themselves to volunteer to go to prison, only to be turned down by the organisers with the advice that they would be called upon when they were a little older.

Mbeki recalls a later occasion, in 1953, by now attending school in Butterworth back in the Transkei, when he was called in by the village headman, C.W. Monakali, who was a friend and colleague of this father.

The headman wished to consult him about what the response of the village should be to the then plans of the apartheid regime to cull the stock of the peasants, to deal with the problem of overgrazing and the consequent soil erosion.

The reality must have been that the headman merely sought to see the child of an old acquaintance who had come to attend school in his village, and he spoke to the child as village elders would, in loud reverie. But to the child, barely in his teens, this represented one of the earliest occasions when he had to face the challenge of taking a difficult political decision.

But how did he end up outside his village of eMbewuleni, spending four of his primary school years in Queenstown and Butterworth?

In the early 1950s the leadership of the South African liberation movement, including the Mbekis, knew that sooner or later they would be arrested, charged with sedition and sent to long terms of imprisonment by the new National Party government, regarded as neo-Facist. (These arrests ultimately took place in 1956, with the arrested leaders being charged with treason.)

Thabo's parents decided that it would be better that their children should, as early as possible, learn to live without their parents. All four children were therefore farmed out to relatives and friends while they were attending primary school.

Thabo lived in Queenstown with his uncle, Michael Moerane, in 1951 and 1952, and moved to the Lavisas in Butterworth in 1953, where he stayed until he completed his primary education in 1954. He subsequently attended Lovedale High School in Alice in the Ciskei from 1955 to 1959, this time at boarding school. This life experience helped to reinforce the attitude of self-reliance and sufficiency which Mbeki would need as he became involved in the struggle to liberate his country.

Undoubtedly, the four-and-a-quarter years he spent at Lovedale were critical to the Thabo Mbeki that our country and the world has come to know. It was there that, in 1955, he experienced his first involvement in organisational politics. During that year, he participated in the activities of the school branch of the Society of Young Africans (SOYA), which was affiliated to the Non-European Unity Movement. The following year he joined the school branch of the ANC Youth League and in 1958 he was elected to the branch executive.

Long before the ANC was banned in 1960, Mbeki and his comrades at Lovedale had to work clandestinely as the white school principal, a Mr Benyon, was hostile to the organisation.

Ultimately, Mbeki was expelled from Lovedale in 1959 after he and his colleagues in the Youth League had paralysed the school in a student strike provoked, in part, by the unsatisfactory living conditions of African students at this kind of school. This strike was supported by the ANC Youth League at the University College of Fort Hare, a close neighbour of Lovedale across the Thyume River.

The high school years afforded Mbeki and his fellow members of the

Youth League an opportunity to preoccupy themselves with the study of the history of the South African struggle – focusing on the ANC, its philosophy, strategy and tactics – and to see themselves as being tied to the rest of the continent, inspired by such events as the independence of Ghana in 1957 and the towering personality of Kwame Nkrumah.

Among these students, at various times, were people like the late Chris Hani; Sipho Makana, now South Africa's ambassador to the Russian Federation; Njongo Ndungane, the present Anglican archbishop of Cape Town; Barney Pityana, currently chairperson of the Human Rights Commission; and Sigqibo Dwane, bishop of the Ethiopian Order.

Lovedale Institution, established and run by Scottish Presbyterian missionaries from 1841, was one of the leading schools throughout Southern Africa. It attracted students from as far afield as Uganda and, at times, was attended by young people drawn from all of South Africa's racial groups, including whites.

Here Thabo Mbeki studied mathematics, biology, physics, chemistry, Latin, English and history. This was described as the 'academic' stream, to distinguish it from other streams which sought to prepare and condition the students for a life of workers by hand as opposed to workers by brain.

The particular challenges of this stream confronted Thabo Mbeki and his colleagues when they had to write their Joint Matriculation Board examination, which Mbeki wrote at St John's High School, Umtata, in 1959. To matriculate, students had to pass all their English subjects, which comprised an essay, grammar and literature.

Thanks to the two years he had spent with his uncle, Mike Moerane, a qualified and practising musician, Mbeki was able to write an essay 'On learning to play the piano', the only subject he felt competent to write about out of six topics listed in the examination paper.

Apart from the youthful erudition this required, he had been prepared for writing this essay by the rest of his education at Lovedale under teachers who taught mathematics in part as philosophical concepts and theoretical constructs capable of comparison with musical compositions.

There were other teachers at Lovedale who inspired the students to immerse themselves in Latin texts by Julius Caesar, Livy and Catullus, and obliged them continuously to seek to comprehend the complex world of life and dynamic interaction, whether expressed in the poetry of Mqhayi,

Shakespeare's plays, Virgil's *Aeneid*, the mating of plants, the rebellion of the Boers against English domination or the Pythagoras theorem.

Mbeki's transfer to Johannesburg in 1961 for further education also marked his continued involvement in the struggle against apartheid. He participated in organising youth and students around the then Pretoria-Witwatersrand-Vereeniging (PWV) area. He was also involved in establishing the African Students Association (ASA) and was elected secretary of ASA at its founding conference in Durban in December 1961.

It was during this period that he began to work with leaders of the ANC, such as the late Duma Nokwe, Bram Fischer and J.B. Marks, as well as Nelson Mandela and Walter Sisulu.

Mbeki's work among the students enabled him to get to know more about the rest of the country – which was quite rare among the young Africans of his day – travelling to places such as Cape Town, Durban, Kimberley, Port Elizabeth, Pretoria and Bloemfontein.

At the same time, he became ever more exposed to struggles elsewhere in the world – whether in favour of nuclear disarmament and world peace, the independence of the Belgian Congo – or in intense debates about the nature of the United Nations in the aftermath of the assassination of Patrice Lumumba in the Congo.

During this period he was also introduced by the late Michael Harmel to the Irish people's struggle for liberation, as well as to Irish literature, from which he developed a great fondness for the poetry of W.B. Yeats.

Mbeki's stay in South Africa was cut short when the ANC leadership decided that he should proceed to the United Kingdom to enter the University of Sussex. This formed part of the ANC's programme, which it started in 1962, to send some of its students to foreign universities to prepare the cadre that would be required to help run a free South Africa.

The choice of the United Kingdom was made by a Mrs Anne Welsh (later Anne Yates) who helped run the South African Committee for Higher Education (SACHED), which enabled Mbeki to study for his British A-levels in 1961– qualifying him to enter British universities – and the University of London junior degree in economics from 1961 to 1962.

Herself educated in England, Welsh was convinced that young Mbeki could only end up in prison as a result of his political activities. To her a university degree was preferable by far.

Reaching out to her former fellow students, she secured a scholarship for Mbeki and a place at the then one-year-old University of Sussex, encouraged to choose this university by the fact that it had attracted some of her former student colleagues, such as Professor Asa Briggs, now Lord Briggs. Thus Mbeki left South Africa in September 1962.

Arriving in Dar es Salaam, Tanganyika, Mbeki and his group met Oliver Tambo and Julius Nyerere. Mbeki was then put on a flight to London, having been entrusted to Kenneth Kaunda, who was on the same flight to continue negotiations with the British government for the independence of his own country, Northern Rhodesia.

Mbeki was to spend four years at the University of Sussex, where he attained a Bachelor of Arts degree in 1965 and a Master of Arts in 1966, in both instances majoring in economics. During this period he twice tried to terminate his studies so that he could be an active participant in Umkhonto we Sizwe. On both occasions Oliver Tambo vetoed this decision.

This attempted flight from academic pursuits did not arise because of any difficulty that Mbeki experienced at the university. But during these years, many among his generation were confident that a hard and determined push against the apartheid regime would soon topple it. These young people strained at the leash to be part of this final drive to liberation. Indeed, before he left South Africa, Mbeki and other young leaders of the ANC had been forced, much against their will, to continue mobilising a youth constituency fired to take up arms to continue the pedestrian work of peaceful political mobilisation and agitation instead.

At the University of Sussex, Mbeki was exposed to a distinguished galaxy of British academics who sought to ensure that the young intellectuals they produced would be competent in their fields of specialisation without being so confined to those narrow worlds that they became nothing more than artisans or craftsmen and -women.

The university exuded an outward atmosphere of relaxed and casual dabbling in the acquisition of knowledge. In reality, it imposed on the students and teachers a very strict and hard-driven process of education, based on the notion that the students had to know enough to be able to question whether what they knew was, in fact, knowledge.

During the later years, a problem arose when some male students were found at a women's residence well after midnight, contrary to university regulations. The rules had been broken! The university disciplinary committee sat to consider the case, with the threat of rustication hanging over the heads of the culprits.

The local newspapers, including *The Brighton & Hove Albion*, reported the incident with great vigour, denouncing the university as a centre of promiscuity, leftist rebellion, opposition to a British nuclear deterrent, drunkenness, indulgence and general anarchy among a spoilt, long-haired and unwashed generation which knew nothing of and did not respect the sacrifices of an older generation.

Of course, the students took precisely the opposite view. They argued that sharing of a cup of coffee between young men and women after midnight could never be used to justify that they should be denied education by sentencing them to be excluded from the university, even for a limited period of time.

Mobilisation started to call the students to strike if the offending students were in fact suspended. Serious attempts had to be made by the humanities students to overcome the resistance and political apathy of the science students and the sports enthusiasts.

Contrary to what *The Albion* thought, many of these were as straight-laced as any ordinary member of the British middle and upper class.

The crisis at the university and in the Brighton and Hove community was resolved in a manner typical of the young and somewhat irreverent centre of learning that Sussex was in the early 1960s.

The dean of students and professor of philosophy, Patrick Corbett – who was also the driving force behind the campaign to convince the students to develop educated and critical minds – subverted the disciplinary process by proclaiming in public, to the chagrin of *The Albion*, that: 'If a boy and a girl cannot do it before midnight, I would not worry about them after midnight.'

So simple was this logic and so obvious the conclusion, that the disciplinary case collapsed, with the affected students embarrassed by having to explain to their peers whether they could indeed 'do it' before midnight.

When the Rivonia trialists – among them Govan Mbeki, Thabo's father – were found guilty of conspiracy to overthrow the apartheid state in 1964, both the university and the community of Brighton and Hove participated in a massive campaign to save their lives.

One of the greatest influences on young Mbeki at this time was the brilliant Hungarian-born Tibor Barna, professor of economics and head of department. When Mbeki sought to explain how callous the apartheid

regime was and how determined it would be to execute its leading opponents, Professor Barna admonished him by asking the simple question:
'Therefore, what are you asking us to do? Are you saying we should do
nothing, simply because the enemy is vicious?'

The students, supported by the university and the town, responded by
marching 60 miles through a rainy night to Trafalgar Square in London,
where they demonstrated in front of the South African embassy, demand-
ing the release of the convicted leaders.

The unity between the town and the university had been re-established
in the face of a threat to the lives of decent people, pursuing a just cause
– a threat which the British public, like many other across the globe, felt
they could not countenance.

Soon after this Mbeki was to meet Bram Fischer in London when the
latter came to defend a corporate case in the British courts. Fischer told him
that after they had been found guilty and before sentence was passed, the
Rivonia accused had turned down all his pleas to appeal to a higher court if
the sentence of death was handed down. Fischer urged the young Mbeki
that his generation of ANC activists would have to strive hard to emulate
the courage and dedication to principle demonstrated by the leaders who
were his colleagues and whom he also served as defence counsel.

Thirty-one years later, in 1995, Professors Barna and Corbett, Lord
Briggs and others who had helped form Thabo Mbeki were present in the
academic procession which accompanied him at the University of Sussex
when the university, with the distinguished actor and director Richard
Attenborough as its chancellor, awarded Mbeki the degree of Doctor of
Laws (*Honoris Causa*).

The years that Mbeki spent in the United Kingdom were not only devoted to the attainment of knowledge, but also to the pursuit of the struggle to
free his people. He was active in the effort to build the worldwide anti-
apartheid movement, occupying positions of leadership among the South
African youth and students in exile and gaining exposure to other countries,
especially in Europe, as well as the world student movement, which took him
to cities such as Oslo, Moscow, Sofia, Ulan Bator, Algiers and Khartoum.

He knew many of the student leaders who participated in the student
uprisings in Western Europe in 1968, once during this exciting period of
change sharing a platform in Amsterdam with Rudi Dutschke. 'Red Rudi'
was counted at the time as part of a new generation of revolutionary lead-

ers, together with his colleague, Daniel Cohn-Bendit, who exemplified the daring of Che Guevara and what the followers of the Vietnamese revolutionary patriarch, Ho Chi Minh, should be.

Within the United Kingdom, together with the members of the ANC Youth and Student Section, on whose leading committee he served, Mbeki also busied himself with the struggle for nuclear disarmament, the protest against increases in fees for foreign university students, and solidarity struggles with the peoples of Zimbabwe, Greece, Cyprus, Spain, the Portuguese colonial territories, Iran, Iraq and, in particular, Vietnam. Together with other South African students at Sussex, such as Essop Pahad, he organised a party in Brighton with the extraordinary touring West Indian cricket team of 1966, led by Gary Sobers.

This was the element of a life which exposed the young Mbeki to the arts, culture, sports, couture and lifestyle of the European 1960s of the flower children, the 1966 Soccer World Cup, the mini skirt, the Kennedy years, the Beatles and the Rolling Stones, the South African Blue Notes and the outstanding South African sculptor and painter, the late Dumile Feni. In Brighton, and as a member of the university's Socialist Society, he was also involved in the campaign in 1964 to defeat 13 years of Tory rule, which resulted in the victory of the Labour Party led by Harold Wilson.

After completing his studies at Sussex, Mbeki worked at the London office of the ANC from 1967 to 1969. Whilst in London, he worked closely with leading ANC and SACP figures, most notably Dr Yusuf Dadoo. He then went to Moscow in the then USSR, where from 1969 to 1970 he studied at the Institute of Social Sciences. A fellow student here was Ahmed Timol, who was killed by the South African Security Forces in 1971. From 1970 to 1971 Mbeki trained as a guerrilla regimental chief of staff. During these years he matured as a politician and a theoretician with an eclectic appreciation of different forms of art and culture.

Thabo Mbeki returned to Africa in 1971, nine years after he had left the continent of his birth. He travelled with Oliver Tambo from London, England, to Lusaka, Zambia, paying a working visit along the way to Lagos, Nigeria, in West Africa *en route* to Southern Africa and the country of Kenneth Kaunda, whom he had last seen when both flew to London in 1962. This was the place, Africa, which Professor Tibor Barna and his economist colleague at the University of Sussex, Professor Guy Routh, a South African émigré and Mbeki's 'personal tutor', had urged and trained him to understand in its full complexity, and not merely as a technician.

Mbeki started working in Lusaka in 1971 as assistant secretary of the ANC's Revolutionary Council, briefly returning to England in 1974 to marry his wife, Zanele Dlamini. After their marriage she was the sole breadwinner until their return to South Africa. She was instrumental in the formation of Women's Development Banking, a micro-enterprise financing programme for poor women.

During the early 1970s, the external leadership of the ANC devoted a lot of attention to the re-establishment of its links with the members and supporters of the ANC inside South Africa. The possibilities of success in this regard improved significantly when the then president of Botswana, Sir Seretse Khama, himself a former member of the ANC, agreed with Oliver Tambo that the ANC could place an official representative in Botswana. This took well over a year to accomplish. Mbeki was given the responsibility to maintain contact with the government of Botswana to pursue this project, which would put the ANC in a position in which it would have easier access to its people inside the country.

Mbeki ended up spending the greater part of 1973 and 1974 in Botswana, during which period this contact with South Africa did indeed improve, with new links being established with the Black Consciousness Movement. The work begun during this period contributed to the majority of the members and supporters of this movement joining the ANC after their organisations were banned in 1977.

Ultimately, the representative of the ANC, Isaac Makopo, arrived in Botswana. Soon after, the government of Salazar in Portugal was overthrown, opening the way to the independence of its African colonies, including Mozambique.

The ANC saw this as opening the possibility to establish itself officially in Swaziland in the same way it had just done in Botswana. Mbeki was therefore sent to Swaziland at the beginning of 1975, where he spent that year and the first few months of 1976 while also paying regular visits to Mozambique to help establish an ANC presence in that country too, as well as construct the channels of communication for people and material between Mozambique and Swaziland.

By this time, Chris Hani had also been sent to Lesotho. It now became possible to attend to the work of internal organisation from

Lusaka, Gaborone, Maseru, Manzini and the then Lourenço Marques.

The first new cadres for Umkhonto we Sizwe to be recruited inside South Africa since the early 1960s began passing through Swaziland and Mozambique, as did military material from Tanzania, through these two countries, to South Africa.

At the same time, the structures of the ANC within South Africa were expanding rapidly and contact with the people was picking up speed. In addition, the level of interaction between the internal and the external ANC had improved to such an extent that the leadership of the ANC outside the country was able to participate at the very beginning of the process which ultimately led to the formation of the Congress of South African Trade Unions (COSATU).

By 1976, the Pretoria regime came to understand what the ANC representatives in Swaziland, where Mbeki had been joined by Jacob Zuma and Albert Dhlomo, were up to. The apartheid security forces attempted to lure these three into South Africa and were so convinced that their scheme had succeeded that they told other activists of the ANC, then in detention in South Africa, that at last they were going to have Mbeki in their hands. However, the plot failed. The three representatives were then detained, under what the government described as 'protective custody', in Swaziland for a month. After this they were escorted out of the country by the Swaziland police and delivered across the border into the hands of the government of Mozambique.

Thus Mbeki missed by a few months the intimate involvement in the Soweto uprising of 16 June 1976, which he would undoubtedly have experienced if he had remained in Swaziland.

Nevertheless, as some of the student leaders of that historic challenge against apartheid – such as Tsietsi Mashinini and Khotso Seatlholo – left the country to go into exile, they carried instructions with them to meet Mbeki outside the country to plan their future. Soon after they left South Africa, Mbeki met these young activists in London.

It was also during the early 1970s that Mbeki participated in discussions with Dr M.G. Buthelezi which led to the establishment of the Inkatha Freedom Party (IFP).

Back in Lusaka, Mbeki, since 1975 also a member of the National Executive Committee (NEC) of the ANC, continued his work in the Revolutionary Council.

He accompanied Oliver Tambo to the tenth anniversary celebrations of Botswana's independence in 1976 for a very special reason: Arrangements had been made for the late Steve Biko to fly to Botswana to hold a secret meeting with Tambo, directed at establishing a partnership between the ANC and the Black People's Convention. Mbeki would participate in the arrangements which would bring Tambo and Biko together in what would have been a historic meeting.

In the end, Biko did not arrive. He had found it impossible to get away, because as the day approached for him to travel to Botswana, the police increased visible surveillance around him.

A number of years later, the ANC concluded that the projected meeting had been betrayed to the South African Security Police by Craig Williamson, who knew of the arrangements being made to take Biko to Botswana.

At the end of 1976, Mbeki was directed to return to the international work of the ANC, which had been reduced when he came to Zambia in 1971. Accordingly, from the end of 1976 to the beginning of 1978, he worked in Nigeria as the representative of the ANC, establishing a bond between the people of this country and those of South Africa which survives to this day. Whilst in Nigeria he led the South African delegation to the Festival of African Culture (FESTAC). More than 70 000 artists from around the globe attended that festival in Lagos. Here he once more came into contact with cultural figures such as Jonas Gwangwa, Louis Moholo, Dudu Pukwana, Julian Bahula and Churchill Jolobe. Mbeki gave political direction to the South African participants in a festival strewn with political minefields. Later he was to influence the script of the Richard Attenborough film, *Cry Freedom*. Without his intervention the film could have reflected a reality that would have done a disservice to black South Africans and the memory of Steve Biko.

Back in Lusaka in 1978, as political secretary to Oliver Tambo, he was to work closely with Tambo until he passed away in 1993.

During his years as secretary for publicity and information and secretary for international affairs, Mbeki had to participate in a serious effort to raise the public profile of the ANC both in South Africa and internationally. Having spent many years in the shadows in many respects, the ANC required that new measures should be adopted to raise its profile. Thus it was that during this period the organisation started its broadcasts to South Africa through its Radio Freedom, having been granted the facility by the government of Zambia to broadcast through the Zambia Broadcasting Service.

From 1979, on the initiative of Oliver Tambo, the ANC began the practice of issuing 'January 8 statements', issued on the day of the establishment of the ANC in 1912 and containing the ANC leadership's directives for the year to its members, followers and the people of South Africa as a whole. The first of these was drafted by Mbeki who, from then onwards, had the responsibility to prepare the January 8 statement.

The ANC also began to interact with the mainstream press in South Africa and internationally, having to overcome the fear that journalists in general worked for intelligence services, many of which were hostile to the organisation.

One of the first major results of this change of posture was the airing of the pace-making television documentary by the United States CBS, *The Battle for South Africa*, which predicted that the future of South Africa would be decided by the battle between the apartheid regime and the ANC.

Oliver Tambo worked to ensure that Mbeki's positions as his political assistant and the head of information gave him the latitude to probe new ideas, to communicate virtually without limitation with everybody, and to find the best ways to place the ANC and its agenda at the centre of the national and international struggle to end the system of apartheid. It was for this reason, as one of the most visible public faces of the ANC, that Mbeki came to interact with many of the players – both South African and international – who were relevant to the solutions of the South African question.

But before this, Mbeki had to return to his work of opening doors for the ANC to gain direct access to its constituency within South Africa.

After Zimbabwe's independence in 1980, Mbeki accompanied Oliver Tambo as he held discussions in the then Salisbury with Prime Minister Robert Mugabe, also accompanied by only one of his ministers, to determine the ways in which the ANC could use liberated Zimbabwe to intensify its own struggle in South Africa.

This committee of four having determined the framework, it was left to Mbeki and the Zimbabwean minister to work on the details and implement the agreed programme. When everything was in place, Mbeki handed over to Chris Hani, going back to his work, which still included the responsibilities which derived from his membership of the NEC and the Revolutionary Council.

By this time, the burdens on the ANC as well as its possibilities had increased many times over, relative to the time when Mbeki returned to Africa a decade earlier.

Umkhonto we Sizwe had expanded greatly as a result of the post-1976 influx into its ranks. Here was an army which needed to be housed, clothed, fed, trained and sent into South Africa to conduct a military struggle.

The possibilities for united mass struggle inside South Africa, for the expansion of the internal orgnisational structures of the ANC and the intensification of the international campaign, had similarly increased radically.

The ANC, a liberation movement, had become a mini-state with additional responsibilities to look after refugees, build and run schools and hospitals, set up fully fledged 'departments of state', adopt formal military and judicial codes, and generate and manage relatively large resources to finance all this, including all elements of the struggle inside the country.

The debate within the movement about issues of strategy and tactics blossomed, ultimately leading to the elaboration of a comprehensive document called 'the Green Book', drafted by a six-member task team of the ANC, which was led by Oliver Tambo and included Thabo Mbeki.

To discuss this new situation and further to enhance unity within the organisation, the ANC convened its Kabwe conference in 1985, adopting decisions which were to guide the organisation through the complex period into which the struggle against apartheid had entered. The Kabwe conference was characterised by heated debates, intense discussions, profound analysis and criticism and self-criticism – more so as it took place after there had been a mutiny in one of the MK camps and 13 South Africans had been killed in Botswana in a callous cross-border raid. Thabo Mbeki played a pivotal role in helping to cement the unity of the organisation and in the drafting of conference documents and resolutions.

This conference resolved that non-Africans could serve on the NEC of the ANC. Non-Africans elected to the NEC for the first time were Joe Slovo, Aziz Pahad, Ronnie Kasrils and James Stewart. It also elected Oliver Tambo, who had served as acting president from the time of the death of Chief Albert Luthuli, as president. Once more, Mbeki was also elected on to the NEC with others of his generation, such as Chris Hani.

This leadership faced the challenge of continuously enhancing the impact of the ANC with regard to directing the internal and international struggle against the apartheid regime.

Visits to Lusaka both by South African and foreign delegations increased, with the white sector of the population joining these processes from 1985, when Gavin Relly, then chairman of the Anglo American Corporation, led a group of business people to Zambia to meet the ANC. Yet other, similar meetings took place elsewhere in the world, including London, New York and Frankfurt.

These processes had two results which were important with regard both to the conduct and the outcome of the struggle in South Africa.

They helped to consolidate the unity of the democratic movement in South Africa behind the leadership of the ANC, making it possible to wage a co-ordinated and truly mass campaign against apartheid. They also helped to create the broad framework and consensus with regard to the shape of the future South Africa which facilitated the advance towards a negotiated resolution of the South African question.

Mbeki was at the centre of all these processes, leading many of the ANC delegations that met both South Africans and members of the international community, and helping to formulate many of the strategic and tactical positions that had to be evolved to meet the changing situation.

Desperate to disrupt all this, and having failed to capture Mbeki in 1976, the apartheid regime sent a captain of the South African Defence Force to Lusaka in 1986 with instructions to blow up the Mbeki residence, ensuring that Mbeki was inside the house.

The assassin failed to carry out the operation. He was arrested, charged and convicted, but was then pardoned by President Kaunda, seemingly because, though serving in the SADF, he was a national of New Zealand, a country with which Zambia had friendly relations.

The meetings we have spoken of included the series of interactions which took place in the United Kingdom between a delegation of Afrikaner opinion-makers, led by Professor Willie Esterhuyse, and a group of members of the ANC, led by Mbeki and including Aziz Pahad and Joe Nhlanhla.

As has become public knowledge, with Tambo and Mbeki's approval, these meetings served as an unofficial channel of communication between the ANC and the Pretoria regime, leading to the point in 1989 when Professor Esterhuyse informed Mbeki that this regime was now willing to meet the ANC directly.

The first of these encounters, the first ever direct negotiations between the ANC and the Pretoria authorities, took place in Switzerland in 1989 under conditions of great secrecy. The ANC delegation consisted of Thabo Mbeki and Jacob Zuma. The South African government was represented by Mike Louw, deputy head of the National Intelligence Service (NIS) and Maritz Spaarwater, a senior NIS official.

Prior to these meetings, but during the same period when the ANC was making important advances on other fronts, it also made the greatest strides in its campaign for the international isolation of apartheid South Africa and the recognition by the major powers of the ANC as the legitimate alternative to the apartheid regime which the CBS documentary had argued.

For the first time ever, the president of the ANC, Oliver Tambo, accompanied by Mbeki, was received at the Kremlin by the Soviet head of government, Mikhail Gorbachev, in November 1986. Again, for the first time ever, Oliver Tambo, once more with Mbeki in his delegation, was received at the State Department, Washington, by the United States secretary of state, George Schultz, in January 1987.

Apart from the Third World and the socialist countries, the governments of the smaller countries of the West had grown into major supporters of the ANC and the South African liberation struggle.

Sweden was prominent among these. Having taken courageous positions under the leadership of the late Olof Palme to oppose United States aggression against Vietnam, Palme insisted that genuine support for any national liberation struggle meant that those who gave this support included recognition of the right of those in struggle to determine their methods of struggle and the nature of the society they sought to build.

Mbeki visited Sweden for the first time in 1974 and engaged in some of the earliest discussions which led to the Swedish government and people evolving into some of the strongest supporters of the South African liberation struggle.

To this day suspicions persist that Olof Palme was assassinated because of this support for the ANC, which also opened the way for other Western governments to recognise and support this liberation movement and its struggle.

The gains of the struggle, the changing international situation and the impending independence of Namibia in particular led the ANC to discuss the possibility of a negotiated resolution of the conflict in South

Africa. Mbeki was in the forefront of those who argued within the ANC leadership that if this became necessary, it was obligatory that the ANC should take the lead in defining the objectives and parameters of those negotiations.

Subsequently, Mbeki was to lead the process of preparing the document which, after approval by the Organisation of African Unity at a meeting in Harare, came to be known as the Harare Declaration.

Later in the same year, 1989, Mbeki led a delegation of the ANC to the United Nations General Assembly, which also adopted the same document, with slight amendments, as its own consensus position. Most important for the ANC, this meant that it was also adopted by all members of the Security Council.

By September 1989 the discussions in Switzerland between the Mbeki delegation and the South African government delegation, now led by Fanie van der Merwe, director-general for constitutional affairs, had reached agreement on a number of important points.

It was agreed that all political prisoners, including Nelson Mandela, would be released, political parties unbanned, exiles allowed to return, subsequent to which negotiations for a new South Africa would begin, as visualised in the Harare Declaration.

Until these actually happened, there were many within the ANC and its supporters in South Africa and internationally who thought it was impossible for the apartheid regime to agree to all these things. They were therefore convinced that Mbeki and his team had betrayed the struggle by holding out the illusion of a negotiated settlement, a sentiment which had had to be dealt with also at the time that the very concept of a Harare Declaration was under discussion.

Later, at the December 1990 Consultative Conference of the ANC, Mbeki had to present to the delegates another controversial position of the ANC leadership: the decision to suspend the armed struggle. He did so unflinchingly. The disquiet and dissatisfaction of a number of delegates was forcefully expressed. But by his impeccable logic, reasoning and explanations he convinced the delegates of the correctness of that decision.

At the Durban conference in 1991 the call for a phased lifting of sanctions against South Africa became controversial. After interminable discussions, Mbeki took the floor at 3 a.m. Conference had been sitting for the whole day and the delegates were tired. But when Mbeki spoke for about an hour, you could hear a pin drop. His mastery of the subject matter, his depth of understanding of the international context, all conveyed in measured tones, won over the sceptics. His interventions at these two conferences also demonstrate his political courage. He is not afraid to tackle the most difficult and controversial issues confronting the ANC.

Mbeki and his colleagues were to face similar challenges during the course of the negotiations when they first floated the idea of 'sunset clauses' and the subsequent Government of National Unity (GNU).

Having understood that it was necessary to open some space for the National Party to participate in government after the elections, as an act of assurance to the white population, Mbeki first raised the question of a GNU at a bilateral meeting of the ANC and the NP in Cape Town in 1992, explaining that the position was unmandated, but inviting the meeting to 'brainstorm' the idea.

The phrase 'sunset clauses' was used for the first time during these negotiations, and at the same meeting, by Barend du Plessis, at the time minister of finance in the apartheid regime.

The final ANC formulation of this proposal was worked out by Mbeki and Sam Shilowa, currently general secretary of COSATU, who were part of a small group delegated to negotiate issues of governance with the NP. Mbeki's ability to listen to other voices, even if they are seriously dissenting, and to put himself into his opponents' shoes so that he can better understand their views, contributed to the negotiated settlement with the IFP and the Freedom Front.

Mbeki also led the ANC delegations which negotiated with the IFP and Afrikaner Volksfront to bring them into the peaceful settlement and the elections, and avoid the eruption of a violent confrontation which would have destroyed the possibility of a peaceful transition to democracy at that time. The process of international mediation having failed to take place, new negotiations with the IFP took place.

Before all this happened, Mbeki and some of his colleagues in exile returned to South Africa in 1990, flying in a Zambia Airways plane provided by the Zambian government.

They came to continue the discussions which had started in Switzerland the year before, described as creating the conditions conducive to negotiations, their arrival having been prepared by a smaller advance delegation led by Jacob Zuma.

Mbeki had been away from the country of his birth for almost 28 years. He has said that as they circled over the sea to land at Cape Town Airport, he felt very sad that it had taken so many years, and so much death and destruction, to arrive at the point where he and his colleagues could do what he felt would be a rather simple thing: to land at a South African airport without fear of being arrested, tortured and possibly murdered in police cells.

Mbeki has since been elected chairperson of the ANC in 1993, deputy president of the ANC in 1994, and president of the ANC in 1997, and currently serves as the deputy president of the republic.

Still inspired by the hope for the reconstruction of Africa he gleaned from reading about Aggrey umAfrika, he has spoken of the need for and the possibility of an African renaissance, evoking a positive response throughout Africa and in other parts of the world.

Undoubtedly, as the challenge of this renaissance is met step by step in South Africa and elsewhere on the continent, Mbeki will still have reason to feel sad that the force of inertia will make it impossible to achieve these goals without some persistence of the ills which have destroyed the lives of millions of Africans.

However, his has always been a life dedicated to inquiry and the discovery of the new. He will remain involved in the struggle for the liberation of all humanity.

Hopefully the speeches contained in this book will help the reader to gain some understanding of what their author, Thabo Mbeki, might seek to contribute to the birth of the new world towards which all of us must strive.

Mbeki is not a populist and consequently his speeches do not contain rhetorical flourishes. They are firmly constructed and well argued. They are meant to be taken seriously and deserve close and critical scrutiny. A man of vision, hope and reason, Mbeki displays what the philosopher Søren Kierkegaard so aptly described as 'a passion for the possible'. He does not regard the present as being cast in concrete, but as a fountain of possibilities which need to be creatively utilised in order to build a meaningful future.

Editorial Board
October 1998

PART ONE

Prologue

1

Voice against Persecution

Statement before a delegation of the United Nations Special Committee Against Apartheid, London, United Kingdom, 13 April 1964

I FEEL IT MY DUTY to introduce myself to you, Mr Chairman, inasmuch as this might help you in your task. Born on 18 June 1942, I was christened Thabo Mbeki. Since starting school at the age of five, the rest of my life has been taken up with acquiring education of one sort or another. During that time I have been at schools in the Transkei and in the Ciskei in the Cape Province. Expelled from school in 1959, I finished my secondary school education as a private student and qualified at the end of the year for entry into any South African university. As the system of Bantu Education had been introduced, however, after consultation with my father, I felt obliged to seek a university place outside South Africa.

After staying for another year in Johannesburg studying as an external student of the University of London, I left South Africa in September 1962, together with and leading 27 other African students who were going out to study overseas. Owing to the delay occasioned by our arrest in Southern Rhodesia, we finally reached Dar es Salaam in November through the efforts of the African National Congress.

While I was in South Africa I had participated extensively in anti-apartheid youth activities, during which time I had the fortune of enjoying constant contact with, among others, Nelson Mandela, Walter Sisulu and Duma Nokwe.

My father, Govan Mbeki, now in the Rivonia Trial, on whose behalf I am here primarily, was by some curious coincidence born on 4 July 1910, the year that South Africa became the Union of South Africa and the date of the independence of America. Born of a family of peasant farmers in the Transkei, he went to school in his village and later to the Healdtown

3

High School, where he matriculated. After this he went to the University College of Fort Hare. Working as a newspaper seller during holidays in Johannesburg, he went through his BA degree and then took up teaching in Durban. He was later to be awarded a BEcon degree by the University of South Africa, after he had studied as an external student for a number of years.

From his early years my father took an interest in the welfare of his people, finally getting elected to the Transkei Territorial General Council in the early 1940s. He was not to stay long, however, as soon afterwards the government of the day began taking unto itself the tasks that the council had previously regarded as falling under its jurisdiction. After a spirited fight he felt obliged to go back to his constituents to tell them that, as the character of the council had changed, he felt he could not claim that he was representing the people by attending it, and therefore was obliged to resign and call on the people to resist the gradual whittling away of their rights by the government. That fight met with an intransigent government, but it heightened the respect of the people for his courage.

In 1943 he was to sign the document 'The African Claims' – the African version of the Atlantic Charter. In later years he continued to work with renowned leaders and others, gradually emerging as a man of powerful intellect and absolute dedication to the cause of freedom. After a number of business ventures by which he tried to secure his independence from a government salary, he was forced to go back to teaching in 1954. He was expelled at the end of the year for his hostility to government policies. He then joined the staff of the newspaper *New Age* which, together with its predecessors and its followers, acted as the newspaper of the liberation struggle.

In 1957 he played a prominent part in a national conference called by African ministers to discuss the Tomlinson Report, the government's Bantustan blueprint. In 1960 he attended the meeting of African leaders called to discuss the then plans of the South African government to declare South Africa a republic. The committee elected at that meeting, of which he was a member, was later to organise the conference that elected Nelson Mandela as its leader, which action has subsequently led to his being sentenced to five years' imprisonment. During this time he had become one of the prominent leaders of the ANC, recognised by his colleagues as an expert on the problems of the reserves, the so-called Bantustans.

At the beginning of 1962 he was arrested and detained for five months on a charge of sabotage. The case was however withdrawn and he was released to be arrested again, at Rivonia. If he is hanged he will leave behind his wife, whom he married in 1939, three sons and a daughter; the two boys at school in Basutoland, their mother and sister still in South Africa and myself in my second year at the University of Sussex in this country.

It has been necessary that this introduction be made so as to explain the calibre of one of the men whom the South African government seeks to hang today. I believe that the years of his political activity have derived their inspiration from his love for his people. During these years, as his older associates would testify, he has earned the respect of his people and his colleagues. Not a single one of the many South African courts has found him guilty of a petty or indictable crime. Yet today he stands accused, and his accusers, who only yesterday found glory in Nazi Germany, stand in the full twilight of their cynical and inhuman power. For decades he, together with the rest of the African people, has appealed to the white governments of South Africa, not for the exaltation of the African people to a position of dominance over the white, but for equality among the peoples. The only reward he has earned, that we have all earned, is the brutal might of South African law which has sought to bend human reason and feeling to the barbarity of madmen. By the profane and demented reasoning of the government, Dr Percy Yutar, well known for the murderers and thieves he has sent to prison or to the gallows, is now prosecuting in the Rivonia Trial.

Though much has been said on this subject, I should also like to add my testimony about the character of the men that the South African government would have the world believe are criminals. They are not only men of the greatest integrity that responsibility to their families and friends would demand, men who could be welcomed by any civilised country, but also men who would grace any government in which they served. Activated by the noblest of motives, they have acquired through the years an understanding of leadership that would be a valuable contribution to the common human experience.

Today these men stand accused of treason, of plotting to overthrow the government by violent means. If it is so, they have acted in defence of the people that the government has sought to silence and subjugate with a

5

whip and the instruments of war. The fact is inescapable that the trial is not only their trial as individuals, but it is a trial of all that they have stood for, which was not and is not war but peace among free and equal men. The government has replied with more brutality, sentencing only last month three respected ANC leaders to death. By so doing that government has declared freedom from poverty, from suffering and from degradation, and human equality without discrimination on grounds of colour of race, to be illegal and criminal in its eyes. And by the Rivonia Trial the government intends to make ten times more its case that freedom is illegal.

The crimes that the South African government has committed are of a magnitude that baffles the human mind. The continued existence of apartheid with the support of the governments of, particularly, the United Kingdom, the United States, France and West Germany, cannot but be seen as an act of violence, not only against the whole African people but also against that portion of humanity which is trying so hard to remove racialism in the intercourse between men. Anybody therefore who, having the power to stop the decapitation of the men on trial in Pretoria, fails to use that power to the fullest extent is by omission an accomplice in the act.

If, sir, I may be so presumptuous as to seize the opportunity, I beg to ask you humbly, and in awareness of the immodesty of the request, to be so kind as to take this message to the nations of the world from one who may be about to lose a noble father and a noble leader.

He acted in defence of the principles on which the civilised human community so firmly stands, and so did his brothers who stand together under the sinister noose of the hangman. They were spurred on by the inspiration of the victorious struggles to their north, no less sacred among these the Algerian revolution. They drew strength from the respect accorded them by their people and the example that their forefathers had set them.

For our part, if the butchers will have their way, we shall draw strength even from the little crosses that the kind may put at the head of their graves. In that process we shall learn. We shall learn to hate evil even more, and in the same intensity we shall seek to destroy it. We shall learn to be brave and unconscious of anything but this noblest of struggles.

Today we might be but weak children, spurred on by nothing other than the fear and grief of losing our fathers. In time yet we shall learn to die both for ourselves and for the millions.

6

Mr Chairman, through you and through the esteemed members of your committee, I wish, in the name of my mother, my brothers, my sister and myself, in the name of Mandela's, Sisulu's, Mhlaba's, Goldberg's and the other families, and in the name of the South African people, to make this appeal to the world.

In the name of humanity the South African government must be stopped. That government has criminally taken up arms against my people. Was any gang of butchers so powerful as to defy the whole world? The leaders at the Rivonia Trial cannot be allowed to die at the hands of the South African government.

2

The Historical Injustice

Speech delivered at a seminar held in Ottawa, Canada, 19 to 22 February 1978

MODERN POLITICAL SCIENCE recognises the fact that social systems are founded on definite historical origins.

If the saying,'Out of nothing, nothing comes' is true, then it must follow that the future is formed and derives its first impulse in the womb of the present.

All societies therefore necessarily bear the imprint, the birthmarks of their own past. Whether to a greater or lesser extent must depend on a whole concatenation of factors, both internal and external to each particular society.

The latter consideration has often led many observers of the process of social development to over-emphasise the particularity of each society, to deny that this social development is in any way reducible to a science founded on observable facts, a science which has general laws, definitions and categories.

In this way, the relative is credited with the features of the absolute. Each society is thus presented as unique, its birth and development products of accidental collisions and interconnections and therefore incapable of scientific prediction and cognition.

We consider that this position constitutes a dereliction of intellectual duty. Those of us who claim to be revolutionaries obviously cannot proceed in this manner. Indeed we must resist all attempts to persuade us that our future lies in the hands of an ungovernable fate. For the imperative of our epoch has charged us with the task of transforming ourselves from the status of objects of history to that of masters of history.

We must, by liberating ourselves, make our own history. Such a process by its nature imposes on the activist the necessity to plan and therefore requires the ability to measure cause and effect; the necessity to strike in correct directions and hence the requirement to distinguish between essence and phenomenon; the necessity to move millions of people as one man to actual victory and consequently the development of the skill of combining the necessary and the possible.

All this becomes attainable if we have succeeded to discover the regularities of social development, if we have studied our own society critically and in depth to discover the interconnections, the dynamic links that knit together and give direction to what might at first appear to be a chaos of facts, incidents and personalities thrown up by this particular society. For, to repeat: Out of nothing, nothing comes.

Therefore, to eliminate the speculative element as much as possible when talking about the policies of a new South Africa, it is necessary to examine the principal feature of the predecessor of that future reality, namely present-day South Africa.

But again, a penetrating understanding of our country today requires also that we look at its past. We hasten to assure you that we shall not drown you in a plethora of historical detail.

The first category of social science that we want to use tonight is that of class. To understand South Africa we must appreciate the fact and fix it firmly in our minds that here we are dealing with a class society.

In South Africa the capitalists, the bourgeoisie, are the dominant class. Therefore the state, other forms of social organisation and the 'official' ideas are conditioned by this one fact of the supremacy of the bourgeoisie. It would therefore be true to say that in its essential features South Africa conforms to other societies where this class feature is dominant.

Yet a cursory comparative glance around the world would seem to suggest that such a statement is hardly of any use in helping us to understand the seemingly unique reality of apartheid South Africa. More and perhaps better explanation is called for. We return therefore to the category of a class society and step back into history.

The landing of the employees of the Dutch East India Company at the Cape of Good Hope 326 years ago, in 1652, represented in embryo the emergence of class society in our country. And that class society was bourgeois society in its infancy.

The settlers of 1652 were brought to South Africa by the dictates of

9

that brutal period of the birth of the capitalist class which has been characterised as the stage of the primitive accumulation of capital. Of this stage Marx wrote:

> The discovery of gold and silver in America, the extirpation, enslavement and entombment in the mines of the aboriginal population, the beginning of the conquest and looting of the East Indies, the turning of Africa into a warren for the commercial hunting of black skins, signalled the rosy dawn of the era of capitalist production. These idyllic proceedings are the chief momenta of primitive accumulation.[1]

He continued:

> The transformation of the individualised and scattered means of production into socially concentrated ones, of the pigmy property of the many into the huge property of the few, the expropriation of the great mass of the people from the soil, from the means of subsistence and from the means of labour, this fearful and painful expropriation of the mass of the people forms the prelude to the history of capital. It comprises a series – of forcible methods... The expropriation of the immediate producers was accomplished with merciless vandalism, and under the stimulus of passions the most infamous, the most sordid, the pettiest, the most meanly odious.[2]

Such indeed was the slave trade. (Such also, incidentally, the eviction of the Scottish Highland peasants, many of whom came to settle here in Canada – vandalism of the most merciless kind.) Such indeed was the expropriation of the African peasantry.

It should therefore come as no surprise that, six years after the arrival of the Dutch settlers in 1658, the first group of slaves arrived in the Cape Colony. In 1806, when England seized the Cape Colony from Holland by force of arms, there were 30 000 slaves in the Colony as against 26 000 settlers. There were also another 20 000 'free Coloured, Nama and in white employ...'[3]

Equally, it should come as no surprise that these 20 000 African wage-earners had been compelled into this position by the process, described by Marx and other historians of the period, of the 'expropriation of the great mass of the people from the soil, from the means of subsistence and from the means of labour...'

Described as 'free' in relation to the 30 000 slaves in the Colony, they were also 'free' in so far as they had been liberated by force of arms, disease and starvation from their status as independent producers with their own hunting, grazing and arable land, their livestock and their working implements.

Writing of a British governor-general in India, Marx says:

> His favourites received contracts under conditions whereby they, cleverer than the alchemists, made gold out of nothing. Great fortunes sprang up like mushrooms in a day; primitive accumulation went on without the advance of a shilling.[4]

And there we have the reason why Europe carried out this early accumulation at home and abroad with such merciless enthusiasm and passion – because the process assured men of property stupendous and immediate profit. Brought up in this European hothouse of rapine, the settlers in South Africa could not but continue this process in their colony. The result was that when England abolished the slave trade in 1834, nearly two centuries after the arrival of the first batch of slaves, the descendants of the original colonists rebelled against this decision.

Judging themselves too weak to re-impose slavery by arms, the Boers resolved to take themselves out of the area of British jurisdiction. Thus began the so-called Great Trek of the Boers into the interior of our country.

Of course, all along the Boers were determined that again they would have to seize our land and livestock and enslave our people. We see therefore that the methods and practices of primitive accumulation, which represented a transitional phase in the development of capital in Europe, assumed permanence in the South African economy and lifestyle of the Boers. They acquired a fixity characteristic of feudal society, legitimised by the use of force and sanctified by a supposedly Calvinist Christianity.

The South African settlers of 1652 had themselves been the expropriated of Europe. But as in America, here in Canada, in Australia and elsewhere, after a little while they were able to re-establish themselves as independent producers, acquiring land in the manner we have described,

11

on the basis of the expropriation of our people, despite the most fierce resistance of the indigenous people.

It was exactly the blissful regaining of their status as masters of their own house, their re-emergence as independent producers, that froze the Boer community at a particular moment of historic time and thereby guaranteed their regression.

Thrown up by the birth of a higher social system, they reverted precisely to that natural economy which capital was so vengefully breaking up. But capital had already taught them that in the pursuit of a better life, everything, including murder, was permissible and legitimate.

A natural economy presupposes the absence of accumulation, 'consisting of the petty dealings of peasants and craftsmen in the small market town, where industry is carried on for the subsistence of the household and the consumption of wealth follows hard upon the production of it, and where commerce and finance are occasional incidents rather than the forces which keep the whole system in motion.'[5] Thus it is the direct opposite of a capitalist economy even when the latter is at its primitive stage of accumulation.

When they reverted to a patriarchal economy, the Boers therefore abandoned all that was dynamic and revolutionary in the formation of bourgeois society and transmuted the rest into something stultified and reactionary.

Nowhere is this clearer than in the fate that befell Calvinist theology. Tawney has said that:

> Calvinism was an active and radical force... [Its adherents were] disposed neither to idealise the patriarchal virtues of the peasant community, nor to regard with suspicion the mere fact of capitalist enterprise in commerce and finance... Calvinism was largely an urban movement... [Its teachings were directed primarily] to the classes engaged in trade and industry, who formed the most modern and progressive elements in the life of the age...[6]

The Boers had brought this Calvinism with them from Holland and were joined later by the Calvinist French Huguenots. But when they grafted this eminently bourgeois theology on to their patriarchal economy, they in fact transformed its content into a species of Lutheranism, which was essentially a theological school which sought to idealise feudalism and save it from destruction by the capitalist mode of production which was springing up all around it.

From Calvinism the Boer took the doctrine of predestination and perverted it. For Calvin, the chosen of God were those who survived the jungle of capitalist enterprise in industry and trade and emerged as successful men of business, without regard to race or nationality. In the patriarchal economy this was transmuted to read: The chosen of God are those who are white.

For his part, Luther had said: 'An earthly kingdom cannot exist without inequality of persons. Some must be free, others serfs, some rulers, others subjects.'[7] Racism, today so much part of South African reality, constituted a justification, an attempt to rationalise, to make acceptable the enslavement and expropriation of the black people by the white.

In Boer society and in the end among almost all the whites, racism as an ideology squired the attributes of a psychological fixation, with the characteristic of fixated behaviour that an ineluctably irrational perception of a particular set of relationships coexists with and distorts the perception of all other sets of relationships. In the circumstance that, in any case, ideological formations bear a complex rather than a simple relationship with the material world, generating a momentum which carries them beyond the material conditions that created them, we could expect that this racism would in time present itself as an autonomous force, God-given or nature-given, as an incontrovertible condition of human existence.

To go back to Calvin, where his theology had sanctified individualism to detach the bourgeoisie from the narrow and rigid world of feudalism and thrown him, unhampered by old prejudices, into the world market, the Boers sang praises to a stultified individualism even narrower than that of the feudal epoch, an individualism which drew its strength from the economic self-sufficiency of each Boer family, the isolation of the homesteads from one another and the isolation of a whole community from the rest of the world; an individualism which became truly itself and complete only to the extent that it despised and set itself in contrast to everything that was black: an individualism, therefore, which was and is characterised by a rabid racism.

British capital subdued this petrified and arrogant individualism during the Anglo-Boer War. In 1910 Boer and Briton entered into a social contract in which the Briton undertook to help ease the Boer out of the Dark Ages while promising to respect his traditions. For his part, the Boer pledged not to resist the advance and domination of British capital.

Between them, Boer and Briton agreed that they would share political power and, finally, that the indigenous African population would not be party to this contract but would be kept under the domination and at the disposal of the signatories, to be used by them in whatever manner they saw fit.

There were therefore written into this agreement, the so-called Act of Union of 1910, the continuation of the methods and practices of exploitation characteristic of primitive accumulation of capital which had remained fossilised in the Boer economy but which British capital had outgrown, certainly in Britain.

Why did the British ruling class, having won the war against the Volksraad, thus regress?

One reason, of course, is that we are here dealing with the post-1885 Berlin Conference period. It could therefore be argued that the predominant colonialist practices and attitudes of the time made it natural and inevitable that the British ruling class would do in South Africa what it was doing in other colonies.

Yet this explanation would not be complete. For Britain had maintained an uninterrupted colonial hold on South Africa, to one extent or another, since 1806.

The decisive point to bring to the fore is that British capital, throughout the 100 years before 1910, had itself, in South Africa, clung tenaciously to the methods and practices of primitive accumulation.

Thus while in 1807 the British administration prohibited the importation of slaves into the Cape Colony, in 1909 it introduced a Vagrancy Act directed at the Khoi people.[8] Under this law, all Khoi people not in the employ of a white person were declared vagrants. Vagrancy was made an offence. To prove that one was not a vagrant one had to produce a pass. To get the pass you had to enter into a written labour contract with a white employer.

This measure was introduced to meet the labour shortfall created by the non-importation of slaves. It was therefore used to drive those Khoi people who still maintained an independent existence off the land, to turn them into permanent wage-earners and to create the means to direct this labour where it was needed.

In the end, it was the British armies which defeated the African people, the British who drove us off our lands, broke up the natural economy and social systems of the indigenous people. It was they who imposed taxes on the African peasants and, starting with the Masters and Servants Act of 1856, laid

14

down the labour laws which govern the black worker in South Africa today.

In Europe, the economic freedom of the worker to hire himself out freely to the highest bidder, which came with and was part of the bourgeois revolution, was of course connected with, accompanied and enhanced by the political freedom of the workers to represent themselves in matters of state through the vote, itself an integral part of the victory of the bourgeoisie over feudal society.

In South Africa this was not to be. Here the capitalist inherited the rights of the feudal lord and appropriated to himself the right to determine where, when, at what price and under which conditions the African shall sell his labour power to the capitalist. He also appropriated to himself the right to decide 'what is good for the native'.

It is therefore clear that British capital in South Africa differed from the Boer patriarchal economy with relation to primitive accumulation in two major respects. The first of these was that it outgrew chattel slavery and therefore abolished it; the second, that *as* capital its aim continued to be that of greater and greater accumulation, through the pursuit of maximum profit.

It was therefore inevitable that British capital would be all that more thorough in the expropriation of the African peasant, all that more brutal in the exploitation of African labour, more scientific and less wasteful.

The historic compromise between the British bourgeoisie and the Boer peasantry represented hence not an historical aberration but the continued pursuit of maximum profit in conditions of absolute freedom for capital to pursue its inherent purposes.

British capital had at other times and in other circumstances made other compromises. One of the most important of these was undoubtedly that made with the British working class.

In its struggle against its feudal predecessors, the British bourgeoisie had called upon and received the support of the working people. It therefore had to take cognisance of the fact that its political victory did not belong to it alone. It further took note of the fact that the denial of political freedoms to its ally while claiming them as a natural right for itself posed the danger that these working masses would pass beyond the struggle against the feudal lords and take on the bourgeoisie itself. While convincing the workers of the sacredness of private property – especially its own, bourgeois property – it nevertheless conceded them their political democracy. Thereby and mainly because of this concession, it destroyed

15

the possibility for capital to continue using primitive methods of accumulation within Britain.

Capital in South Africa never had to contend with such a situation. Historically, it owes the working class nothing and has therefore conceded to it nothing (excepting, of course, the white workers, about whom later).

It is clear that during its war with the so-called Boer republics, the British ruling class consciously avoided putting itself in a state of indebtedness to the black people. For instance, in January 1901 Lord Milner, the British high commissioner, 'told a Coloured deputation ... that he could not accept their offer to take up arms against the republican forces.'[9] The same thing happened when another Boer rebellion had to be put down in 1914.

That the bourgeoisie was aware that the denial of democratic rights to the workers was in the interests of capitalism was evident when indentured labour was imported from China after the Anglo-Boer War.

Then, the mine bosses stated that a big body of enfranchised white workers 'would simply hold the Government of the country in the hollow of their hand' and 'more or less dictate not only on the question of wages, but also on political questions'.[10]

Translating the advantages of black worker disenfranchisement into cash, the Chamber of Mines stated in its 1910 annual report that it 'viewed the native purely as a machine, requiring a certain amount of fuel'. It decreed accordingly that the diet of the African miners living in the mine compounds should be determined in terms of the formula 'the minimum amount of food which will give them maximum amount of work'.[11]

Of the bourgeois countries, South Africa is unique to the extent that profit maximisation is the overt, unhidden and principal objective of state policy, and can therefore be regarded with respect to this characteristic as an almost perfect model of capitalism, cleansed of everything that is superfluous to its essential characterisation; a model which displays to all, in their true nakedness, the inner motive forces of this social system and its fundamental interconnections.

The position that black people occupy in this model can be defined as follows:

- They are the producers of wealth.
- They produce this wealth not for their own benefit but for its appropriation by the white population.

16

- They are permitted to consume part of this wealth, but only in that proportion which will 'give the maximum amount of work' on a continuing basis.

This may sound harsh and anti-human but it characterises 'pure capitalism'. For instance, in his studies of Max Weber, Marcuse said:

> The 'formally most rational' mode of capital accounting is the one into which man and his 'purposes' enter only as variables in the calculation of the chances of gain and profit. In this formal rationality, mathematisation is carried to the point of the calculus with the real negation of life itself...[12]

If this sounds too abstract, the white South African member of Parliament, G.F. Froneman, translates it into the concrete when he says:

> [Within white society, Africans] are only supplying a commodity, the commodity of labour... It is labour we are importing [into the white areas] and not labourers as individuals...[13]

Froneman went on to say that the numbers of Africans to be found in the so-called white areas therefore make no difference to the composition of Society – society with a capital S – precisely because the African is not an individual, comparable to a white individual. Rather, he is the repository of the commodity labour power, which can and must be quantified in a profit and loss account to the point of the very 'negation of life itself'. In that very real sense the African therefore belongs to the category of commodities to an equal extent as gold, diamonds and any other commodity you care to mention, to be bought and sold, hoarded and even destroyed, depending exclusively on the state of the market.

The denial of the humanity of the slave which occurred during the period of primitive accumulation of capital is therefore repeated here but at a higher and more rational level. That rationality demands that, to ensure maximum profit, that portion of the national wealth which accrues to the black people as consumers should be kept at the barest minimum. Consequently, the real wages of the African miners are today lower than they were in 1911.[14] Note also the almost total absence of social security benefits for the African people. To provide these benefits would be to increase the cost of reproduction of the producer and conversely to decrease capital's share of the national cake.

It might be argued that our thesis might begin to collapse when we tackle the question of the white workers.

Appearance would have it that in maintaining a white labour aristocracy, capital is behaving in a most irrational fashion, that capital itself has become so impregnated with racial prejudice that it cannot seek to extract maximum profit from a white worker. Yet we must bear in mind that the capitalist class does not view itself solely as the appropriator of wealth in contradistinction to our being the producers. The capitalist class is also heavily burdened with matters of state administration. It has taken on itself the task of ruling our country. As early as November 1899, Lord Milner had said: 'The ultimate end [of British policy] is a self-governing white Community, supported by well-treated and justly governed black labour from Cape Town to Zambesi [sic].'[15] A principal preoccupation of this self-governing community must therefore be to ensure that the 'well-treated and justly governed' do not one day rise up and transform themselves also into a self-governing community.

From the very beginning, British capital knew that it had to face this possibility and that if it fought without any allies, it would lose in such a confrontation. The historic compromise of 1910 has therefore this significance that in granting the vanquished Boer equal political and social status with the British victor, it imposed on both the duty to defend the *status quo* against especially those whom that *status quo* defined as the dominated.

The capitalist class, to whom everything has a cash value, has never considered moral incentives as very dependable. As part of the arrangement, it therefore decided that material incentives must play a prominent part. It consequently bought out the whole white population. It offered a price to the white workers and the Afrikaner farmers in exchange for an undertaking that they would shed their blood in defence of capital.

Both worker and farmer, like Faustus, took the devil's offering and, like Faustus, they will have to pay on the appointed day. The workers took the offering in monthly cash grants and reserved jobs. The farmers took their share by having black labour, including and especially prison labour directed to the farms. They also took it in the form of huge subsidies and loans to help them maintain a 'civilised standard of living'. The indebtedness of these farmers to the profit-making bourgeois in 1966 was equal to $1,25 billion, amounting to nearly 12 per cent of the gross national product.[16]

In 1947 a commission of the Dutch Reformed Church included in its report the prophetic words: 'In the country, one feels dependent on God; in the towns on men, such as one's employer.'[17] In the struggle that marks the growing onslaught of the black producers on the society of the parasites, the white worker will have to pay for that dependence on the employer-industrialist, the white farmer for that dependence on the employer-creditor.

The God of Calvin is a jealous God, visiting the iniquity of the fathers upon the children to the third and fourth generation of those who hate him: The God of Capital will, after all, have his pound of flesh!

Engels wrote in 1895 that:

> When Bismarck found himself compelled to introduce [universal] franchise as the only means of interesting the mass of the people in his plans, our workers immediately took it in earnest and sent August Bebel to the first constituent Reichstag. And from that day on, they have used the franchise in a way which has paid them a thousandfold and has served as a model to the workers of all countries. The franchise has been ... transformed by them from a means of deception, which it was before, into an instrument of emancipation... And so it happened that the bourgeoisie and the government came to be much more afraid of the legal than the illegal action of the workers' party, of the result of elections than those of rebellion.

Engels continues:

> Of course, our ... comrades do not thereby in the least renounce their right to revolution. The right to revolution is, after all, the only really 'historical right', the only right on which all modern states without exception rest...[18]

Yet it came to pass that in large measure the working class of Western Europe and North America did in fact, for some time anyway, renounce its right to revolution.

Some of the mass parties of the workers became parties of order and reform. And to the extent that bourgeois law and order was the basis on which the proletariat founded its trade unions and secured for itself higher wages, better working conditions and the right to strike, this was an inevitable outcome. That bourgeois law and order also gave the proletariat the right to form its own political party and the right to install that party in power, all within the legal framework of bourgeois democracy.

In the work from which we have just quoted, Engels says:

> The irony of world history turns everything upside down. The Parties [of the property-owning class] ... are perishing under the legal conditions created by themselves. They cry despairingly ... legality is the death of us; whereas we, under this legality, get firm muscles and rosy cheeks and look like life eternal... [There] is nothing left for them to do but themselves break through this fatal legality.[19]

The condition of the black workers of South Africa, the place in society allocated to us by the capitalist class, demands that we must assert our right to revolution.

Capital in its South African mould turns things right side up again. We are perishing under the legal conditions created by the bourgeoisie whereas they, under this legality, get firm muscles and rosy cheeks and look like life eternal. We have no choice but to break down this fatal legality. For the burden of our argument has been exactly this, that in the totality of the social relations that describe the apartheid system, we have a place only and exclusively in so far as we are 'the ragged-trousered philanthropists' – the exploited producers. We are otherwise the outsiders, the excluded – on our own continent, in our country!

In this context, take the Bantustan programme. In its objectives stated by the creators of this policy, the black producers will have the right to be complete human beings only in these areas which have been set aside as our so-called homelands. Otherwise, when we enter so-called white South Africa, we have the following *dramatis personae*: 'He who [is the] money-owner ... strides in front as capitalist; the possessor of labour power follows as his labourer. The one with an air of importance, smirking, intent on business; the other, timid and holding back, like one who is bringing his own hide to market and has nothing to expect but – a hiding.'[20]

The Bantustan policy is therefore not a *deus ex machina*, a contrived and inartistic solution of a difficulty in the drama of South African life. Rather, it is but the legal codification, the pure representation, in juridical form, of the centuries-old socio-economic reality of the alienation of the black producer from the society which he daily produces and reproduces.

At the level of abstraction, there are two alternatives out of this condition available to the black workers.

One of these is to cut the umbilical cord that ties us to bourgeois South Africa, for us to cease to be producers on somebody else's account. What would then happen?

We could then join the demimonde of the thieves and murderers, the pimps and prostitutes and, by becoming true and complete outcasts, recast ourselves in the parasitic model of our bourgeois progenitor, outside the bounds of bourgeois legality. Such an alternative is obviously absurd.

The racist regime is on the other hand pushing us into the Bantustans. This constitutes a death sentence for thousands of our people. For South Africa's land policy, of which the Bantustans are the historical outcome, is founded precisely on the land dispossession of the African people which ensures that hunger compels us to bring our own hides to market.

The second and, in fact, the only historically justifiable and inevitable alternative is that we cling very firmly to our position as producers, that we hoist the bourgeoisie with its own petard.

The irony of the South African situation is that exactly because capital permits us to enter the city, to pass through the sacred portals of a white church and set foot in the even more sacred sanctuary of madame's bedroom, but only as workers, capital thereby indicates to us daily that it is in fact our labour that makes the city to live, that gives voice to the *predikant*, the preacher, and provides the necessary conditions for procreation.

Since then we are, in a very real sense, the creators of society, what remains for us is to insist and ensure that that society is made in our image and that we have dominion over it.

Inasmuch as the producer and the parasite who feeds on the producer represent antithetical forces – the one working, the other idle; the one wanting to escape the obligation of the nursemaid and the other striving to ensure that he is for ever the fed – inasmuch therefore must a South Africa over which we have dominion be the antithesis of a present-day South Africa.

That free South Africa must therefore redefine the black producer or rather, since we, the people, shall govern, since we shall through our own struggle have placed ourselves in the position of makers of history and policy and no longer objects, we shall redefine our own position as follows:

- We are the producers of wealth.
- We produce this wealth for our own benefit to be appropriated by us, the producers.
- The aim of this production shall be the satisfaction, at an increasing level, of the material and spiritual needs of the people.
- We shall so order the rest of society and social activity, in education and culture, in the legal sphere, on military questions, in our international relations, and so forth, to conform to these goals.

In my view, this redefinition contains within it the theoretical basis of the Freedom Charter, the political programme of the African National Congress adopted in 1956.

It should be of some interest to point out that this programme was written exclusively on the basis of demands submitted by thousands upon thousands of ordinary workers, peasants, businessmen, intellectuals and other professional people, the youth and women of all nationalities of South Africa.

It is a measure of their maturity that these masses should have so clearly understood the fundamental direction of their aspirations. It is a demonstration in practice of how much the bourgeoisie, by refusing to temper its greed, did ultimately teach us to identify our true interests without any equivocation.

Whenever we stand up and say: 'South Africa belongs to all who live in it, black and white, and no government can justly claim authority unless it is based on the will of all the people...',[21] we always meet with three different reactions.

There are those, naturally, who agree with us. There are those who howl in derision – these are the white supremacists who are confident of the everlasting power of the repressive force of apartheid South Africa.

But perhaps more important, there are those, themselves the offspring of the black producers of our country together with their sympathisers, who, in anger, throw at us the epithet, traitor!

Yet this is what a free South Africa will be like. For as the masses themselves long discovered, the antithesis to white supremacy, exclusiveness and arrogance is not a black version of the same practice.

In the physical world, black might indeed be the opposite of white. But in the world of social systems, social theory and practice have as much to do with skin pigmentation as has the birth of children with the stork. To connect the two is to invent a fable with the conscious or unconscious purpose of hiding reality.

The act of negating the theory and practice of white apartheid racism, the revolutionary position, is exactly to take the issue of colour, race, national and sex differentiation out of the sphere of rational human thinking and behaviour, and thereby expose all colour, race, nation and sex prejudice as irrational. Our own rational practical social activity – rational in the sense of being anti-racist and non-racist – constitutes such a negation; it constitutes the social impetus and guarantee of the withering away of this irrationality.

Consider the circumstances in which we might position 'black capitalism' as the antithesis to 'white capitalism'. Fortunately, Fanon has already warned us that one of the results of imperialist domination is that in the colonial middle class:

> The dynamic pioneer aspect, the characteristics of the inventor and the discoverer of new worlds which are found in all national bourgeoisies are lamentably absent.
> In its beginnings, the national bourgeoisie of the colonial countries identifies itself with the decadence of the bourgeoisie of the West. We need not think that it is jumping ahead; it is in fact beginning at the end. It is already senile before it has come to know the petulance, the fearlessness or the will to succeed of youth.[22]

Thus black capitalism, instead of being the antithesis, is rather confirmation of parasitism with no redeeming features whatsoever, without any

23

extenuating circumstances to excuse its existence. If you want to see a living example, go to the Transkei.

Even more, by thus expelling racism to the realm of the irrational by our own practice, we would help to deny those who want to exploit and oppress others, including our very selves, the possibility of finding justification for their actions in such prejudices.

We particularly, who are the products of exemplary capitalist exploitation, must remember that when German capital found opportunity, especially during the Second World War, to revert to primitive forms of accumulation under the stimulation of passions the most infamous, the most sordid, the pettiest, the most meanly odious, it used exactly these prejudices literally to enslave and slaughter millions of people.

We must remember that the exploitation of the so-called *Gastarbeiter* in Western Europe today is founded, in part, on contempt for their nationality; that in the United States and Northern Ireland the black and Irish worker respectively is oppressed and exploited on the basis of colour and national prejudice.

The charge of traitor might stick if we were to advance a programme of equality between black and white while there remained between these two communities the relations of exploiter and exploited.

But we have already said that our victory presupposes the abolition of parasitism and the reintegration of the idle rich as productive members of society, as well as our writing off the debt of the white worker and farmer so that they can start again afresh, as equals with other producers in law and in every other respect, without the heavy weight of blood money in their pockets and on their consciences.

The Freedom Charter itself says that 'the national wealth of our country, the heritage of all South Africans, shall be restored to the people'. It also goes on to say 'all the land [shall be] redivided among those who work it to banish famine and hunger'.[23]

We believe sincerely that it is only in conditions of such an equality as is underpinned by these provisions that we shall each be able to discover and unfold our true individuality, re-acquire the right to be human and thereby create the conditions for the creative realisation of the considerable talent of our people, both black and white, which today is so firmly stifled by the suffocating purposes of a small, exploiting and oppressive minority.

To transcend the status of mere producer to that of human being, capital has taught us by negative example that we must guarantee ourselves the right to work and to social security, good housing and health services, education, culture, pride and joy in the multiplicity of languages and progressive national traditions among ourselves and among the people of Africa and the world.

We must therefore preface our own system of accounting with the provision that our rational calculations must serve to enlarge human life and not to negate it.

We therefore have to strive to banish war and the use or threat of force in the settlement of international disputes. We must work to abolish the use of fear against individuals and communities as an instrument of policy, and therefore uphold and fight for the right of all peoples to true self-determination, for friendship and mutually advantageous co-operation among the peoples of the world.

We are convinced that in this way we would restore our country to its rightful position in the world as a steadfast friend and ally of all who struggle for peace, democracy and social progress, and not the repugnant predator that she is today.

In 1953 one of our outstanding leaders, Nelson Mandela, wrote:

> To talk of democratic and constitutional means [to achieve liberation] can only have a basis in reality for those who enjoy democratic and constitutional rights... We cannot win one single victory ... without overcoming a desperate resistance on the part of the Government... [Therefore] no organisation whose interests are identical with those of the toiling masses will advocate conciliation to win its demands.[24]

This is a call to revolution. This revolution is necessary, as Marx and Engels once said – 'not only because the ruling class cannot be overthrown in any other way, but also because the class overthrowing it can only in a revolution succeed in ridding itself of all the muck of ages and become fitted to found society anew.'[25]

We have tried to convey to you our own view, as scientifically as possible, of our past, our present and our national democratic future and the organic connection between these.

Let us leave you with a few more words from Nelson Mandela:

In South Africa, where the entire population is almost split into two hostile camps ... and where recent political events have made the struggle between oppressor and oppressed even more acute, there can be no middle course. The fault of the Liberals ... is to attempt to strike just such a course. They believe in criticising and condemning the Government for its reactionary policies but they are afraid to identify themselves with the people and to assume the task of mobilising that social force capable of lifting the struggle to higher levels... The real question is: in the general struggle for political rights, can the oppressed people count on the Liberal Party as an ally?[26]

That question, posed 25 years ago, has reached a broader audience today, including this audience. Can the oppressed people count on you as allies?

PART TWO

Nation-building and Reconciliation

MBEKI'S WELL-KNOWN 'I am an African' speech, delivered on the occasion of the adoption of South Africa's Constitution in May 1996, sets the scene for what is dealt with by the seven speeches contained in this section. In poetic phrases he declares his roots, identifications and commitments, while at the same time developing an inclusive understanding of concepts such as 'nation' and 'African'.

His much talked-about 'Two Nations' speech, delivered in Parliament two years later, asks incisive questions about nation-building and has to be read in conjunction with 'I am an African'.

A careful reading of the speeches in this section shows that Mbeki does not refrain from talking frankly about the problems facing South Africa. 'Breaking with the past' (March 1996), a moral and strategic necessity for South Africa, is not going to come easily. Neither will it happen without pain and sacrifice. However, the break has to take place. The transition to 'a better life for all' is unavoidable and impossible to postpone. Transformation and structural change is South Africa's destiny.

What transformation entails becomes clear from the speeches assembled in this and other sections. It is linked to a view Mbeki mentioned during an interview:

> Within the ANC, the cry was to 'catch the bastards and hang them'. But we realised that you could not simultaneously prepare for a peaceful transition while saying we want to catch and hang people. So we paid a price for the peaceful transition. If we had not taken this route, I don't know where the country would have been today. Had there been a threat of Nuremberg-style trials over members of the apartheid security establishment we would never have undergone the peaceful change.[27]

3

I am an African

Statement on behalf of the African National Congress on the occasion of the adoption by the Constitutional Assembly of The Republic of South Africa Constitution Bill 1996, Cape Town, 8 May 1996

ON AN OCCASION such as this we should, perhaps, start from the beginning.

So let me begin.

I am an African.

I owe my being to the hills and the valleys, the mountains and the glades, the rivers, the deserts, the trees, the flowers, the seas and the ever-changing seasons that define the face of our native land.

My body has frozen in our frosts and in our latter-day snows. It has thawed in the warmth of our sunshine and melted in the heat of the mid-day sun.

The crack and the rumble of the summer thunders, lashed by startling lightning, have been causes both of trembling and of hope.

The fragrances of nature have been as pleasant to us as the sight of the wild blooms of the citizens of the veld.

The dramatic shapes of the Drakensberg, the soil-coloured waters of the Lekoa, iGqili noThukela, and the sands of the Kgalagadi have all been panels of the set on the natural stage on which we act out the foolish deeds of the theatre of our day.

At times, and in fear, I have wondered whether I should concede equal citizenship of our country to the leopard and the lion, the elephant and the springbok, the hyena, the black mamba and the pestilential mosquito.

A human presence among all these, a feature on the face of our native land thus defined, I know that none dare challenge me when I say: I am an African!

I owe my being to the Khoi and the San whose desolate souls haunt

31

the great expanses of the beautiful Cape – they who fell victim to the most merciless genocide our native land has ever seen, they who were the first to lose their lives in the struggle to defend our freedom and independence and they who, as a people, perished in the result.

Today, as a country, we keep an audible silence about these ancestors of the generations that live, fearful to admit the horror of a former deed, seeking to obliterate from our memories a cruel occurrence which, in its remembering, should teach us not and never to be inhuman again.

I am formed of the migrants who left Europe to find a new home on our native land. Whatever their own actions, they remain still part of me.

In my veins courses the blood of the Malay slaves who came from the East. Their proud dignity informs my bearing, their culture is part of my essence. The stripes they bore on their bodies from the lash of the slave-master are a reminder embossed on my consciousness of what should not be done.

I am the grandchild of the warrior men and women that Hintsa and Sekhukhune led, the patriots that Cetshwayo and Mphephu took to battle, the soldiers Moshoeshoe and Ngungunyane taught never to dishonour the cause of freedom.

My mind and my knowledge of myself is formed by the victories that are the jewels in our African crown, the victories we earned from Isandhlwana to Khartoum, as Ethiopians and as the Ashanti of Ghana, as the Berbers of the desert.

I am the grandchild who lays fresh flowers on the Boer graves at St Helena and the Bahamas, who sees in the mind's eye and suffers the suffering of a simple peasant folk: death, concentration camps, destroyed homesteads, a dream in ruins.

I am the child of Nongqause. I am he who made it possible to trade in the world markets in diamonds, in gold, in the same food for which my stomach yearns.

I come of those who were transported from India and China, whose being resided in the fact, solely, that they were able to provide physical labour, who taught me that we could both be at home and be foreign, who taught me that human existence itself demanded that freedom was a necessary condition for that human existence.

Being part of all these people, and in the knowledge that none dare contest that assertion, I shall claim that I am an African!

I have seen our country torn asunder as these, all of whom are my people, engaged one another in a titanic battle, the one to redress a wrong that had been caused by one to another, and the other to defend the indefensible.

I have seen what happens when one person has superiority of force over another, when the stronger appropriate to themselves the prerogative even to annul the injunction that God created all men and women in His image.

I know what it signifies when race and colour are used to determine who is human and who subhuman.

I have seen the destruction of all sense of self-esteem, the consequent striving to be what one is not, simply to acquire some of the benefits which those who had imposed themselves as masters had ensured that they enjoy.

I have experience of the situation in which race and colour is used to enrich some and impoverish the rest.

I have seen the corruption of minds and souls as a result of the pursuit of an ignoble effort to perpetrate a veritable crime against humanity.

I have seen concrete expression of the denial of the dignity of a human being emanating from the conscious, systemic and systematic oppressive and repressive activities of other human beings.

There the victims parade with no mask to hide the brutish reality – the beggars, the prostitutes, the street children, those who seek solace in substance abuse, those who have to steal to assuage hunger, those who have to lose their sanity because to be sane is to invite pain.

Perhaps the worst among these who are my people are those who have learnt to kill for a wage. To these the extent of death is directly proportional to their personal welfare.

And so, like pawns in the service of demented souls, they kill in furtherance of the political violence in KwaZulu-Natal. They murder the innocent in the taxi wars. They kill slowly or quickly in order to make profits from the illegal trade in narcotics. They are available for hire when husband wants to murder wife and wife, husband.

Among us prowl the products of our immoral and amoral past – killers who have no sense of the worth of human life; rapists who have absolute disdain for the women of our country; animals who would seek to benefit from the vulnerability of the children, the disabled and the old; the rapacious who brook no obstacle in their quest for self-enrichment.

All this I know and know to be true because I am an African!

Because of that, I am also able to state this fundamental truth: that I am born of a people who are heroes and heroines.

I am born of a people who would not tolerate oppression.

I am of a nation that would not allow that fear of death, torture, imprisonment, exile or persecution should result in the perpetuation of injustice.

The great masses who are our mother and father will not permit that the behaviour of the few results in the description of our country and people as barbaric. Patient because history is on their side, these masses do not despair because today the weather is bad. Nor do they turn triumphalist when, tomorrow, the sun shines. Whatever the circumstances they have lived through – and because of that experience – they are determined to define for themselves who they are and who they should be.

We are assembled here today to mark their victory in acquiring and exercising their right to formulate their own definition of what it means to be African.

The Constitution whose adoption we celebrate constitutes an unequivocal statement that we refuse to accept that our Africanness shall be defined by our race, colour, gender or historical origins.

It is a firm assertion made by ourselves that South Africa belongs to all who live in it, black and white.

It gives concrete expression to the sentiment we share as Africans, and will defend to the death, that the people shall govern.

It recognises the fact that the dignity of the individual is both an objective which society must pursue, and is a goal which cannot be separated from the material wellbeing of that individual.

It seeks to create the situation in which all our people shall be free from fear, including the fear of the oppression of one national group by another, the fear of the disempowerment of one social echelon by another, the fear of the use of state power to deny anybody their fundamental human rights, and the fear of tyranny.

It aims to open the doors so that those who were disadvantaged can assume their place in society as equals with their fellow human beings without regard to colour, race, gender, age or geographic dispersal.

It provides the opportunity to enable each one and all to state their views, promote them, strive for their implementation in the process of governance without fear that a contrary view will be met with repression.

It creates a law-governed society which shall be inimical to arbitrary rule.

It enables the resolution of conflicts by peaceful means rather than resort to force.

It rejoices in the diversity of our people and creates the space for all of us voluntarily to define ourselves as one people.

As an African, this is an achievement of which I am proud, proud without reservation and proud without any feeling of conceit.

Our sense of elevation at this moment also derives from the fact that this magnificent product is the unique creation of African hands and African minds. But it also constitutes a tribute to our loss of vanity that we could, despite the temptation to treat ourselves as an exceptional fragment of humanity, draw on the accumulated experience and wisdom of all humankind to define for ourselves what we want to be.

Together with the best in the world, we too are prone to pettiness, petulance, selfishness and short-sightedness. But it seems to have happened that we looked at ourselves and said the time had come that we made a superhuman effort to be other than human, to respond to the call to create for ourselves a glorious future, to remind ourselves of the Latin saying: *Gloria est consequenda* – Glory must be sought after!

Today it feels good to be an African.

It feels good that I can stand here as a South African and as a foot soldier of a titanic African army, the African National Congress, to say to all the parties represented here, to the millions who made an input into the processes we are concluding, to our outstanding compatriots who have presided over the birth of our founding document, to the negotiators who pitted their wits one against the other, to the stars who shone unseen as the management and administration of the Constitutional Assembly, the advisers, experts and publicists, to the mass communication media, to our friends across the globe: Congratulations and well done!

I am an African.

I am born of the peoples of the continent of Africa.

The pain of the violent conflict that the peoples of Liberia, Somalia, the Sudan, Burundi and Algeria experience is a pain I also bear.

The dismal shame of poverty, suffering and human degradation of my continent is a blight that we share.

The blight on our happiness that derives from this and from our drift to the periphery of the ordering of human affairs leaves us in a persistent shadow of despair.

This is a savage road to which nobody should be condemned.

This thing that we have done today, in this small corner of a great continent that has contributed so decisively to the evolution of humanity, says that Africa reaffirms that she is continuing her rise from the ashes.

Whatever the setbacks of the moment, nothing can stop us now!

Whatever the difficulties, Africa shall be at peace!

However improbable it may sound to the sceptics, Africa will prosper!

Whoever we may be, whatever our immediate interest, however much we carry baggage from our past, however much we have been caught by the fashion of cynicism and loss of faith in the capacity of the people, let us say today: Nothing can stop us now!

4

At the Helm of South Africa's Renaissance

Inaugural address as chancellor of the University of Transkei, Umtata, 18 May 1995

I ASSUME THIS POST [of chancellor of the University of the Transkei] with a sense of duty, because I believe that an institution such as this should be an intellectual and academic champion of the momentous transformation process taking place at many levels of our society.

As chancellor of this institution, I believe that my primary responsibility will be to contribute to the creation of an atmosphere within which the ethos of the freedom of intellectual activity and academic excellence can be promoted, protected and guaranteed. I believe, however, that intellectual and academic freedom can only find its full expression if it places itself within the larger context of the pursuit of the greatest good for the greatest number of people.

As a consequence of this recognition, it is difficult to conceive of intellectual and academic freedom committed only to its own protection and pursuit, without reference to what those who enjoy this freedom should do about the vast economic, social and cultural disparities which derive from the apartheid legacy of race, ethnic and gender discrimination. Indeed, it is difficult to talk of full academic freedom where many institutions of learning still bear physical and ideological features bestowed on them by many decades of apartheid and racial oppression.

For intellectual and academic freedom fully to blossom, the majority of disadvantaged sections of the community must be empowered with equal opportunities to enter the academic world. It is for that reason that our task to promote, protect and guarantee the process of the expansion of knowledge within the University of Transkei (UNITRA) should be seen in conjunction with the larger agenda of the reconstruction and development of our society. It should be seen within the context of political, economic and social emancipation of the people.

I believe that we should not confine the achievement of intellectual and academic excellence to the narrow realm of individual success. Rather, we should link that excellence to the objective of the emancipation of the people from the darkness that derives from ignorance and poverty, for the spiritual and material fulfilment that is the prerogative of all human beings.

Our country is going through a revolution. It is experiencing a national renaissance. As a generation, we have been thrust into the forefront of that revolution and placed at the helm of that renaissance.

On the shoulders of that generation rests a dual responsibility. Firstly, we have the responsibility to complete the political and constitutional revolution. Both in the larger society and in the chambers of Parliament and the Constitutional Assembly, lively democratic political and constitutional debates are indicative of a mature democracy emerging.

Secondly, we are charged with the responsibility of safeguarding an accelerated as well as sustainable social, economic and cultural renaissance.

Indeed, as we sit here today, we are witnesses to an intellectual generation upon whose shoulders history has conferred unprecedented responsibilities and for whom it has opened the way to the possibility of great opportunities. We can therefore say that, in good measure, the destiny of the country is in your hands as we are pursuing the national dream of social emancipation.

At no time in the history of our country has education been so critical to the task of building a new society. In the past you struggled against apartheid and sharpened your educational skills primarily in order to deliver our society from political oppression and socio-economic dispossession. Today your social and intellectual endeavours should be informed by the use of people's power to deracialise our country, to ensure the emancipation of women, to uplift our youth, to free the people from poverty, and to guarantee democracy and peace.

As an institution of higher learning, which should always seek to narrow the gap between our academic pursuit and the struggle of the larger community to free itself from the shackles of political oppression, socio-economic deprivation, illiteracy and cultural underdevelopment, we have an important role to play in addressing the legacy of apartheid. Deliberately we must put in place structures and programmes designed to achieve this objective.

Those structures and programmes should, in a very practical way, begin by addressing themselves to the conditions of the workers in our academic institutions. I am talking about the workers who clean our hostels, cook our food and make our gardens.

It is equally important to acknowledge that our educational institutions, as well as the theoretical framework in which educational thought is constituted, are linked to the apartheid past by a myriad of threads. There is an urgent need for the transformation of all our academic institutions. There is a need to reorient both the theoretical paradigm and the idiom of our curriculum.

Tertiary institutions should set in motion processes which affirm in favour of those sections of society which were disadvantaged by apartheid rule. There is a dire need to affirm the national and gender character of our society. Affirmative action should also take into account the unequal social and economic opportunities open to urban as against rural communities.

We have the noble responsibility to defend the unity and integrity of the new South African state. We must encourage the vibrancy of its democracy. It should be a democracy where neither race, ethnicity, gender, religion nor creed performs any discriminatory role in the individual or collective pursuit of human fulfilment.

We have a responsibility to work for a South Africa where there is peace, stability and ever-increasing overall wellbeing of the people.

Furthermore, our country should place itself within the context of the Southern African region and define its place on the continent of Africa and the world.

As a university which does not fear change but seeks to immerse itself in the process of contributing to the determination of the form and content of that change, we must surely welcome with the greatest enthusiasm the challenge so as to act that history can record that UNITRA was part of the spearhead in the struggle to give birth to a nation of South Africans.

5

Breaking with the Past

University Forum, University of Natal, Howard College Campus, 7 March 1996

IN HIS POEM 'Sailing to Byzantium', the great Irish poet William Butler Yeats says:

> That is no country for old men. The young
> In one another's arms, birds in the trees
> – Those dying generations – at their song,
> The salmon-falls, the mackerel-crowded seas,
> Fish, flesh or fowl, commend all summer long
> Whatever is begotten, born, and dies.
> Caught in that sensual music all neglect
> Monuments of unageing intellect.[28]

Yeats had no thought of South Africa as he composed these beautiful lines, but perhaps we can borrow them to say something about our country today.

What that is would be that the new South Africa should indeed be a country for the young, the joyful young in one another's arms, birds in the trees at their song, caught in their sensual music, oblivious of the old because of their celebration of the future.

Surely none can contest the vision that we stand at the threshold of the evolution of a new and beautiful South Africa, which should see us advance step by step towards the creation of the material and spiritual conditions which should gradually free all our people from poverty, ignorance and human degradation, from fear and needless violence, progressing towards the true emancipation of the human being.

To entertain such a vision one should be young, not necessarily in years, but young in one's ability to break with the past, in one's capacity to remove from oneself the shackles of old thinking, allowing oneself to be inspired by the notion that where there is no vision, the people perish.

But neither can we, as Yeats decries, neglect our own monuments of unageing intellect. Because indeed, out of the horrible disaster that was the system of apartheid, of racial division, racial oppression, despair and human degradation, we have through our efforts created freedom and given hope to millions both in our country and throughout the world, there being no greater monument to unageing intellect than this.

Inspired by a wonderful wisdom, our people have fully grasped the concept of reconciliation, nation-building and national unity. They have understood that unless we make a determined and sustained effort to achieve these objectives, we would both destroy the monuments of the magnificence of the human spirit and remove the conditions which enable us to build the new South Africa.

The challenge ahead of us is to achieve reconciliation between the former oppressor and the formerly oppressed, between black and white, between rich and poor (who, in our own conditions, are also described by colour), between men and women, the young and the old, the able and the disabled.

When our president, Nelson Mandela, spoke of a new patriotism, he was projecting such a vision according to which, as South Africans seeking to reconcile ourselves with one another, we would be moved to act together in pursuit of common goals, understanding that we not only cannot escape a shared destiny but should indeed celebrate the prospect of a shared destiny of democracy, non-racialism, non-sexism, national unity, prosperity and peace.

Consequently, such reconciliation as the president spoke about has embedded in it the fundamental concept of change. To create a society of democracy, non-racialism, non-sexism, national unity, prosperity and peace means that we must radically change the old order.

Simultaneously as we speak of national reconciliation so must we speak of transformation. As we vigorously strive to realise the first national objective, so must we understand fully that we have a responsibility also to pursue this second and equally important goal of fundamental change.

Both strategically and tactically, perhaps one of the biggest challenges we face in the struggle to build a better South Africa is the challenge of understanding and managing the dialectical relationship between reconciliation and transformation.

I believe that, in this regard, the first thing to understand is that these concepts belong together. They are interdependent and impact upon each other. None is capable of realisation unless it is accompanied by the other.

Consequently, I would make the strong assertion that it is as wrong to argue that the only challenge we face is transformation as it would be to say that the sole task ahead of us is reconciliation.

Similarly, it would be mistaken to treat these two objectives as though they could be separated one from the other, with one capable of being secondary to the other, except in the context of a dynamic equilibrium in which precedence is determined by transient and therefore tactical circumstances.

I am certain that if you asked the overwhelming majority of our people if they were in favour of reconciliation, they would answer in the affirmative, in the same way as they would if you inquired about their attitude towards transformation.

And yet in the practice this matter is not as easy as this might suggest. To borrow a phrase, the devil is in the implementation.

If we understand that reconciliation is more than the ability to share a cup of tea or to greet each other in the morning and that it is an inherent part of a process of social change, then it will be easy to realise why it is easier to accept the twin concepts of reconciliation and transformation in principle, while their implementation is not necessarily comfortable for anyone of us.

Consider, for instance, the great challenge we faced of achieving reconciliation among the political forces in our country which had engaged in a life and death struggle, the one to defend the system of apartheid and the other to ensure the destruction of this system.

Needless to say, the reconstruction and development of our society was impossible as long as this conflict persisted. Its transformation could not begin until reconciliation had been achieved between the mortal enemies.

And yet that reconciliation also could not be attained until the political conditions in our country had themselves been changed. No reconciliation was possible outside the context of the establishment of a democratic system, outside the context of the abandonment of the system of white minority rule.

Let us take perhaps a more controversial example. This is the issue of language.

As everybody knows, for decades this country had two official languages, English and Afrikaans, reflecting the political domination of South African society by the white minority.

On the other hand, the new Constitution provides for 11 languages, to assert the equality of all national groups in our country as part of the creation of a democratic and non-racial society.

There can be no gainsaying the fact that the realisation of reconciliation among the different national groups in our country is among the most noble of our objectives. This has, as one of its elements, respect for the language, culture and identity of each of the national groups on the basis of equality. The achievement of these goals would be both an expression of the objective of national reconciliation and an instrument for the accomplishment of this aim.

To return to the issue of language, the question must be posed: Is it possible to achieve reconciliation between the former two official languages and the rest of the languages of our country without also effecting a transformation in the relationship among all these languages?

If the answer is no, then we have to deal with the question of how to end the relationship of domination of the two over the others, so as to ensure the termination of the conflict which is inherent to the relationship of domination on the one hand and subservience on the other. This clearly has to be done in a manner that does not undermine but enhances the other objective we have already stated, of respect for the language, culture and identity of each one of our national groups on the basis of equality.

I believe it would be dishonest to pretend that the process of achieving an equitable relationship among our languages can be achieved without the former official languages feeling some pain, if we can put the matter thus. But similarly, no reconciliation among our languages can take place unless the old relationship among them is changed and transformed.

Let us, again, take another delicate matter. This relates to the question of the distribution of wealth and income.

Nobody in this room needs educating about the fact that in our country the incidence of wealth and poverty is, in large measure, defined by race and colour. I am certain that all of us would also agree that it would not be possible to say we have created a better life for all and that we can be certain of social stability, unless we have dealt successfully with the problem of poverty, which affects so many millions of our people. The peculiar challenge we face is, as we have said, the fact of the identification of prosperity and deprivation with race and colour.

The matter therefore does not rest merely with the upliftment of the poor. It also relates to closing the gap between black and white, which implies what some treat as a dreaded prospect, namely the redistribution of wealth as an important part of the struggle to create a non-racial and non-sexist South Africa.

We would argue that this is one of the fundamentals in terms of the pursuit of the goal of reconciliation between black and white in our society. We can never hope that there would be social stability while the economic arrangements in our country continue to be characterised by the apartheid patterns of the past.

The conclusion therefore cannot be avoided that we must indeed embark on the transformation of our economy to achieve a radical departure from the past of the inequitable distribution of wealth, income and opportunity based on racial discrimination and domination.

Let me also add that this, of course, must be accomplished in a way that does not threaten the important objectives of economic growth and development on a sustained basis.

But the point we are making is that there can be no permanent reconciliation between the haves and the have-nots if their social relationship continues to be defined by the patterns of the past, if we fail to attain the transformation of that relationship. The maintenance and perpetuation of the past can only be a recipe for conflict, and more, for an explosion in future which would arise from anger fuelled by the continued existence of the master-and-servant relations of our apartheid past.

You will remember the remarks that the president made recently in this regard when he opened Parliament, when he said that all of us are called upon to make sacrifices and that reconciliation does not consist merely in the disadvantaged forgiving the erstwhile oppressor.

The challenge confronting the haves is themselves to define the contribution they should make to achieve the economic transformation we are talking about in pursuit of the goal of reconciliation, which is directly in their own interest, as opposed to taking a position which seeks to defend privilege, which, in the long term, the haves must surely realise is against their own interests.

Once more we would argue not only that economic transformation is necessary to achieve reconciliation, but also that a common commitment to the pursuit of that reconciliation is itself an important condition for the realisation of the necessary condition of transformation.

Whether we can achieve this in practice, in the context of the 'new patriotism' which the president spoke about, remains to be seen.

Here we clearly and without doubt need reconciliation. To achieve it we also need transformation. But what is it that needs transformation?

I believe that we need transformation around the question of the practice of politics. Over time, the situation arose in this province that the use of force became established as an instrument in the conduct of politics under any and all circumstances, perpetuating the assumption that one of the goals of the practice of politics was for one political formation to achieve permanent domination over the other and over the people.

The process of transformation must therefore in KwaZulu-Natal focus on the elimination of the capacity of all political forces to conduct violent campaigns. Clearly this would best be achieved in circumstances in which all the political formations in the province agree genuinely to the achievement of this objective and actively co-operate to ensure its realisation.

To reiterate, I believe that the understanding and management of the dialectical process of reconciliation and transformation is one of the principal challenges of all who occupy positions of leadership in the country.

Reconciliation is as important to the formerly oppressed as it is to the former oppressor. Equally, transformation is as important to the disadvantaged as it is to the privileged. They cannot be positioned one against the other or treated as though the one was separate from the other.

It is in the art of fostering and managing the interaction of these two objectives that the calibre of the broad leadership of our people will be tested.

I believe that the challenge this and other universities face is as much to achieve reconciliation and transformation within themselves as it is, as centres of learning and research, to make their input into the realisation of this objective in all spheres of social life.

By so doing they will define themselves as among the young whom Yeats wrote about, but who also, by their activity, would help to create new monuments of unageing intellect, monuments to the magnificence of the creativity and ingenuity of the great people of our rainbow nation.

6

South Africa: A Workable Dream

Keynote address, Europe–South Africa 1995 Business and Finance Forum, Montreux, Switzerland, 27 June 1995

AT 3 A.M. ON SUNDAY, the Council of Foreign Ministers of the Organisation of African Unity (OAU) was still in session, working to complete its preparations for the summit meeting which opened yesterday in Addis Ababa, Ethiopia.

At that early hour, the South African foreign minister rose on a point on the agenda, but decided to preface his remarks by announcing the results of the Rugby World Cup final, which had been concluded less than 12 hours before.

He never did get to announce the result. As soon as he mentioned the words 'Rugby World Cup', the African foreign ministers, who were already aware of the Springbok victory, broke into a spontaneous ovation which lasted for a while.

The wonder of this moment of celebration was, of course, that except for half a dozen countries at most, the African continent does not play rugby. Indeed many, like some in our own country, would probably consider rugby a barbaric game.

The celebration by Africa's first diplomats was not about the victory of one clutch of barbarians over another. What they rose to rejoice about was an African success, the fact of so decisive a break with a recent past in which it seemed that the African dream would forever be deferred.

As they clapped fervent hands, their hearts and ours were enveloped by an affirmed conviction that ours, as Africans, had become a workable dream.

After all, was it not true that in the history of modern international sport the entire African continent had never, until this moment, brought a

single world cup to our shores? Despite all that had been said and predicted, there it was – a world cup in the firm grasp of African hands.

In any case, were we not, as Africans, the ones who had caused
humankind to triumph when we defeated the system of apartheid, despite
all that had been said and predicted: that we would need a divine and miraculous intervention to defeat so vicious and powerful a conspiracy?

As the souls of Africa's first diplomats sang and louder sang, the question must have crossed their minds: Was it not in Africa that, in contemporary history, a new and startling process of reconciliation between
erstwhile foes emerged, took shape, found a home and inspired an almost
mystical hope for peace and human solidarity – across the globe?

What I am addressing is the African reality that is obvious to the leaders who are gathered in Addis Ababa: that our continent is and has been
victim to a litany of human catastrophes which have included bad governance, war and violent strife, the absence of development, and hunger on
an enormous scale.

And yet the millions of Africans throughout our continent continued
to dream of peace and stability, of democracy, of respect for human
rights, of freedom from hunger and ignorance, of a future when the continent would no longer be the object of humanitarian assistance and the
charitable attention of the rest of the world.

What has happened in South Africa in the recent past says to our continent, including the people of South Africa themselves, that this indeed
is a workable dream.

For this dream to have full meaning, however, and indeed for it to be
fully workable, it has to address itself to the total objective of all-round
human fulfilment.

It has to relate to the creation of enough jobs, the provision of basic
formal education to the majority, the construction of enough clinics, the
drastic reduction of the high rate of unemployment, the provision of houses
to the homeless, and the establishment of a clean and healthy environment.

For the overall wellbeing of the people to improve, this dream has to
include social stability, personal security and the maintenance of peaceful relations between our country and the rest of humanity.

In the first year of democracy in South Africa, our government has
been preoccupied with the need to broaden and consolidate a national
consensus with regard to two important issues.

47

Firstly, we started the process of democratising our country, fully cognisant that we were coming from a past torn apart by political and social conflict. That meant that we urgently needed to reconcile our divided society and to fashion a new sense of a shared destiny.

This national consensus, epitomised by the first democratic elections of 27 April 1994, is premised on a common vision of a South Africa we want to build. There is a common understanding and a general acceptance in our country that we cherish a future South Africa which is united in its composition, democratic in its character, non-racial in its political complexion and prosperous in its socio-economic objective. It is a vision which seeks to safeguard and promote the rich diversity of our languages and cultural expression.

We have managed to establish a national consensus on the need to defend this young democracy and to make it work.

Secondly, we have begun to lay the foundation for political, economic and social transformation of the entire fabric of social life. In South Africa the national agenda for the achievement of this transformation is familiarly known as the Reconstruction and Development Programme.

There is general acceptance in our society that any form of development which is not accompanied by the transformation of the fabric of life would only help to entrench and widen distortions and disparities created by apartheid.

This programme of reconstruction and development constitutes our paramount national project. It is an agenda which is agreed to and supported by all political parties in the Parliament as well as all important national and regional organisations of civil society.

The pursuance of the national agenda of reconstruction and development is taking place within a national and international climate which offers many possibilities and formidable challenges. The objective of a thoroughgoing transformation and a complete democratisation process can only succeed if the economy of our country grows on a sustainable basis. We need an economy which can locate itself within the world economy, adapt to its positive major trends and benefit from its dynamism.

The Government of National Unity, the business sector, major trade union formations and a multiplicity of community structures are generally agreed on the main elements that are necessary for the restructuring and development of the economy. We are seriously involved in efforts aimed at creating a situation in which domestic and international confidence in the management of our economy is firmly established.

Steps have been taken in the direction of reducing protective tariffs in line with our commitment to the Uruguay round of the General Agreement on Tariffs and Trade. We are seriously committed to opening our economy to more effective trade. In the same context, we have signed on to the World Trade Organisation and are fully committed to extensive though gradual tariff reforms, we are taking steady steps towards the removal of exchange controls, and are also introducing changes in our monetary and fiscal policies with the objective of creating a climate conducive to local and foreign investment.

As this august audience is well aware, South Africa is endowed with a multiplicity of natural resources. However, this reservoir of natural resources in existing mines is diminishing. For example, the reserves of key resources such as gold in some of our mines are fast deteriorating. Although there are indications that there are still large reserves in other areas, these are located too deep and are thus too expensive to exploit. We need more technologically advanced and cost-effective methods in order to break into the depths of these reserves.

Our economic experience has also brought to sharp focus the fact that it is difficult and risky to build and anchor your economy on potentially volatile commodity markets. For this reason, we are committed to shifting our resources steadily from the extraction and processing of primary products towards the production of competitive manufactured goods and services as a basis for our economy as we enter the twenty-first century.

We are also committed to exploiting the strengths of our economy in the reconstruction and development of our country. These strengths include a diversified economy, a very good physical infrastructure, a sophisticated financial sector, potentially high levels of domestic investment and growth which we are beginning to demonstrate, access to markets in the region and beyond, and abundant supplies of labour, some of which is highly skilled and most of which is competitively priced.

In line with the need to empower the majority of our people and to redress racial and gender imbalances created by apartheid rule, we give special attention to the development of small, medium and micro enterprises. We believe that this is one of the effective ways in the war against underdevelopment, poverty, underemployment and joblessness among disadvantaged communities. It is a way of spreading the base of the economy and widening the door for economic opportunities.

Women from these disadvantaged communities constitute the bulk of those whose conditions cry out for urgent attention.

We encourage foreign and local investors to enter into partnership with local small, medium and micro enterprises, especially with the emergent black business sector. Such partnerships should be geared at injecting capital, transferring technology, imparting entrepreneurial skills and developing human resources.

We sincerely believe that foreign investment will be a critical catalyst in the process of reconstruction and development. It will bring new technologies to our economy, it will demonstrate new forms of work organisation, it will provide access to new markets, and it will raise the competitive temperature of our economy.

We are also well aware that the success of our reconstruction and development strategy depends on enlisting domestic investors in the cause of competitive twenty-first century economic development. Indeed, in the last year we have witnessed an increase in the level of gross domestic fixed investment. Figures indicate that gross domestic fixed investment is still growing well this year and is forecast to continue growing in 1996.

We also situate the task of reconstruction and development within the broader context of the Southern African region and the world. We have already joined the Southern African Development Community – largely because we are convinced that the time has arrived for the region to join hands, as equals, in the reconstruction and development of the region as a whole in order to offer its people a better standard of life, social stability and peace. We are also currently renegotiating the Southern African Customs Union which provides border-free trade across the five southernmost countries of the region, namely South Africa, Lesotho, Swaziland, Botswana and Namibia.

The legacy of apartheid rule is still reflected in human anguish, social dislocation and economic underdevelopment throughout the Southern African region.

We are greatly encouraged by peaceful negotiations as regards political and social conflicts in the Southern African region. We believe that the immediate settlement of these questions will contribute hugely in the promotion of economic and security co-operation, tourism, social stability and peace in the region. The return of social and political stability to the region, we believe, will contribute to the creation of an investor-friendly climate.

We believe that our region needs a radical expansion of the frontiers of democratic participation if it is to tap the initiative and intellect of its citizens, limit any tendency towards arbitrary rule and accelerate the integration of their regional economy into the economy of the world.

I want to state with all humility, and within the context of equality and mutual respect among the countries of the Southern African region, that South Africa possesses some advantages which can make it act as a bridgehead of development in the region. For instance, our geographical location on the southernmost tip of the continent, with seaports on both the Indian and the Atlantic oceans, affords our country the possibility to function as a bridge in South–South trade and general socio-economic interaction. It also provides the possibility of bringing together, in a mutually beneficial way, the aspirations of the developing world (especially Southern Africa) and the technological and financial capacities obtainable in the developed economies of the world.

Europe is South Africa's largest trading partner. We are highly appreciative of the fact that the European Union's programme for reconstruction and development is one of the largest support programmes we have. At the same time, we are keen to see the negotiations we are soon to begin with the European Union concluded as soon as possible. Happily, all indications are that the member states of the union are interested to enter into an agreement with us which will assist in our process of reconstruction and development while taking into account the need for development throughout the region of Southern Africa.

Let me conclude by saying that a democratic, non-racial, non-sexist and prosperous South Africa is indeed a workable dream. The very convening of such an august business and finance forum is an eloquent statement that the world actually believes that South Africa is a workable dream. To the majority of our people this forum is a statement of confidence in our young democracy.

I am convinced that I speak on behalf of the majority of our people when I say that, as South Africans, we have rolled up our sleeves and are seriously getting down to work on this, so glorious a dream.

7

Alliances and Allegiances:
Rebuilding South Africa

1995 Global Cultural Diversity Conference, Sydney, Australia, 27 April 1995

WE RECOGNISE AND appreciate the sterling role that Australia and its people played in the struggle to end the apartheid crime against humanity. That sustained involvement, expressive of a common allegiance to a set of values which binds all humanity, demonstrated the possibility to agree and act upon an international agenda for change, involving not only governments and institutions, but also the ordinary citizens of all countries, including those which themselves had their own serious domestic challenges.

We say all this to make the point also that it may be that the matters you are discussing at this important conference may help all of us to evolve a common plan of action to encourage universal peace, freedom, prosperity and stability in our extremely diverse but interdependent world.

Ours is also a country characterised by a diversity of cultures and people – what President Mandela has described as a 'rainbow nation'.

It was out of a particular form of social interaction within this diversity that the system of apartheid was born. Put in other words, the all-pervasive system of racial domination in South Africa was the result of an historically evolved effort to manage this diversity. That, in the end, the United Nations (UN) characterised the system of apartheid as a crime against humanity showed the extent to which what resulted was not management but criminal mismanagement.

The question therefore arises: What went wrong?

I believe that one word is enough to answer this question, and that word is 'domination'!

From the very beginning of the process of the colonisation of South

Africa, 340 years ago, the occupying European peoples and governments sought to achieve domination over the rest of South African society. Imbued with the certainties of the seventeenth century, they saw themselves as endowed with the right to be the masters, a gift granted to them by God, a privilege accorded to them by their definition of what constituted civilisation, an imperative which attached to the colour of their skin and a prerogative dictated by the superiority of their weapons of war.

One of the consequences of the processes which resulted from this arrogance was an early terrible outcome, little mentioned in South African history, of the decimation of the Khoi and the San people, pejoratively called 'Hottentots' and 'Bushmen' by the colonisers. As a result these have ceased to exist as peoples within the territory of South Africa and can now only be found in Namibia and Botswana, perhaps representing an early example of the crime of 'ethnic cleansing'.

It is from these grim origins that the cascade of wretchedness took place which led us to the abyss of human abuse which, in the end, energised all humanity to cry out: Enough, no more! – giving birth to the extraordinary international mobilisation that led to the South African Freedom Day, which we are happy to observe and celebrate today.

Along that gloomy path stands a whole series of bollards which act as signposts of what it is that in the cumulation constitutes an explanation of what went wrong, and should therefore be avoided. On the rough face of those monuments of a past we cannot deny and which we dare not forget is inscribed a litany of the things that do not make for the free, diverse and tolerant societies to whose creation this conference is dedicated. On these signposts you will find inscribed, among others, the following record which describes our past:

- The different races cannot live together in peace unless one dominates and maintains dictatorship over the others.
- The dominant race owes it to itself to ensure that resources are distributed in a manner which benefits all who belong to that race at the expense of those whom it dominates.
- The dominated must be stripped of their self-worth, their cultures debased, their languages mocked, their histories presented as the antithesis of civilised behaviour and their value systems decried as the very expression of savagery.

- Accordingly, these, who therefore have neither culture, nor language, nor history, nor morality, should be taught to believe that they are not quite human, and persuaded by all means possible to convince themselves that their subservient position is an expression of a preordained and natural order of the human world.
- In the end, should they dare to question their condition with all that it means, they should be taught most severely that the master truly means it when he thinks and says that he has little regard for the life of him or her who is born to live and die as an underling.

In such a situation, conflict, confrontation and war were inevitable. This is a war which could have been fought until one side or the other emerged as the clear victor, capable of imposing the terms of surrender on the vanquished.

The full story of the processes and conditions which led to a negotiated resolution of the South African question, rather than a war to the finish, still remains to be told. This clearly is not the occasion when we should try out our skills as a storyteller. The point should however be made that, fundamentally, the decision by the belligerents to negotiate arose from the fact that after a protracted conflict, these belligerents arrived at a situation of what could be described as an armed equilibrium.

Neither side had defeated the other. The corollary of this, of course, is that both sides continued to dispose of sufficient strength to inflict casualties on each other, to use the language of military conflict. Equally important, each side understood clearly that because the other had these possibilities, continuation of the conflict meant that whoever sought to assume a militant posture, summarised in the slogan 'The Struggle Continues', would have to accept that they too would be severely bled and weakened, to the point where any victory they secured might very well result in them as victors having to preside over a wasteland.

I believe that we drew two important conclusions from this particular experience which became important with regard to reaching an acceptable accommodation of the different interests that are inherent in the culturally diverse societies that this conference is discussing.

One of these was that it was critically important that each of the stakeholders in our society should have the sovereign possibility and the space to identify, elaborate and propagate its interests – to place these within the complex of issues for which a regime of mutually beneficial coexistence has to be evolved.

The second of these conclusions, which derives from the first, was that all these stakeholders must accept that compromise is an inherent part of the process of arriving at what we have described as a regime of mutually beneficial coexistence of the different interests that would be put on the agenda by the different players.

To arrive at such a regime, it was however also necessary that the players agree on what colloquially could be described as 'the rules of the game'. Here we refer to the elaboration of a consensus on a set of values which then constituted the framework within which we sought to accommodate the identified and conflicting interests.

The accommodation we are talking of is, of course, what we have also designated as reconciliation. Arising from what we have already said, it is clear that the pursuit of the objective of reconciliation became one of the basic driving forces in our search for a just and lasting negotiated settlement.

I believe it would be true of all multicultural societies that peace, stability and good neighbourliness must necessarily be based on such a striving towards reconciliation.

But inevitably, because we invariably have to deal with societies in which inequality and frustrated aspirations already exist, we have to twin the concept of reconciliation with the equally critical objectives of transformation.

Certainly, in our case we could not approach the matter of reconciliation purely on the basis of the biblical injunction to love thy neighbour as thyself, as a voluntary outpouring of goodwill by a multitude of individuals who happened to be moved by the spirit. Reconciliation has and had to be based on the removal of injustice. This is precisely why, in our case, it is impossible to achieve reconciliation, an accommodation of different interests, without effecting fundamental transformation.

I believe we can now answer more directly the questions that arise from the topic we were given, namely 'Alliances and Allegiances: Rebuilding South Africa'.

Proceeding from the position that the people of our country had to achieve reconciliation on the basis of redressing past wrongs, one of the first steps we had to take was to build an allegiance of all forces around a set of values that would become part of a permanent national consensus. That set of values would necessarily have to be transformative in character.

Accordingly, to achieve political reconciliation, our starting point was the acceptance by all political and other social forces that South Africa had to be transformed into a united, non-racial, non-sexist and democratic country. Inherent in this, and arising directly from our determination to end the racial oppression and racial and ethnic divisions imposed on our people by the system of apartheid, are the concepts of national unity and nation-building which would, at the same time, recognise, respect, defend and honour the cultural diversity of this one nation.

It is a matter that remains little known that the discussion between the oppressed and the oppressor, between the advantaged and the disadvantaged, to come to an agreement about a common set of political values took no less than a decade and included extensive discussions that Nelson Mandela held with the representatives of the apartheid regime while he was in prison.

Agreement became possible because the national liberation movement, the ANC, had from its inception espoused the goal of an equitable settlement that would recognise the cultural diversity of South African society.

The very consistency of these positions over a period of three-quarters of a century of the life of the ANC at the time itself served as reassurance and, indeed, an eye-opener – that the cultural majority in our society genuinely did not seek to dominate, but was committed to a just and stable settlement responsive to the fact of the diversity of our country.

To return to our narrative, with a national allegiance around a common set of political goals having been achieved, it then became possible for all the political players to put on the agenda their various interests, without let or hindrance.

Accordingly, to give some examples, we were then able to deal with diverse issues tabled by different parties, such as federalism, what was described as the self-determination of the Zulu people on a territorial basis, what was similarly described as the self-determination of the Afrikaner people on a territorial basis, the question of property rights and a Bill of Rights, affirmative action, the place of traditional leaders in a democratic society, religion and family law, and so on.

One of the fundamental points we are trying to make is that our experience teaches us that it is impossible to bring peace and stability to divided societies unless conditions are created for democratic, open and meaningful participation by all role players, however small, in the determination of the destiny of the country. In our case, the elaboration of a national consensus on our basic political values was the outcome of such a process.

That same democratic, open and meaningful participation in the process of determining the future of our country also enables all role players, however small, to put their concerns on the national agenda. In the process of the evolution of the democratic settlement which came into force one year ago today, once more we relied not on the power of the powerful to dictate this settlement, but on engaging in a process characterised by democratic, open and meaningful participation by all, regardless of their size.

What we are trying to describe is an alliance of the people and their organised formations around the important matter of 'process' which, because it is inclusive, should lead to an outcome that enjoys legitimacy and therefore inspires the allegiance of the people as a whole. Consequently, it should follow that even those who might feel that they did not obtain what they sought in this process would nevertheless be prepared to live with this outcome.

If 'the South African miracle' has, so far, derived from our ability to build both a national allegiance to common basic goals and therefore a national alliance for change, it does not necessarily follow that in the further process of rebuilding South Africa we shall be blessed with this happy outcome.

As we proceed from the general to the particular, the challenge of allegiances and alliances will become more complex. This will bear particularly on the task of effecting fundamental transformation while persuading those who will lose their privileged positions that this is necessary in terms of a process of reconciliation that serves their interests as well.

But to return to the beginning of our argument – the struggle to deal correctly with the challenge of global cultural diversity, with its twin elements of reconciliation and transformation – we have to confront the issue of domination and counterpoise, an approach which, in politics, affirms the rights of the democratic majority while empowering the minorities.

This is an approach which would also give democratic space to all groups in multicultural societies to participate in a meaningful way in the country's policy. Such goals as participatory democracy, human rights and the recognition of cultural diversity therefore become both an end in themselves but also a precondition for peace, stability and development.

The things we have said impact on a great variety of issues. Let me mention only three.

One of these is that we can no longer describe democracy merely in terms of regular multiparty elections with the winner exercising exclusive power until the next elections. The appropriate institutions and processes have to be found to give expression to the perspective of an inclusive exercise of power by the greatest number of citizens in all their formations – both cultural and other.

The second of these is that this multiplies a millionfold the challenge of ensuring that the masses are empowered by their access to information, their capacity to inform society of their views, and their ability to participate in open debate to influence the evolution of the societies in which they should no longer be the objects but the makers of history. This has important implications with regard to the role of the media, which in many instances disempowers those to whose views, culture, values and being it is insensitive.

The third of the issues we would like to mention relates to the distribution of resources. The success we seek with regard to our own country depends not only on the opening of our democratic space to give voice to all forces that are part of our culturally diverse society. It rests also on our ability to create a situation in which there is an equitable access to material resources, both for the individual and the community, to address any sense of grievance that some are discriminated against and to work towards the situation in which the inalienable dignity of the individual is not compromised by poverty and deprivation.

Our history teaches us that to dominate is to buy short-term security and stability. It informs us that, in the end, domination and inequality invite counter-action which will also threaten the comfort of even those who are firmly mired in the certainties of seventeenth-century Europe.

We believe this to be self-evident: that neither the successful management of conflicts anywhere in the world nor the construction of the new world order can be achieved on the basis of domination.

The handmaiden that will give life to our common projects for peace and good neighbourliness is none other than that of real respect for democracy and human rights.

We have met here to discuss the important questions that are on our agenda. But we also meet to mark the fiftieth anniversary of the UN.

Perhaps the answer we seek to the challenge of global cultural diversity lies in the serious and determined implementation of the vision contained in the many serious documents which have emanated from the world body, including the Universal Declaration of Human Rights.

But, finally, that answer must surely be found in our willingness as individuals and as countries to refuse to acquiesce in the oppression, marginalisation and deprivation of any person, regardless of their cultural origin, gender, colour, race, creed, age or physical condition.

8

South Africa: A Year of Democracy

Bruno-Kreisky Forum, Vienna, Austria, 28 August 1995

THE TOPIC WE HAVE been asked to address is 'South Africa's First Year of Democracy', a year which, for us as South Africans, has been one of new challenges and exciting developments, starting with the moving inauguration of Nelson Mandela as president of the democratic Republic of South Africa and the installation of the rest of the Government of National Unity.

We could not avoid noting the fact that as we marked our first year of liberation from apartheid tyranny, the peoples of the world, and those of Europe in particular, celebrated 50 years of their own emancipation from Nazi tyranny.

Many of the architects of the apartheid system in South Africa had drawn direct inspiration from German Fascism and had sought both to advance the fortunes of the Nazis and to implement their terrible vision of race domination and tyrannical rule over our country as well.

As we marked our first anniversary of democracy, we hoped that our victory had helped to bring to its final close a period of history when it had been possible for racists to seize power, impose a system of racial and ethnic domination on the peoples, and engage in the crime of ethnic cleansing. Events in various parts of the world, including Europe, Africa and Latin America, would however suggest that our common task, to end the barbarism of the notion and practice of racial and ethnic superiority, has not yet been completed.

As a country and a people, one year after our emancipation, we continue to be confronted by the challenge of overcoming the legacy of the system of apartheid which imposed on our country:

- racial and ethnic divisions, antagonisms and mistrust;

- gross racial, gender and geographic imbalances in terms of distribution of wealth, income and opportunity;
- terrible levels of poverty;
- a stagnant and malformed economy;
- a largely illegitimate machinery of state; and
- a national budget locked into minimal capital outlays, being swallowed up mainly by consumption expenditure.

In reality, it is impossible successfully to reconstruct and develop a society afflicted with so many ills and functioning within a democratic political order, without deliberate and conscious co-operation among its main political and social players.

In our case, the stage for such deliberate and conscious co-operation was set both by the process of negotiations which resulted in an agreed process of transition to democracy, and the establishment of a Government of National Unity (GNU) which drew into a coalition government the main political players identified as such by the first democratic elections of 27 April last year.

In a sense, and without underestimating the genius of our people, we can say that in this instance, as in many others, necessity became the mother of invention.

To reflect on this matter properly, we might perhaps say that that genius consisted in the practical application of the philosophical principle that freedom is the recognition of necessity. It was in the exercise of that freedom that we elected to convene an all-party conference to negotiate our transition and agreed to form a multiparty government to preside over that transition.

The necessity to proceed in this manner resulted from the fact that neither of the main belligerents in the struggle for the future of our country achieved its principal goal of completely defeating the other. The ruling forces of apartheid failed to defeat and destroy the movement for national liberation and democracy. For their part, the latter did not succeed to overthrow the apartheid regime and seize power from it.

This situation did not result in a stalemate. Rather, it created a new, dynamic and unstable equilibrium which necessarily had to be addressed within the context of its own specifics, even as some among the contending forces might still pine or contend for a result which they had failed to accomplish.

It was a result of the practical expression of the latter consideration that throughout the process of negotiations, political violence in the country continued with varying intensity, and the negotiations themselves occasionally came to a halt, only to resume when it became clear that the equilibrium achieved at the beginning continued to hold.

I believe that even now, as the country develops in the context of a negotiated and agreed settlement, led by a GNU, we must expect that elements of co-operation and competition will continue to characterise the relations among the main players in our society.

This is an observation that we can quite easily substantiate from both a theoretical and an empirical basis.

We are, therefore, happy to advise this audience that it should not be stampeded to read crisis each time the element of competition among the leading players in our society asserts itself, even as these players continue to participate in the process of deliberate and conscious co-operation that we have spoken of.

To take this matter one step further, the argument remains yet to be substantiated as to why and under what conditions the minority parties participating in government would find it in their interest to withdraw from government, go into opposition and deny themselves the possibility to share the accolades for the success of the process of reconstruction and development which will, inevitably, make South Africa a better place to live in for all its citizens.

If we have so far been discussing questions of form, let us now turn to the important matter of content and substance.

Occupying the centre stage in this regard are the twin concepts of reconciliation and transformation. What underpinned the dynamic equilibrium we have spoken of was the common realisation that no constituency or interest would benefit from a protracted struggle that would turn our country into a wasteland of destruction, poverty and insecurity. Most of those called upon to play a role realised that nobody could lose and everybody would gain from sharing a common nationhood and joining hands to determine a shared destiny.

Of enormous importance in this regard was the fact that throughout the decades of its existence the liberation movement had consistently and unequivocally espoused the principle of non-racialism and a common South African nationhood, even in the face of the harshest forms of racial tyranny and racist bigotry and insult that the apartheid system was capable of.

Taking all these factors into account, it became obvious that national reconciliation and national unity indeed had to belong among the principal results of the resolution of the South African conflict. Without that reconciliation, the conflict and the war from which nobody would profit would never come to an end. It would never be possible to embark on a programme of reconstruction and development. Reconciliation that merely sought to reassure the former rulers by forgiving them their sins and legitimising their positions of racial privilege could never be sustained.

Similarly, and as part of the process of reconciliation, we have thought it important that human rights abuses that occurred during the struggle should be exposed and acknowledged. Accordingly, a Truth and Reconciliation Commission will be established to discover the truth about these abuses, enable those involved to obtain amnesty and those affected to receive reparation. We believe that in this way we will avoid the possibility of people seeking vengeance against those who persecuted them, and create a climate for healing of wounds and true reconciliation among those who were enemies.

But the reconciliation also had to be situated within the context of a vigorous process of transformation.

As an example, political reconciliation among the contending political forces could only be achieved on the basis of the transformation of the political order, creating the conditions in which the formerly disenfranchised could participate as equals in the new dispensation, while the formerly enfranchised lost their exclusive control of political power.

If you consider the breadth and depth of the transformation project on South African society as a whole, then you will understand the enormity of the challenge we face to transform South Africa into what our Constitution describes as a non-racial and non-sexist country.

This is so because that process of transformation must encompass everything else in addition to the political, including the economy, the public service, the security organs of the state, education and the social services, the language issue, access to resources for the promotion of arts and culture, and so on.

In this regard, consider a few statistics. The income differential between whites and Africans in our country remains in the range of 8 to 1. More than 80 per cent of the economy is controlled by the whites, who constitute 13 per cent of our population.

Between eight and nine million Africans are classified as destitute. Only 30 per cent of African women participate in the formal economy, with the majority trapped in poverty and destitution.

To change all this is going to take a gigantic effort of national will and application. If these conditions are not addressed, if the people's dream for a better life is deferred for ever, then surely must we expect that at some point in future South Africa will be torn apart by a major and catastrophic racial explosion.

It should therefore be clear why we describe reconciliation and transformation as twin elements of our process of reconstruction and development.

Transformation requires that all the major constituencies in our country should join hands in conditions of peace and stability to bring about the changes, especially the deracialisation of our society, which are the necessary prerequisites for true and permanent peace and stability. That investment in transformation itself creates the conditions for the true and permanent reconciliation we will attain when, by ceasing to define ourselves in politics and economics in terms of race, colour and ethnicity, we finally make a break with a past of three centuries of colonialism and apartheid when race and colour were a fundamental, all-encompassing condition of existence.

In a sense, what we have said so far encapsulates our experience one-and-a-quarter year after our liberation.

The process has also continued to put in place institutions of the democratic order that will further entrench and strengthen the democratic system. These include historically new institutions such as a Constitutional Court, a Human Rights Commission and the office of the Public Protector.

Legislation is also being processed which will create a Gender Commission and a Youth Commission to ensure that we deal effectively with the two important questions of the emancipation of women and youth development.

The transformation of the public service, including the security organs, is also moving apace, addressing in particular the questions of race and gender imbalance within the management echelons of this service, as well as the reorientation of the public administration so that it serves the people rather than act as an instrument for their oppression.

A distinct feature of the practice of democracy in the country has been the serious attempt to involve the people in governance as an expression of what has been described as a people-driven process, to help ensure that we achieve and maintain a national consensus with regard to all major elements of our transformation.

In this regard, we should mention the establishment of a statutory body called the National Economic Development and Labour Council, which brings together government, labour, business and the non-governmental sector in an organ which helps to develop policy on the major socio-economic issues facing our country.

As part of the same process of seeking national consensus and involving the people in governance, all major pieces of legislation have been subjected to extensive public scrutiny through consultations, carried out both by the executive and the legislature. In this regard, mention should also be made of an Open Democracy Bill that will soon be tabled to ensure the greatest possible access of the public to government information, both as a means of protecting the rights of the individual and enabling the people to impact on the process of governance.

Undoubtedly, one of the greatest challenges we have faced in this period has been the implementation of programmes that would impact directly on improving the quality of life of the people by way of the creation of new jobs, provision of housing, expanding primary health care, supplying clean water, especially in rural areas, and so on. Success in this regard rests on three principal pillars, these being the capacity of the government to generate the necessary resources, the willingness of the private sector to participate in the provision of these resources and the institutional capacity actually to implement policy.

We do not have time to dwell on the detail of this matter, save to say that 15 months on we are in a better position to achieve greater progress than has been the case to date. This is not to say nothing has happened, as various programmes have already been started, including the provision of free health care for mothers and children, school feeding, a public works programme and the supply of clean water.

Similarly, the period we are talking about has seen positive development with regard to the economy, including the growth of fixed investment, increased inflows of foreign capital and a limited advance towards the creation of new private-sector jobs.

Of great importance has been a sustained interest by the international investor community in the South African economy, as well as significant confidence in the future of the country, exemplified in part by two successful government bond issues and investment ratings issued by United States and Japanese rating companies.

We believe that it is also important that we remind ourselves of the location of South Africa in the region of Southern Africa and the African continent.

Our region, for many years affected by wars of liberation, civil wars and a campaign of aggression and destabilisation by apartheid South Africa, is moving towards establishing peace for itself.

The last country in the region in which the guns have finally been silenced is Angola. Our region as a whole is keenly interested that the Angolan peace agreement be implemented in full as soon as possible. Among other things, we look forward to the completion of the deployment of United Nations Angola Verification Mission (UNAVEM) personnel to assist the government and people of Angola finally to bring peace to a country which has suffered greatly as a result of armed conflict which has persisted for over two decades.

The point should also be made that the region of Southern Africa is also characterised by the establishment of democratic systems in all our countries, with successful multiparty elections having taken place in at least seven countries in the region in the last 18 months, the next one being due in Tanzania in October.

The countries of the region continue to strengthen the relations among themselves in various areas, including the political, economic and security fields. Even as we speak, a summit meeting of the 11 member states of the Southern African Development Community (SADC) is taking place in South Africa, hosted by President Mandela.

The processes bode well for the region, which has already been able to take joint action to begin clearing the considerable number of illegal weapons that are available in various countries and to deal with the problem of drugs that are being brought into the region from various parts of the world.

One of the important events that have occurred in the period since our liberation was the beginning of discussions between SADC and the European Union in a conference held in Berlin last June to look at the question of region-to-region co-operation between these two entities.

The period since the liberation of South Africa has confirmed the importance of Southern Africa in terms of making a contribution to ending what has been described as 'afro-pessimism', according to which the larger part of the continent is seen as an area afflicted by endemic conflict, permanent underdevelopment and military rule.

The reality of the region is that it is transforming itself into a zone of peace, building stable democratic systems, positioning itself productively to exploit its considerable human and natural resources, and organising itself to make a contribution to the challenge of peace, democracy, development and stability in the rest of our continent.

We firmly believe that Austria, which for decades took sides in favour of independence and a democratic Southern Africa, will continue to maintain its interest and involvement in our country and region because there is concentrated a process of development in which you, as Austrians, are surely interested, namely:

- the creation of non-racial societies in an area which has known the worst excesses of racism;
- the construction of a future of peace in an area which has had to experience war over a protracted period;
- the strengthening of economic growth and development in a region which knows very well the experience of famine for millions of people; and
- the building of relations of friendship, co-operation and solidarity in a region which has known aggression and destabilisation emanating from within the region.

One year after its emancipation, South Africa is proud to play its own humble role in these developments and looks forward to your support in the struggle to sustain the miracle of the transformation, not only of South Africa, but of our region as a whole.

9

South Africa: Two Nations

Statement at the opening of the debate on reconciliation and nation-building, National Assembly, Cape Town, 29 May 1998

THE 1993 CONSTITUTION of the Republic of South Africa ends with an epilogue entitled 'National Unity and Reconciliation'. Among other things, it says:

> This Constitution provides an historic bridge between the past of a deeply divided society characterised by strife, conflict, untold suffering and injustice, and a future founded on the recognition of human rights, democracy and peaceful coexistence and development opportunities for all South Africans, irrespective of colour, race, class, belief or sex.

It continues:

> The pursuit of national unity, the wellbeing of all South African citizens and peace require reconciliation between the people of South Africa and the reconstruction of society.

For its part, the 1996 Constitution of the Republic of South Africa has a preamble which, among other things, says:

> We, the people of South Africa, recognise the injustices of our past ... [and] believe that South Africa belongs to all who live in it, united in our diversity.
> We therefore ... adopt this Constitution as the supreme law of the Republic so as to heal the divisions of the past ... [and] to improve the quality of life of all citizens and free the potential of each person.

In its 'Founding Provisions', this Constitution also says that our republic has as one of its values 'commitment to promote non-racialism and non-sexism'.

I believe that as we discuss the issue of national unity and reconciliation today, we will have to do a number of things.

The first of these, to which I am certain we will all respond in the same manner, is that we should commit ourselves to the pursuit of the objectives contained in the two constitutions for a democratic South Africa.

The second is that we will have to answer the question honestly as to whether we are making the requisite progress:

- to create a non-racial society;
- to build a non-sexist country;
- to heal the divisions of the past;
- to achieve the peaceful coexistence of all our people;
- to create development opportunities of all South Africans, irrespective of colour, race, class, belief or sex; and
- to improve the quality of life for all citizens.

Thirdly, we will have to answer the question, again as honestly as we can, as to:

- whether our actions have been and are based on the recognition of the injustices of the past and
- whether our actions have genuinely sought to promote the integrated constitutional objectives of:
  - national unity;
  - the wellbeing of all South Africans;
  - peace;
  - reconciliation between the people of South Africa; and
  - the reconstruction of society.

In the light of these prescriptions contained in the two constitutions to which I have referred, let me declare some of the matters to which the government I represent is committed.

We are interested that, as a people, we move as rapidly and as consistently as possible to transform South Africa into a non-racial country.

We are interested that our country lives up to its constitutional commitment to transform itself into a non-sexist society.

We are interested that together, as South Africans, we adopt the necessary steps that will eradicate poverty in our country as quickly as possible and in all its manifestations, to end the dehumanisation of millions of our people, which inevitably results from the terrible deprivation to which so many, both black and white, are victim.

We are interested that we must deal with our political past, honestly, frankly and without equivocation, so that the purposes for which most of us agreed to establish the Truth and Reconciliation Commission (TRC) are achieved.

We are interested that our country responds to the call to rally to a new patriotism, as a result of which we can all agree to a common national agenda, which would include:

- a common fight to eradicate the legacy of apartheid;
- a united offensive against corruption and crime;
- concerted action to advance the interests of those least capable to defend themselves, including children, women, the disabled and the elderly;
- an agreement about how we should protect and advance the interests of all the different cultural, language and religious groups that make up the South African population;
- a commitment to confront the economic challenges facing our country in a manner that simultaneously addresses issues of high and sustained growth, and raising the living standards of especially the black poor;
- an all-embracing effort to build a sense of common nationhood and a shared destiny, as a result of which we can entrench into the minds of all our people the understanding that however varied their skin complexions, cultures and life conditions, the success of each nevertheless depends on the effort the other will make to turn into reality the precept that each is his or her brother's or sister's keeper; and
- a united view of our country's relations with the rest of the world.

We believe that these are the issues we must address when we speak of reconciliation and nation-building. They stand at the centre of the very future of South Africa as the home of a stable democracy, human rights, equality, peace, stability and a shared prosperity.

Accordingly, we must attend to the question whether, with regard to all these issues and at all times, all of us behave in a manner which promotes the achievement of the goals we have mentioned, and therefore take us forward towards the realisation of the objectives of reconciliation and nation-building, without which the kind of South Africa visualised in our Constitution will most certainly not come into being.

So must we also pose the questions: What is nation-building? and Is it happening?

With regard to the first of these, our own response would be that nation-building is the construction of the reality and the sense of common nationhood which would result from the abolition of disparities in the quality of life among South Africans based on the racial, gender and geographic inequalities we all inherited from the past.

The second question we posed is: Are we making the requisite progress towards achieving the objective of nation-building, as we have just defined it?

If we elected to answer this question in a polite and reassuring manner, we would answer: Yes, we are making the requisite progress.

However, I believe that perhaps we should answer this question honestly and deal with the consequences of an honest response, however discomfiting it may be. Accordingly, our answer to the question whether we are making that requisite progress towards achieving the objective of nation-building, as we defined it, would be: No!

A major component part of the issue of reconciliation and nation-building is defined by and derives from the material conditions in our society which have divided our country into two nations, the one black and the other white.

We therefore make bold to say that South Africa is a country of two nations.

One of these nations is white, relatively prosperous, regardless of gender or geographic dispersal. It has ready access to a developed economic, physical, educational, communication and other infrastructure. This enables it to argue that, except for the persistence of gender discrimination against women, all members of this nation have the possibility to exercise their right to equal opportunity, the development opportunities to which the Constitution of 1993 committed our country.

The second and larger nation of South Africa is black and poor, with the worst affected being women in the rural areas, the black rural population in general and the disabled. This nation lives under conditions of a grossly underdeveloped economic, physical, educational, communication and other infrastructure. It has virtually no possibility to exercise what in reality amounts to a theoretical right to equal opportunity, with that right being equal within this black nation only to the extent that it is equally incapable of realisation.

This reality of two nations, underwritten by the perpetuation of the racial, gender and spatial disparities born of a very long period of colonial and apartheid white minority domination, constitutes the material base which reinforces the notion that, indeed, we are not one nation, but two nations.

And neither are we becoming one nation. Consequently, also, the objective of national reconciliation is not being realised.

It follows as well that the longer this situation persists, in spite of the gift of hope delivered to the people by the birth of democracy, the more entrenched will be the conviction that the concept of nation-building is a mere mirage and that no basis exists, or will ever exist, to enable national reconciliation to take place.

Over the years, and this includes the period before the elections of 1994, we have put forward and sustained the position that the creation of the material conditions that would both underpin and represent nation-building and reconciliation could only be achieved over a protracted period of time.

I would like to reaffirm this position. The abolition of the apartheid legacy will require considerable effort over a considerable period of time.

We are neither impressed nor moved by self-serving arguments which seek to suggest that four or five years are long enough to remove from our national life the inheritance of a country of two nations which is as old as the arrival of European colonists in our country almost 350 years ago.

Let me digress briefly and say something about the ongoing progress of German unification.

As the honourable members are aware, the two post-war German states united into one country in 1990. After 45 years of division into two states with competing social systems, the German leaders and people understood that, truly to become one country and one people, they too, like ourselves, would have to address the central questions of national unity and reconciliation. This was despite the fact that here we speak of a people who share the same language, colour and culture.

The seriousness with which the German people treated that process of the promotion of German national unity and reconciliation is reflected, among other things, by the extraordinary volume of resources which the richer, developed West Germany transferred to the poorer and relatively underdeveloped East Germany.

During the first five years of unification after 1990, $586,5 billion of public funds were transferred from West Germany to East Germany to underwrite Germany's project of national unity and reconciliation. This exceeded East German tax revenues for the same period by a factor of 4,5 to 1.

Further to illustrate the enormity of this effort, these transfers amount to 75 times the size of the national budget which this House is currently debating.

To help finance this extraordinary expenditure, a 7,5 per cent surcharge on individual income tax was imposed in 1991 and extended in 1995 for an unspecified period of time. Correctly and interestingly, this was designated a 'solidarity tax'.

It might also be of interest to note that despite the huge flow of German public and private funds into the east, at the end of this first five-year period, per capita income in the east still amounted to 74 per cent of income in the western part of the country.

In our case, the reality is that in the last five years the national budget has in real terms increased by a mere 10 per cent. In other words, to all intents and purposes, taking into account the increase in population, we are spending the same volume of money to address the needs of the entirety of our population as were disbursed to address the needs of essentially the white minority before the democratic transition.

Our own 'solidarity tax' was imposed for one year only, accompanied by much grumbling from some sectors of our society.

Before we digressed to Germany, we were making the point that four or five years are not enough to weld the two nations which coexist in South Africa as a consequence of a long period of the existence of a society based on racism.

To respond to all of this, in conceptual terms we have to deal with two interrelated elements. The first of these is that we must accept that it will take time to create the material base for nation-building and reconciliation. The second and related element is that we must therefore agree that it is the subjective factor, accompanied by tangible progress in the creation of the new material base, which must take the lead in sustaining the hope and conviction among the people that the project of reconciliation and nation-building will succeed.

Given the critical importance of the subjective factor, therefore, we must return to the question we posed earlier during this intervention. That question is: Are we all, as the various parties in this Parliament and our society at large, behaving in a manner which promotes the objective of reconciliation and nation-building, without which the kind of South Africa visualised in our Constitution will most certainly not come into being?

Again, my own answer to this question would be a very definite: No!

Clearly, it would be irresponsible for me to make such a statement without substantiating it. Let me therefore cite openly some of the interventions or non-interventions which, over the last four years, have not helped to move us more speedily towards the attainment of the objective of reconciliation and nation-building.

Unlike the German people, we have not made the extra effort to generate the material resources we have to invest to change the condition of the black poor more rapidly than is possible if we depend solely on severely limited public funds, whose volume is governed by the need to maintain certain macro-economic balances and the impact of a growing economy.

What this throws up, inevitably, is the question: Are the relatively rich, who as a result of an apartheid definition are white, prepared to help underwrite the upliftment of the poor, who as a result of an apartheid definition are black?

If we are serious about national unity and reconciliation and treat the obligations contained in our Constitution as more than words on paper, we have to answer this question practically.

The South African Revenue Service (SARS) is engaged in a difficult struggle to ensure that every individual and corporate entity meets its tax obligations. I am informed that so far SARS has established that something in the order of 30 per cent of our corporations are not registered for tax purposes. These are people who, by honouring their legal obligations, could make an important contribution to addressing the material challenges of national unity and reconciliation. They deliberately choose not to but will not hesitate to proclaim that the government has failed to 'deliver'.

Many of us in this House find it very easy each time we speak to demand that the government must spend more on this and that and the other. At the same time, we make passionate demands that taxes must be cut and the budget deficit reduced.

The constant and, in some instances, dishonest refrain for more funds, in many instances incanted for party political gain, re-emerges in our streets as when, only a few days ago, public sector workers marched behind posters which bore the words 'Give Us More', 'Give Us More'.

In the majority of cases, the call for the transformation of both public and private sector institutions and organisations, in particular to address the issue of racial representativity, has been resisted with great determination.

Indeed, one of the issues of great agitation in our politics is the question of affirmative action. To ensure that it does not happen, some of what is said is that 'black advancement equals a white brain drain' and 'black management in the public service equals inefficiency, corruption and a lowering of standards'.

In many instances, correctly to refer to the reality that our past determines the present is to invite protests and ridicule even as it is perfectly clear that no solution to many current problems can be found unless we understand their historical origins. By this means, it comes about that those who were responsible for or were beneficiaries of the past absolve themselves from any obligation to help do away with an unacceptable legacy.

The current situation suggests that the TRC will be unable to complete its work, especially with regard to the full disclosure and attribution of many acts of gross human rights violations. This will leave the law enforcement agencies with no choice but to investigate all outstanding cases of such violations, making it inevitable that our society continues to be subject to tensions which derive from the conflicts of the past.

Some in our country, including some who serve within the security forces, are prepared to go to any length to oppose the democratic order, including the assassination of leaders and destabilisation by all means. These include the now well-known allegation of the involvement of former freedom fighters in plans to carry out a *coup d'état*, as well as other disinformation campaigns which the intelligence services are investigating, involving allegations that Minister Mufamadi is involved in the cash-in-transition robberies, while Deputy Minister Kasrils and myself are responsible for the murder of white farmers.

Last week I mentioned in the House the negative impact of such events as the recent appearance of the president of the Republic in court, the South African Rugby Football Union saga and the matter of the appointment of the deputy judge president of the Natal bench.

I am certain that many of us can cite several examples of interventions which have not contributed to the goal of national unity and reconciliation, including the numerous instances of resistance to pieces of legislation which seek to transform our country away from its apartheid past.

And yet we must make the point that the overwhelming majority of our people have neither abandoned this goal nor lost hope that it will be realised. An important contributory factor to this is that there are indeed significant numbers of people in our society, including people among the white and Afrikaner community, who by word and deed have demonstrated a real commitment to the translation of the vision of national unity and reconciliation into reality.

Again last week, in this House, I said that much of what is happening in our country which pushes us away from achieving this goal is producing rage among millions of people. I am convinced that we are faced with the danger of a mounting rage to which we must respond seriously.

In a speech, again in this House, we quoted the African-American poet Langston Hughes, when he wrote, 'what happens to a dream deferred?'

His conclusion was that it explodes.

PART THREE

Transition, Strategy and Priorities

THE SEVEN SPEECHES comprising this section tie in with those of the previous section. The main thrust of Mbeki's thinking on the issues of transition, strategy and priorities is provided by a speech from 1995, 'A National Strategic Vision for South Africa', in which Mbeki the visionary and strategist takes the podium.

A central theme in this section is Mbeki's emphasis on the need for a national consensus on specified priorities. It is important to note that his occupation with the need for such a consensus is not driven by motives of power or an attempt to bolster the political fortunes of the ANC as a party. What he hopes to achieve is the elevation of certain pressing problems above the party-political scene, getting them recognised as national challenges.

In fact, he goes a step further by linking the need for a national strategic vision to principles embodied in the Constitution.

Mbeki is a devoted constitutionalist. His speeches reflect his commitment to the Constitution as the highest law of the land.

Two speeches in the present section deserve special mention. The one deals with transforming the economy and was delivered in 1995 at the annual banquet of the South African Chamber of Business. The other, presented in 1998 at a convention of the South African Property Owners' Association, treats equity within the property market. These speeches reflect Mbeki's thinking on the economy and his ideas on socio-economic equity.

His strong commitment to socio-economic equity is also manifested in his speech entitled 'Confronting Racism in Our Thinking', delivered at the banquet of the *Cape Times* in 1996.

10

A National Strategic
Vision for South Africa

Address to the Development Planning Summit, hosted by the Intergovernmental Forum, Pretoria, 27 November 1995

AT HIS INAUGURATION in May 1994, President Mandela declared: 'We have at last achieved our political emancipation. We pledge ourselves to liberate all our people from the continuing bondage of poverty, deprivation, suffering, gender and other discrimination.' In *Long Walk to Freedom*, he wrote: 'I have taken a moment here to rest, to steal a view of the glorious vista that surrounds me, to look back on the distance I have come. But I can rest only for a moment, for with freedom come responsibilities, and I dare not linger, for my long walk is not yet ended.'[29]

As South Africans, we have all taken part in the long walk. We all need a space to survey our journey so far, and to absorb the view. And though we have come from diverse starting points, our future destiny is together. As we pause for breath and consult the map, our challenge is to find the common path ahead. And we must start by agreeing on our destination.

As governments and economies globalise, no national state can plan rigidly and precisely for the future. We cannot predict exchange rates or oil prices in 25 years. We can, however, ask one simple question: Do we have a common vision to guide our actions?

Proverbs 29:18 in the Old Testament warns us: 'Where there is no vision, the people perish.' And we are further advised by the prophets, in Habakuk 2:2: 'Write the vision and make it plain, that they who read it may run ... the reckless will lack an assured future.' In our discussions today we must ensure that our actions over the coming months, however well intentioned, will not be reckless, and through adopting a common vision we must do our utmost to assure our peoples' future.

But first let us pause to survey our journey thus far.

In the Interim Constitution we entrenched basic rights and liberties, national unity and equality, the rule of law, accountability and transparency of government, and freedom of expression and association. Our reintegration into the global community has normalised our relations with our neighbours in Southern Africa and presented new opportunities and challenges in international trade.

The Reconstruction and Development Programme (RDP) established a unique national consensus on the need for prosperity, democracy, human development and the removal of poverty. However, despite its almost biblical character, the RDP base document did not provide us with all the answers. We have always known that its many, many priorities and programmes need to be distilled into a series of realistic steps, guided by a long-term vision and our resource constraints.

This distillation process is not straightforward. It started with the policy reviews which have been undertaken by most national departments and the development planning which is under way in the provinces. This has exposed the particular challenges facing each sector and area of our country.

As the particular constraints and opportunities became clearer, we recognised the urgency of setting a clear framework to guide our decision-making. And so in the RDP White Paper we said: 'Government will co-ordinate the development of a national strategic framework. This will set out a long-term vision, which includes goals and critical success factors, macro-economic and expenditure guidelines, and priority focus areas. The framework will set parameters on what must be done, define inter-governmental relationships, and set guidelines for the utilisation of government resources.'

We also said: 'Provinces will have to work out a rolling three-year programme and an annual business and spatial plan.' Through participation in the Forum for Effective Planning and Development, most provinces have now produced initial perspectives which identify the key issues and constraints. These will feed into our national vision and will form a sound basis for provincial strategies.

Our six-pack of critical measures announced in November 1994, and the cabinet *bosberaad* [workshop in the bush] in January of this year identified the most urgent short-term priorities for the government.

Before we look ahead, it is important to recognise a number of imperatives in the current environment.

First is the challenge of unemployment and poverty. We need to ensure that every strategy and action we decide on has as its starting point the need to tackle this momentous task.

Second is our trade opportunity with the European Union. Our export capacity will be a critical component of our growth path, and we have a particular window of opportunity to take advantage of the European market. Some economists believe that maximum penetration of the European market was the deciding factor in the economic success of the East Asian Tigers. And trade is not just in goods, but also people. Increased and innovative tourism presents a major opportunity for growth and development.

Third is the challenge posed by AIDS. Recent studies in a number of African countries suggest that, at current rates of infection, AIDS will be one of the major impediments to sustained growth and prosperity. The scale of our own problem is only just becoming known and requires serious attention and action.

Fourth is our need to ensure that we are investor friendly. The confidence which exists in our political system and economy has not been matched by high levels of fixed domestic and inward investment. Our many comparative advantages need to be better marketed and understood both at home and around the world. In addition, we need to implement simple mechanisms to facilitate investment, such as the proposed national one-stop investment centre, which has been agreed by Cabinet, linked to economic development units in provinces and local authorities.

Fifth is the role of information in the global economy. Knowledge is increasingly recognised as a valuable resource, and effective information collection and dissemination has become a defining feature of the economy. The information superhighway can enable us to further our development needs in a new way and to empower our citizenry through a two-way exchange of information.

Sixth is the concern about the speed of delivery. During the winter the media began to suggest that the RDP was failing to deliver. In fact, we knew that the lead times in our projects and the fundamental transitions in many of our institutions would mean that the RDP projects could not materialise overnight. Over the past three months we have seen major progress with the Presidential Lead Projects and we have turned the tide of media criticism. We must now ensure that this pace of delivery is sustained and communicated.

Seventh is the work under way within the National Economic Development and Labour Council to formulate an accord of growth and development between government and our social partners. It is crucial that our long-term vision informs this accord.

Finally we must recognise the danger of fragmentation. In our race to meet all the challenges and ensure visible progress, we have not always made time to examine our priorities. We must guard against unrealistic wish lists by picking out the critical success factors. We must take the time to ensure that each department, province and local authority develops compatible policies and plans. We cannot afford to waste resources through contradictory actions.

Now that we have paused to survey our journey so far and looked at the current environment, we are able to turn our attention to the future.

We have said that we need to agree on a vision to guide our future actions. And that is our business today. In other words, today's meeting provides us with an opportunity to review our progress and agree on our future direction.

Let us dwell for a moment on what we have to achieve during the day.

First, we must agree on the central pillars of our Growth and Development Strategy.

Second, we should begin to establish realistic targets, based on current information. These are the basis of our vision.

Third, we must commit that all future policies, plans and activities will contribute to the vision.

Fourth, we must ask our directors-general to produce a more detailed Growth and Development Strategy by February 1996. This strategy will guide the allocation of public sector resources in the budget, spatially and sectorally. It will also guide personnel planning and will provide a framework for private sector investment. In order to guide the 1997/1998 budget process, departments must finish this work in time for us to finalise the Growth and Development Strategy by February 1996.

Let us start with the vision itself.

The RDP identifies *growth with development* as the South African growth path. That is, economic growth cannot be separated from the need to reduce poverty and improve the quality of life. Development resources should be allocated in ways that optimise economic growth aspects. For instance, programmes to provide new infrastructure should also foster local production, employment, innovation and regional trade and should aim to reduce spatial inefficiencies. Economic expansion is a result of and a means to share wealth more evenly amongst our people. High growth will permit us to achieve much greater equity in incomes and raise living standards for all.

To succeed, this strategy requires that every government department – national, provincial and local – review its policies to ensure that they align with the national strategic vision and the national Growth and Development Strategy.

We can already define the six pillars of our Growth and Development Strategy. They are not new. In fact, they have emerged by clustering the key areas identified in departmental and provincial policies and plans. Their power is their simplicity. Although not every issue of importance to every department is covered explicitly, these pillars aim to encompass and crystallise all our work. They are as follows:

- investing in people, especially the poor majority, as the productive and creative core of the economy;
- creating employment on a massive scale, while building a powerfully competitive South African and Southern African economy;
- investment in household and economic infrastructure, both to facilitate growth and to improve the quality of life for the poor;
- a national crime prevention strategy to protect the livelihood of our people, secure the wealth of the country and promote investment;
- building efficient and effective government as a responsive instrument of delivery and empowerment, able to serve all South Africans while directing government resources primarily to meet the needs of the poor majority; and
- welfare safety nets which aim to draw the poorest and most vulnerable groups progressively into the mainstream of the economy and society.

On the basis of these pillars, we are able to set medium-term cross-sectoral targets. These targets are not set in stone, and we may need to review them as we gather information and develop more detailed strategies. However, they provide an important collective yardstick against which to measure the outputs of all government programmes. Moreover, they permit the public to monitor our progress.

We must now quantify these targets. It is essential to put in numbers and time frames which challenge us and the whole society. Once we have completed the October 1996 census and analysed the results, we may need to further review the targets. However, we can already begin to use the draft targets to evaluate all our programmes.

Finally, the vision recognises the need for a stable macro-economic framework for employment creation and growth. Monetary policy will combine with supply-side measures, including reforms to improve agricultural productivity, to hold down inflation. We will finalise a policy on the value of the rand to maintain our international competitiveness. Exchange controls will be steadily removed to achieve the aim of attracting increased long-term capital inflows to supplement domestic savings. The government will specify clear targets for deficit reduction by the year 2000.

We believe that this vision provides the basis to critically refocus all our efforts. The key now is to develop coherent strategies in all departments and provinces which support the vision and contribute tangibly to its targets. This will mean proposing that certain existing programmes be phased out to free up resources for the new priorities. The directors-general must prioritise this work to complete it by February. In the meantime the directors-general will report on their progress to the Ad Hoc Presidential Committee on Growth and the Intergovernmental Forum.

In closing, let me say that none of this will be possible unless we have efficient, effective and accountable government. Our fundamental challenge, then, is to construct a truly developmental state. International experience demonstrates that government driven by a vision and measured by results is far more effective than a rule-governed state. In addition, government which is empowered at all levels and which is able to ensure the active participation of citizens in decision-making is critical. Finally, government must be enterprising. If our efforts are constrained by the extensive system of rules we have inherited, we will achieve nothing. We must replace any unnecessary regulations with clear objectives and performance measures.

Thus the fundamental role of our vision – which I might call 'South Africa 2020' – is to unleash the creativity of our people in government and throughout South African society.

In the words of US General George Patton: 'Never tell people how to do things. Establish what you want to achieve and they will surprise you with their ingenuity.'[30]

11

Our Common Vision:
A Non-racial and Non-sexist Democracy

Address to the National Assembly on the occasion of the budget vote for the office of the deputy president of the majority party, Cape Town, 22 September 1994

A VERY HUMAN AND anti-racist cry resonates throughout and dominates the drama contained in Shakespeare's *Merchant of Venice*.

That cry is expressed in the vexed words of the merchant of Venice, Shylock the Jew, who says of Antonio:

> [He hath] laughed at my losses, mocked at my gains, scorned my nation, thwarted my bargains, cooled my friends, heated my enemies. And what's his reason? I am a Jew.

And then he asks:

> Hath not a Jew eyes? Hath not a Jew hands, organs, dimensions, senses, affections, passions, fed with the same food, hurt with the same weapons, subject to the same diseases, healed by the same means, warmed and cooled by the same winter and summer, as a Christian is?
> If you prick us, do we not bleed? If you tickle us, do we not laugh? If you poison us, do we not die?

And ominously he adds:

> And if you wrong us, shall we not revenge? If we are like you in the rest, we will resemble you in that... The villainy you teach me I will execute; and it shall go hard but I will better the instruction.

87

I, like the majority of the members of this House, am born of the African and black majority of the people of our country. Because of that, I, together with that majority, found and find a coincidence of voice, of sentiment and of outrage with Shylock the Jew.

At the time, which to the forgiving mind seems so distant now, but which is part of our continuing reality, when race defined everybody's place in South African society, we too asked these questions of those who had the power of life and death over our people: Hath not a black person hands, organs, dimensions, senses, affections, passions... If you prick us, do we not bleed? If you tickle us, do we not laugh? If you poison us, do we not die?

Those who had the authority of state power and the mandate of armed force to make us bleed did indeed deign to answer the questions we posed.

They deigned to answer because so confident were they of the incontrovertible truth of their bigotry and the science of their superstitions!

They took time out to answer because so convinced were they of the actual being of the delusion that they spoke in the name of the creator of all things!

And to us they said that we who bled should indeed bleed.

They proclaimed that the colour of our skins, the shape of our noses, the thickness of our lips and the texture of our hair bespoke an animal form which they judged was not yet, not quite, not theologically human.

Thus they decreed, because they knew that they were the arbiters who had been accorded the right to decide who shall live and who shall die, and who shall be placed where in a descending or an ascending order in the supposed gradation from the ape to the human.

I say all this not to dredge up the past but to draw our attention and to indicate the tasks we face together with regard to the present challenges confronting all of us who sit in this chamber.

These are challenges that we should confront together, in confirmation of the correctness of the decision we took in the negotiation process that, for the first five years of the transition, we must govern the country together.

For we all did, in our various ways and at different paces, decide that we should turn our backs on racism and racial domination.

We assume it to be true that whatever might separate us as different parties, our loyalty to our country's Constitution binds us to the common vision of the creation of a non-racial and non-sexist democracy.

We must assume it to be true that all of us volunteered to serve in the capacities in which we serve because we thought we could contribute a little to the creation of the humane society which must surely be the purpose and definition of good governance.

We are at the beginning of the protracted process that will lead to the creation of that society. Each one of us, as individuals and as parties, has a contribution to make. We are all entitled to expect that when the record is tabulated, we shall each be judged as having been joint architects in the making of a glorious future. Whether that will, in fact, be the case for each one of us, time shall, without mercy, make its own finding!

Despite the welcome reality of the existence of our democratic and non-racial legislatures and executive structures, the fact is that the society over which we exercise the powers of government is one that is deeply enmeshed in its past. To take it forward, we must extricate it from that past of race and gender discrimination and oppression, of the marginalisation of its youth and of inadequate care and concern for the needs and demands of the handicapped and of our mature citizens.

As this Parliament and as the government that is drawn from among its members, we must measure the success efforts by the progress we record in building the non-racial, non-sexist, democratic and humane society which the Constitution mandates and obliges us to create.

All our parties and all of us as members of Parliament shall be judged by the people as having been good or bad or of no meaning, not by our eloquence in this chamber, nor by our agility in parliamentary debate nor yet by the skill with which we outsmart our real or imagined opponents.

We shall be found to have been good or bad or of no meaning by the extent to which we use the positions of power which we occupy, actually to improve the quality of life of all our people.

What is easy to say about non-racialism, non-sexism and a better life for all may not be as easy to achieve. And yet our integrity, judged on the basis of the honesty of our declarations, must in the end be tested against what we do in practice.

One of the institutions available to the country to create that humane society is the public service in all its elements.

As President Nelson Mandela has said and as we all agreed, including the civil servants themselves, we desire that the public service should be dedicated to serving the public good, that it should be sensitive to the needs of the citizenry and that it should be composed in a manner that reflects the make-up of our society.

The reality is that the public service, like so much else in South African society, continues to reflect our apartheid past. The pursuit of non-racialism and non-sexism demands that it should be changed. We must of necessity build this into our thinking and our comprehension: that change cannot be carried out without pain to some. The replacement of a white, male director-general by one that is black and female may indeed be an unpleasant experience to the outgoing incumbent. But the question must be asked: How else shall we produce a representative leadership of the civil service if we do not go through such processes? The questions must also be asked: When will it be the right time to begin these processes? and With what speed should they be executed?

We must also guard against the elevation of such concepts as stability and continuity to the position where they become guiding beacons which lead us nowhere except to the maintenance of an unjust *status quo*.

Similarly, the phenomenon of uncertainty should not be imposed on our thinking as a scarecrow that frightens us away from embarking on a journey of change. All genuine change must, by definition, produce uncertainty. But without change all social organisms atrophy and die. In our case, absence of change will inevitably lead to a destructive explosion.

The act of leadership we are all called upon to exercise is the management of change and not the conservation of the past. It therefore becomes necessary that, as individuals and as parties, we contextualise whatever position we take with regard to any specific act or action and measure its correctness by the degree to which it contributes to the social transformation that is visualised in the Constitution. As such parties, we represent different constituencies, each one as entitled as any other to enjoy the benefits that will derive from the better society we seek to build.

A particular responsibility rests on those who see themselves as being the representatives of the advantaged sections of our population to continue to play a decisive role as change agents within these privileged sectors of our society. The point needs to be made clearly that the guarantee of a better life for these sectors as well depends not only on their acceptance of the necessity for change, but also on their active involvement in bringing about the transformation that our society cries out for, as well as the avoidance of the use of the levers of power in their hands to block the process of change.

We must also accept the corollary that those among us who represent the disadvantaged sections of our people have a similar responsibility to mobilise our constituencies to understand and accept that despite the legitimacy and justice of the demands of the deprived, we have inherited a society which does not necessarily have the means to meet all those demands today.

This is a situation which calls for a balance of sacrifices, including by us who have the honour to sit in this House, to underwrite a sustainable process of change for the better. Success requires that we depart radically from any notion that what must predominate in our thinking is addressing the needs of the haves and decrying the efforts of the have-nots to put their concerns on the national agenda.

In the end, the government, together with the public service trade unions and associations in particular, must elaborate a comprehensive plan and programme focused on the transformation of the structures of governance so that they do indeed become expressive of the vision of the just society to which we must give birth.

It is the acceptance of a transparent, predictable, practical and implementable process of change which will introduce certainty and stability, and not an illusory absence of change.

An exciting and rewarding act of creation, which must inspire all of us with hope and confidence in our future rather than despair and fear in the face of change, lies ahead of us. It is a project which I trust all parties in this House will welcome with great enthusiasm.

A better life for all demands this.

Similar observations can and should be made about property relations in the country. The House needs no educating about the yawning and unacceptable race and gender inequalities in our country with regard to distribution of wealth, income and opportunities. It is self-evident that the objective we pursue of the creation of a non-racial and

91

non-sexist society cannot be achieved outside the struggle to address these disparities.

The fact that the trade union movement has put so firmly on the collective bargaining agenda the issue of racism in the workplace should serve as sufficient warning that the non-racial transformation cannot be confined merely to the political sphere but must encompass the economic as well. The outstanding challenge lies not in the description of existing reality but in answering the question: What is to be done?

In the recent period, the economic debate in the country has been dominated by various matters such as public finances, foreign exchange issues, inflation, interest rates, the international competitiveness of industry and so on.

There is no gainsaying the fact that these are legitimate matters which we must address successfully. But equally, we must bring back to the centre of the public debate the issue of the more equitable distribution of wealth, income and opportunity, focusing in particular on the questions of ending racial and gender discrimination in our society.

The matter of creating opportunities for the vigorous and sustained development of small and medium enterprises cannot be treated as a mere sop to silence the voice of essentially the black entrepreneurs, who demand to enter the economy as other than workers, consumers and minority participants in the retail sector. In this regard, we face the added reality that it is now internationally accepted that to address the issue of job creation, which is a central element of the reconstruction and development of our country, we have to depend on small and medium businesses, understanding that large, capital-intensive enterprises have a different role to play.

Once again, the government, together with the corporate world and the unions, will have to elaborate and implement our detailed policies to address these matters. Over time this must result, among other things, in changing the structure of ownership of productive property and increasing competition within the South African economy, away from its domination by a handful of conglomerates.

Similar considerations bear on the issue of access to and the use of productive land. An element of redistribution in this regard is necessary, desirable and inevitable. This impacts on many issues, including addressing the historic injustice of land dispossession, the betterment and emancipation of women, reducing poverty, ensuring rural development, changing the relationship between the town and the countryside, and attending to the challenge of rural-urban migration.

In both these instances, relating to the economy in general and the land question in particular, the reality is that centuries of a particular history produced a particular system of property relations which benefit some and discriminate against others.

And yet the point needs to be understood that once more it is in the interest of those who were advantaged by the past actively to participate in processes that impact on themselves to ensure that they help to achieve a more equitable spread of ownership, income and opportunity.

Clearly, the government would want to enter into a constructive dialogue on these matters with those who own productive property and land. To the extent that it is possible, this would ensure a united and concerted approach to the matters we have raised.

If we can, we must together manage the process of change rather than allow ourselves to be imprisoned by a *status quo* whose perpetuation can only lead to disaster.

Once more we come back to the issue of our separate and collective responsibilities as the political leadership of all the people of our country. More than in any other area of social existence, it is perhaps in this that we have to try hardest to avoid the temporary ovations where such approval postpones the confrontation of the challenge on our doorstep of dealing with the creation of a more equitable socio-economic order.

In the immediate past, other contentious questions have been raised in this chamber and elsewhere in the country, bearing on such matters as language policy, national symbols and so on. As with other issues, these matters will also need to be handled with all due sensitivity to ensure that they do not exacerbate tensions and prepare the ground for renewed racial conflict.

Nevertheless, the point needs to be raised once again that all of us who join this discussion need to place it in the context of the wider and more enduring national objective of putting away the things that caused racial and ethnic conflict in the past and fostering national unity and reconciliation.

I do not believe that it will ever be possible to discuss and resolve in a just manner such questions as the place of Afrikaans in the official communication system or what to do with the statues of the late H.F.

Verwoerd or what to do with regard to the fact that the airport at George is named after P.W. Botha, unless we place these within the longer-term objective of creating a society which recognises both our diversity and the imperative to build a peaceful and non-racial society of equal and inter-dependent communities.

The question comes back to all of us who sit in this House, who claim leadership of the new South Africa and wish to be seen as the founding fathers and mothers of our democratic society, whether we have it in us to accept the challenge of leadership with regard to these questions as well.

There are many issues of a similar kind and weight that each one of us can raise in a similar vein. Perhaps what we have said is sufficient to establish the point we are trying to make.

We have embarked upon a complex process of the transformation of our society. It would be deceitful to pretend that the tasks ahead will be easy. The late Amilcar Cabral enjoined us to tell no lies and to claim no easy victories. This we certainly need to bear in mind.

It would equally be the height of foolishness to assume a triumphalist posture which would suggest that the struggle for non-racialism and equity can be won without pain and sacrifice by all our people. The policies we have to implement leading to the creation of a truly non-racial and non-sexist society, in conditions of peace, stability and mutual tolerance, do not allow for anyone of us to be instant heroes within our constituencies. We must accept that balanced, fair and equitable change may indeed result in charges of treachery. But then, neither is it an act of heroism either to promise the maintenance of the *status quo* or, as in *Alice in Wonderland,* to hold out the false prospect of jam today.

When all is said and done and we have debated the merits and demerits of what I have said today, this we must remember: that the country we live in, the dear heritage of all our people, is one in which the system of apartheid has not yet been fully dismantled.

If, in time, the reality of the absence of fundamental change convinces the disadvantaged majority that we have created a political democracy which is unable or unwilling fully to dismantle the system of racial oppression and exploitation, then we must expect that the dream deferred will, rather than wilt in the sun, explode!

Then shall these masses revert to Shylock and ask a question which, miraculously, they have not yet asked: If you wrong us, shall we not revenge?

Hardened by their new experience, they will indeed say that the villainy we teach them, they will execute. And, given who they are, ordinary and compassionate and humane people, it shall go hard for them, but they will surely better the instruction that we who sit in this House will have imparted to them.

We must take care to ensure that we, whatever the side of the House on which we sit, do not sacrifice the future of our country to the vanities of short-term political advantage.

12

Transforming the
Economy of South Africa

*South African Chamber of Business Annual Banquet, Carlton Hotel,
Johannesburg, 14 September 1995*

SIXTEEN MONTHS AGO, when we installed Nelson Mandela as the first
democratically elected president of the 'New Republic', millions of our
people, black and white, for the first time joined hands as equals to rejoice
over the end of a past that has separated and oppressed them for generations.

That joyous moment also brought with it great challenges and created
new opportunities. Of necessity, that historical moment enjoined us to initiate the process of addressing the consequences of more than 300 years
of racial oppression and exploitation and thereby transform the conditions of life for the majority of our people.

As we entered the new era in which our people will no longer be at
war with one another, we had to work actively and purposely at defeating
any tendencies that would drive us back to the dark days of conflict and
disunity. As a people and a government we elected to root the transition
to democracy on the noble and correct concepts of reconciliation and
national unity.

We recognised the fact that without such reconciliation and unwavering commitment to the building of a common South African nationhood,
the conflict and the war from which we had just emerged would not come
to an end and that it would never be possible to embark on the important
task of reconstruction and development.

Let me also point out that noble and correct as they are, reconciliation
and nation-building, unless they are accompanied by the fundamental
transformation of the entire socio-economic fabric of our society, would
remain but unrealisable ideals. For those of us who have been the objects
and victims of racial oppression and social and economic deprivation, we

96

cannot but conceive of the two processes as two sides of the same coin, or two interdependent processes, each of which is incapable of realisation if it is not accompanied by the other.

Reconciliation must, therefore, of necessity encompass the transformation of everything else in addition to the political accession to power of the representatives of the formerly oppressed blacks. It must include the transformation and deracialisation of the South African economy. For it is in the ownership, operation and management of the productive resources of our land that black people will begin to contribute to the generation of the country's wealth – no longer as landless, propertyless, unskilled and semi-skilled workers or as street hawkers and marginal retailers in the formal sector.

The challenge of economic transformation demands that the South African Chamber of Business (SACOB) and other business organisations join hands with government in designing innovative policies which will ensure that we broaden the ownership and management of the economy from the privileged few to include those who were marginalised and excluded by apartheid.

We are encouraged by the tentative moves to broaden economic ownership through joint ventures and unbundling that have been made by some sections of the private sector. I am certain that it is common cause among us that as laudable as these may be, they are still far from sufficient.

Moreover, we would agree that it is necessary to move beyond the trend of just swapping paper through portfolio investments at the stock exchange and embark on green-field projects in manufacturing, tourism, the service industry and other sectors, in order to generate high levels of new employment which will enable us to make a dent on unemployment.

Let me emphasise that the responsibility to meet all of these challenges cannot be left to government alone. But as government we have the responsibility to ensure that we manage the transition very carefully and evolve policies which will produce conditions of stability and engender confidence in private investors that we are able to manage the economy in a responsible manner.

Indeed, organisations like SACOB, local and foreign investors are perfectly within their right to expect government to persist in ensuring an investor-friendly environment.

The government is only too aware that without new fixed investment there will be no new jobs, and that in the long run it is mainly the private business sector, and not the government, that can create sustainable employment opportunities.

Yet one of the most gratifying economic developments since South Africa's political transition last year has been the strong revival in private fixed investment.

It is clear that our successful transition to democracy was a precondition for halting the sustained decline in domestic fixed investment and the steady deterioration of most aspects of the economy that marked the last two decades of the old South Africa.

The political transition has also made possible renewed access to the world's financial markets and the multilateral institutions such as the World Bank and the International Monetary Fund. As a government we have been able to successfully place South African bonds on the international markets and the country has received positive ratings from internationally renowned institutions. And for the first time in many more years South African companies have been able to raise finance internationally.

A successful transition to democracy was a necessity, but by no means a sufficient precondition for turning South Africa's economic fortunes around. Economic policies had to change radically as well. The Government of National Unity (GNU) inherited major problems of inequalities, social infrastructure backlogs, poverty and unemployment.

But it also inherited major fiscal constraints on its ability to tackle these problems, which include:

- a relatively high budget deficit;
- a 55 per cent debt to gross domestic product ratio; and
- a government budget that is geared largely to funding recurrent expenditure.

Given this fiscal legacy, the GNU has had to find a difficult balance between early and rapid delivery on basic needs on the one hand, and addressing the fiscal issues in a way which would avoid a crisis in government finances further down the line.

While I am certainly not complacent, we have, in my view, found a fairly good balance so far. The improvement in business confidence, the turnaround in the private sector's fixed investment, the performance of the financial markets and the value of the rand in particular confirm that there is a broadly favourable judgement in the local and foreign business sectors on the government's policy choices up to now.

The 16 months since the political transition have provided many examples which indicate that we are aware of policy imperatives flowing from the need for a dynamic, internationally competitive economy, and that we are to face up to the inevitable trade-offs and difficult choices. Let me note a few of these:

- The sharply rising trend in real government expenditure has been halted, and we are working to shift the mix of government spending away from recurrent to capital expenditure. The rationalisation of the public service is likely to reinforce this trend.
- We have set in train a process of reviewing all aspects of government spending and are moving to a system of multi-year zero-based budgeting.
- In line with our General Agreement on Tariffs and Trade and World Trade Organisation obligations, we have committed the government to the simplification and phased reduction of import tariffs with the specific goal of making South African industry more internationally competitive and reducing the costs of imported foreign capital goods. And to help local industry through the adjustment process that will necessarily follow from this, we are designing supply support measures.
- We recently published a discussion document which spells out the government's approach to the restructuring of state assets. This document makes it clear to all that government favours less rather than more public ownership, and that we are certainly intent on 'reordering' the state assets in ways that promote the Reconstruction and Development Programme and benefit the performance of the economy while addressing socio-economic issues. We will be appointing task teams in the next week or so to undertake a detailed analysis which will, before the end of the year, recommend to the Cabinet the steps needed to implement the restructuring process.
- To the surprise of many who supposed that an ANC-led government would be wedded to direct intervention in the financial markets,

exchange controls over non-residents were abolished within less than a year after the transition and the government has committed itself to the phased removal of the remaining exchange controls over residents.

However reassuring these policy developments are, we are conscious of the fact that some may consider 16 months as being a rather short time to establish a firm track record. Let me assure you that as a government we are committed to staying on the track along which we are proceeding.

The recently established Presidential Ad Hoc Committee on Economic Policy is intended to precisely address some of the critical and difficult questions we need to deal with in the short to medium term in order to ensure that the economic recovery is sustained and we fast-track some of our socio-economic programmes and the restructuring of the state sector.

As this audience is well aware, the GNU places a premium on co-operation and partnership between itself, the private sector, organised labour, the non-governmental sectors and civil society broadly defined.

The institutional expression of this partnership is to be found in the National Economic Development and Labour Council (NEDLAC). It is gratifying to us to note that despite its youth NEDLAC has been able to weather the storm and the difficulties associated with the new Labour Relations Act. It is indeed a tribute to organisations such as SACOB, Business South Africa, the National African Federated Chamber of Commerce, and the Federation for African Business and Consumer Services from the business sector; the Congress of South African Trade Unions, the National Council of Trade Unions and the Federation of South African Labour Unions from the labour side; and, from government side, the minister of labour and his team that we have been able to agree on this important piece of legislation.

We believe that this legislation provides an important institutional framework which allows for certainty, unifies the disparate labour relations in the country, enables the parties to participate in the formulation of industrial policy, encourages productivity enhancement and worker participation in companies, and seeks to reduce adversarialism which has been the hallmark of our industrial relations up to now.

100

There are, however, other key areas in which we would like to see the strengthening of this co-operation between government and the private sector. As an example, let me deal with just two such areas.

Firstly, there is the all too important area of housing and infrastructure development. As far as housing is concerned, as government we believe that the establishment of the subsidy scheme and the Mortgage Indemnity Fund provide an important framework for the delivery of houses to low-income people.

We believe there are other ways in which the private sector can contribute to addressing the housing issue. These could include providing discounts to communities who purchase building materials in bulk, providing material and other support such as construction, bricklaying and other house-building related skills to the community-based housing support centres, and donating or making land available to communities at preferential rates. We are pleased that some of the private sector companies have responded positively in this regard.

Secondly, there is the area of education and training. One of the biggest problems we have inherited from the old South Africa is the enormous shortage of trained and skilled labour. Government officials, private sector representatives and organised labour have been working tirelessly in the last few years to develop a national training and qualifications framework which will enable all of us to tackle this enormous problem.

In this connection, we are pleased that the National Assembly approved the National Qualifications Framework Bill which was jointly prepared by the ministers of education and labour. We have now established the framework within which we can seriously begin to address the problem. Here I refer to Adult Basic Education and Training (ABET). Government has, accordingly, committed an amount of R50 million to ABET.

We would like to take this opportunity to invite SACOB and other business organisations to join hands with us and contribute materially and otherwise to ensure that this initiative succeeds. As business people you know too well that a trained, literate and educated workforce is an asset and is a *sine qua non* for higher productivity.

At the tertiary education level the government is working towards the establishment of a student loan scheme, to make what can only be a modest beginning towards assisting the 70 000 needy students. We hope that the private sector will join hands with us in addressing this matter.

If we have so far been focusing on purely domestic matters, let us now turn, albeit briefly, to our relations with the Southern African region and the world.

Angola is moving towards peace. We would like to believe that the people of this sister country are committed to reconciliation and reconstruction. Thus today we can say, without any fear of contradiction, that the region of Southern Africa is very firmly set on the road to the strengthening of democracy and the guarantee of peace and stability.

In recognition of our shared and common destiny as a region, we have committed ourselves to all-round and mutually beneficial co-operation among ourselves, which itself will be a very powerful factor for the stability and prosperity of our subcontinent.

We in the GNU are very proud of the fact that South African companies are forming partnerships with their counterparts in the sub-region and are therefore leading the investment revival in our region. As you are well aware, the region offers a market base of around 120 million people and great investment opportunities in tourism and eco-tourism, agro-industry, mineral-based industries, infrastructure development, transport and so on.

As a government we are committed to the strengthening of the Southern African Customs Union (SACU) and the Southern African Development Community (SADC). We are presently renegotiating the SACU and are working to reaching an agreement which will benefit all the members, big and small.

The recent SADC summit reached agreements on energy and water which, together with existing agreements on transport and communication systems, form the core of our co-operation in infrastructure development. We hope to build on these agreements as we progress towards a prosperous Southern Africa in the twenty-first century.

In dispensing its responsibility as the co-ordinator of the financial and investment sector within SADC, South Africa is working hard with its partners to ensure that the Community evolves a credible strategy in this sector, including the attraction of investors to the region.

Balanced development, equity and mutual benefit are the watchwords guiding our approach to regional co-operation.

We are also determined to evolve maximum co-operation with regard to crime prevention, including trafficking in drugs, illegal weapons, stolen goods as well as money laundering and violent crime.

One of the most important initiatives with regard to relations beyond the sub-region is the current negotiations between ourselves and the European Union (EU) which are aimed at working out an agreement that, *inter alia*, will allow South African products better access to the EU market.

It will be very important for the private sector to assist our negotiators and continuously interact with them so that you can ensure that the outcome of these negotiations truly benefit our business community and consumers. This will include providing technical backup, research teams and any other assistance that may be necessary to the negotiating team.

Let me conclude by saying that the GNU which you helped put in place has every determination to live up to the dreams of our people, to strive for democracy, empowerment of the disadvantaged majority, human rights, deracialisation of our society and economy, non-sexism, development, prosperity, peace and stability.

We once again call upon SACOB and the general business community to join hands with us to become true partners in all of these.

13

Is There a National Agenda – and Who Sets It?

Prestige lecture delivered at the University of Port Elizabeth, 17 March 1995

TO BEGIN OUR PRESENTATION and to indicate its substance, we would like to pose some related questions. These are: Is there a national agenda around which the whole country should unite?

If there is, the question arises: Who has set that agenda? If there is not, the question remains to be answered: Who shall set that agenda?

In a sense, it is easy to answer these questions. But those easy answers may very well contain within them some other difficult questions which have yet to be addressed.

Let us deal with the easy matters first.

Our national agenda is described as a programme for reconstruction and development, or, to use its more familiar form, the Reconstruction and Development Programme (RDP). This programme contains various objectives, which include achieving sustained economic growth, meeting the needs of the people, redressing the racial and gender imbalances we have inherited from the system of apartheid, transforming the state machinery, and creating the institutions and vehicles we need to ensure a better life for all.

I am certain that there is nobody present here who would wish to distance himself or herself from these goals. In that sense it would therefore be correct to say that there does indeed exist a national agenda around which the whole country is united. Certainly, the parties both in Parliament and in government have all expressed support for the RDP and are presumably engaged in efforts to ensure that the programme is implemented.

As to the question: Who set this agenda? the answer is again relatively simple.

Once more, as you know, this programme originated from the ANC, its allies and the broad democratic movement. The various government initiatives dedicated to the pursuit of the objectives of the RDP have been approved by the government as a whole and have and will find expression in legislation that has been or will be approved by Parliament.

As you can see, so far it has been quite easy to find answers to the questions that we posed.

It is when we go beyond the simple to the complex that it becomes clear that the questions: Is there a national agenda? and Who shall set it? are not in fact that easy to answer.

Let me therefore return to some of the objectives contained in the RDP, taking first the issue of what we have described as redressing the racial and gender imbalances that we have inherited from the system of apartheid. We will focus on this matter to illustrate the burden of our argument tonight.

To redress the racial imbalances we have inherited from the past means a commitment to the creation of a non-racial society. Since the adoption of our interim national Constitution, the attainment of this objective has become a constitutional obligation. All organs of state are therefore legally obliged to work towards the creation of a non-racial society.

So wide is the acceptance of this aim that even as we negotiated the issue of an Afrikaner Volkstaat with the Afrikaner Volksfront during 1993 and 1994, agreement was reached that any arrangement to deal with the issue of 'Afrikaner self-determination' would have to be consistent with the overriding objective of the creation of a non-racial society.

With regard to the matter of non-racialism as an important element of our national agenda, we can therefore say: So far, so good!

Still discussing non-racialism, let us now take what should logically be the next step in the argument.

To create a non-racial South Africa must mean that we do everything in our power for the upliftment of the black majority that was oppressed and discriminated against, so that this majority is brought to a position of equality with the white section of our population. Let me explain here that we are using the word 'black' to include Africans, coloureds and Indians.

Agreement has been reached within government that one of the instruments that should be used to advance towards redressing the racial imbalances in our society is affirmative action.

By affirmative action we understand a process which would, *inter alia*, focus on the preparation of the disadvantaged majority to catch up with its advantaged compatriots. Among other things, this must mean the creation of possibilities for that majority to obtain such education and training as would give them the capacity to compete for jobs as directors-general in the public service, as university professors, as judges, as financial managers in large corporations, as generals in the National Defence Force, and so on. We are therefore not talking of tokenism – of putting black people in positions of responsibility without the necessary ability to carry out the functions which those responsibilities entail.

Let us now take the situation in which a particular business school has a limited number of places for the training of Masters in Business Administration. Consistent with the national objective of creating a non-racial society, the business school should have no problem in deciding that in the allocation of places it will discriminate in favour of black applicants. To deal with the consequences of this, it would institute bridging courses to enable black students to cope with the syllabus. Thus the business school would not impair the objective it will have set itself of attaining excellence in terms of its teaching and the qualified people it seeks to graduate.

We are therefore at the point where what has happened is that a qualified white student was unable to gain entry into the business school, having lost his place to a less qualified black student.

All this results from the pursuit of the objective of the creation of a non-racial society and, consequently, the application of the principle of affirmative action.

Three years down the road, 'Screw It Up Company (Pty) Ltd' will have the possibility to begin changing its management structure by employing the now qualified black MBA to understudy its current white finance manager as part of its own process of deracialising the company.

It should now be clear that there will be some among us who will begin to say that, whatever may be said about the objective of the creation of a non-racial society, they will not accept that this can be described as part of a national agenda which enjoys the support of everybody in the country. This would affect both individuals and sections of various communities who might feel that the pursuit of the objective of a non-racial society discriminates against them and therefore does not deserve their support.

In the event that these might have the capacity to have their voices heard loudly and clearly, through access to the media or by any other means, we could then arrive at the situation where the discussion is reopened as to whether we can in reality claim that the objective of the creation of a non-racial society enjoys the support of the generality of our population.

Coming from where I come, I must at this point make it clear that I am convinced that we cannot turn away from the pursuit of the goal of establishing a non-racial society. If we do not attend to this challenge in a visible, consistent, sustained and practical manner, it is inevitable that we would condemn our country to conflict, instability and insecurity for all our citizens, regardless of their race or colour. Undoubtedly, that conflict would be based on colour. It would force upon all of us a regression to the terrible past from which we have sought to escape through our process of democratisation and the implementation of the programme for reconstruction and development.

But if we assume, as I think we must, that some will make determined efforts to present the process of the deracialisation of our country as being inimical to the interests of the minority that attained positions of privilege as a result of the system of apartheid, perhaps resulting in an increase in racial tensions, then we must return to the question: Is non-racialism part of our national agenda, and who sets that agenda?

Already the process has begun of seeking to diminish the moral weight and the legitimacy of the process of creating a non-racial society by describing it as an 'Africanist' project. According to this argument, which in many instances is presented as analysis, there exists a faction within the ANC which seeks to champion the cause of the Africans in our society for reasons which have to do with power politics both within the ANC and the country at large.

Thus described, the challenge of ensuring the all-round upliftment of the African majority, the most disadvantaged section of our population, ceases to be an issue that should become a critical part of our national agenda, supported by all our people.

The public in general is also encouraged to come to the determination that this matter has been put on the agenda merely by a self-seeking political faction which has as much a right to be listened to, or not listened to, as any other political faction.

Thus we return to the questions: Is there a national agenda? and Who sets it?

To reiterate our own view, the issue of the deracialisation of our society or the creation of a non-racial South Africa is indeed a critical matter on our national agenda. Its direct and immediate implication is that our society as a whole must discuss and adopt practical ways and means by which to attain it.

But the question can legitimately be posed: Who am I to presume that I am the one to set the national agenda? To which I would answer as follows: Indeed I, as an individual, have no such right or power.

The right and obligation to set the national agenda rests with the democratically elected bodies of our country. I would therefore be very interested to see the matter of the implementation of the constitutional provision of the creation of a non-racial society discussed by all our legislatures, both national and provincial, as well as the interim structures established at the local level.

It would make an important contribution to the evolution of a national consensus on so fundamental a matter if such an open debate took place, with each party or political organisation stating where it stands with regard to this issue. Such a discussion would have to go beyond general and ineffectual statements and focus in a forthright manner on what it is that we all have to do to achieve the national and urgent objective of progressing towards a non-racial South Africa.

The second point I would like to make with regard to the question, Who sets the national agenda? is that this debate should also go beyond the institutions I have mentioned.

It should also bring in the public at large, utilising all representative organisations, including non-political ones, from within which our people as a whole can state their own views on the matter we have been discussing. We are, in other words, calling for the involvement of civil society in this and other debates of national importance, so that it too becomes part of the process of setting the national agenda. I further believe that institutions such as this university should join this debate to make their own learned contribution to the remaking of our country.

I believe that if we proceed in this way we shall indeed succeed both to set a national agenda and to ensure that the national agenda enjoys the support of all our people, or at least the overwhelming majority, thanks to the processes we would have followed to set that agenda. An obvious benefit that our country would derive from this is that the country would not then be condemned to addressing agendas set either by particular factions in particular political organisations or by people who have the courage to appoint themselves as spokespersons of the public at large.

Let me also make the point that the arguments we have advanced with regard to the creation of a non-racial society also apply to the equally important challenge of creating a non-sexist society.

I am told that the Chinese have a proverb which says that the felling of one tree makes more noise than the growth of an entire forest.

I believe this interesting observation has relevance to the matters we have been discussing. It bears directly on the issue of the setting of the national agenda.

I am equally certain that, working methodically and systematically and in an atmosphere free of hysteria, we will also make progress with regard to the vision which President Mandela projected a few months ago, of creating a society freed of the pervasive corruption which is a direct result of the apartheid experience.

With regard to the matter of social morality and the kind of society we are trying to create, I would also like to draw attention to what President Mandela said about avoiding a resort to an atmosphere of engineered mass hysteria such as characterised the campaign waged by Senator Joe McCarthy in the United States four decades ago.

In dealing with any problem that our society may face, we believe that it is fundamentally important in ensuring the quality of that society to fight against the phenomenon typical of the European Middle Ages of discovering witches and sorcerers who would then be subjected to public pillory and burning at the stake in circumstances described by the Irish poet W.B. Yeats when he wrote: 'a blood-dimmed tide is loosed, the ceremony of innocence is drowned'.

To return to our Chinese proverb, all around us a great forest of millions of healthy trees is growing quietly but steadily. We owe that process of the renewal of our country to the efforts of millions of our people, including you who are gathered here.

But if we were not participants in this historic process of the birth of a nation which the nations of the world support and watch with great interest and optimism, we might be tempted to believe that all that was happening was that a single tree was being felled, so intense is the absence of focus on all these things that make for the happy and prosperous South Africa for which our people sacrificed.

To respond to the effort to set a national agenda focused on the single tree, all of us as ordinary citizens of our country have an obligation to join together to nurture the forest of the positive reconstruction and development of our country.

It must be a fundamental element of the definition of our democracy that the people shall govern! Let us join our legislators in our millions and together with them say loudly: This is the national agenda which we, the people, have set.

Let us, in a real and meaningful way, take our destiny into our own hands!

14

Confronting Racism in Our Thinking: The Role of the Media

Banquet to celebrate the 120th anniversary of the Cape Times, *Cape Town, 3 April 1996*

IN THE SUPPLEMENT ON the *Cape Times* which this paper carried a week ago, the distinguished editor of the paper, Moegsien Williams, writes:

> A typical South African newsroom is an unhappy place, staffed by demotivated, mainly junior reporters and frustrated sub-editors who are expected to cover and produce newspapers able to reflect accurately an increasingly complex society.

Further on he says:

> We want to redefine the news. We sense it can't be 'journalism as usual' in the new South Africa... In practical terms, redefining the news means getting closer to the readership by engagement, new contacts, new story ideas and a move away from stereotypes.

I believe that the editor deserves our congratulations for the honesty with which he states his views and the courage with which he sets a vision for the *Cape Times* when, in addition to what we have already cited, he says:

> While we will expose society's ills and wrongs, we will be its cheerleaders when things go right and there are successes. While we will be opposed to many things, we are able for the first time to be passionately and uncompromisingly in favour of some things, especially our newborn democracy.

111

It may come to pass that 50 years into the unknown future, those who will be alive then will see this particular period in the history of our country, as we effect the transition from apartheid to non-racialism and democracy, as the golden age of its rebirth.

It will turn almost exclusively on what all of us do, accepting as we must that if we fail to succeed, the fault will not be in our stars but in ourselves.

And what is it that all of us South Africans must do?

While recognising and cherishing the colour, race, language and cultural diversity of our country, we must nevertheless seek to build out of that diversity one nation which shares a common sense of patriotism. Put in other words, we have to do battle with and against the legacy of racial division and conflict which has characterised South African society almost from the beginning of the period of our country's settlement by European peoples.

It is perhaps natural and should be expected that some among us will complain about why we thus continue to recall the past. After all, it is sometimes said: Have we not ended the system of apartheid? Is it not now time that we speak of the future rather than persist in recalling a painful past which is best forgotten, rather than kept alive by constant reference by those who have nothing original to say?

But I do not believe that if we are honest with ourselves we can seriously suggest that, after these long centuries of our actual historical experience, it would be possible in a year or two or three or five to wipe out notions of racism and racial superiority from the consciousness of many. Capable as we might be of achieving miracles, this is one of those that are beyond our abilities.

If we recognise this reality, then surely one of the things we must do is that we, as a people, should deliberately and directly engage this challenge and not pretend that it does not exist.

I would like to hazard the guess that most of us present in this room followed with some interest the debate between two of our bright intellectuals as they crossed swords in the print and electronic media on this vexed issue of racism.[31] I believe that it is important that the discussion took place, whatever the pain it might have caused both to the jousters and the spectators. I would also hope that it would free all of us from the inhibition to debate this matter in public, whether this arises from fear of derision or from concern that by discussing it, we help to fan the propagation of racism.

Over the recent past, including this very day, we have watched as the rand has done somewhat of a mad dance, gyrating to the music of a band of faceless, odourless and non-corporeal musicians who are described as the market. As I tried to listen to the music this band has been playing, I thought I heard lyrics which contained the refrain: This, after all, is just another African country! And the recollection came flooding back of a now forgotten phrase: 'the white man's burden'.

All this happens because there seems to be an accusation that is being made that it cannot be that a majority black government can properly manage an economy as sophisticated as ours. After all, look at the rest of Africa!

And so it must remain the white man's burden – and it was never the white woman's – to preside over the economy, as the black are condemned to a predilection and a hereditary instinct to abuse political power for purposes that are inimical to the objective of a healthy and growing economy!

Cold fear grips my heart even as I say this, because I can hear the deluge of criticism that will wash over me. Some will say that all I did was to make racist remarks. Others will ask: What did you expect from an Africanist?

Yet others will say: Why does he not understand that what the colour-blind market is reacting to is the inexperience of the new government and not its racial complexion?

To which I will probably respond by saying that you are probably correct – and go to bed convinced that the governments that replaced Salazar of Portugal and Franco of Spain inspired new confidence in the economic prospects of those countries rather than gloom occasioned by the inexperience of the new democratic governments and fear that the economies of Portugal and Spain would collapse.

On this matter, those among us who have confidence in the capacity of our government to be as intelligent as any other in the world and to be as literate as any other, as regards the factors that make for sustained growth and development in the modern world in which we live, will laugh best because they will laugh last as practice proves the sceptics wrong.

Whatever my own fate after this evening, I will continue to assert it as one of the challenges our society faces, to confront the issue of racism in our thinking and understanding as an essential part of the building of the one nation towards which so many aspire.

In any case I believe that we have no choice but to deal with the material circumstances in our country which are the consequences of our racist past and whose continued existence is precisely the fodder that feeds racial tensions, resentment and possible conflict in future. I refer here, of course, to the enormous disparities in income, wealth and opportunity between black and white which continue to characterise our society. The new South Africa the millions dream of cannot both be new and continue to carry this feature of a racially advantaged minority and a racially disadvantaged majority.

It used to be only a few years ago, perhaps as a result of what we ourselves said, that there was a genuine fear among those who had something to lose that what we were after was the seizure of everybody's property and its redistribution among the people. I recall distinctly very wise advice being given by one of our major captains of industry that if we nationalised the corporation he heads and handed out its shares to all adult South Africans, all we would achieve would merely be to destroy the company and with it the economy. Happily, we have passed the stage when the spectre of such disastrous adventures still haunted some in our country and the world. At least, I trust that we have passed that stage.

Ahead of us must unfold a programme of work to rebuild and expand our economy on a sustained basis. Clearly, among other things this must include sharply increasing the rate of investment, expanding and modernising our manufacturing sector, developing our human resources, increasing our international competitiveness and changing the patterns of our international trade, especially with regard to the product mix of our exports and imports.

At the end of it all, we want to see an end to the high levels of unemployment we continue to experience, a radical reduction in the incidence of poverty, ignorance and disease – a South Africa in which wealth, income and opportunity are shared equitably and in which the racial divides of today are a thing of the past.

None of us can doubt the enormity of this challenge and the vision, dedication and measured impatience it will require of all of us to achieve this result. But equally, it would be difficult to overstate the excitement that derives from that challenge and the sweetness of the reward which success will bring, as we see one more person employed, one new family properly housed, yet another engineer qualifying and another playhouse built so that the community can gain access to theatre.

I have absolutely no doubt that we will realise this dream, relying on the resources of both the public and the private sectors as well as the creativity and enthusiasm of the masses of our people.

It may be that history will judge these first two or three years of our democratic rule as the period during which we constructed the engine which must pull us forward towards the truly non-racial, non-sexist, prosperous and peaceful South Africa we all desire.

Perhaps the occasion will present itself one day to discuss the component parts of this engine, among which are correct and realistic policies and programmes, reorganised and remotivated government structures, active co-operation between government, labour and business and the involvement of the masses of the people in development.

It may also be that the political, constitutional, economic and social successes we achieve will help to push back the negative assumptions that some make about the African continent as well as contribute something to the worldwide struggles to end racism and to find lasting stability in multicultural societies.

Thus history has granted all of us the privilege to be the midwives of a new nation, to transform the ethos of our society from despair to hope, to be pioneers and Voortrekkers on the road to a glorious future which none of us has ever traversed.

And so we come back to Moegsien Williams. What we want to achieve cannot be achieved without the *Cape Times* publishing according to the dictum with which he ended his article: 'Serve your readers and practise independent journalism.'

But how shall this be realised with newsrooms that are unhappy places, staffed by demotivated, mainly junior reporters and frustrated sub-editors? To this we must also add: How can it be achieved with newsrooms that still desperately need to address the urgent questions of better race and gender representativity?

I believe that we should take example from Moegsien Williams and not fear to criticise ourselves, to change ourselves from what we were and not be satisfied merely to repeat by rote that this or that is the nature of the media, and then run as far and as fast as possible away from confronting the challenge of defining the role of the press in these changing times.

The history of the *Cape Times* must surely serve those who are its producers and owners as an inspiration to do better and set new standards rather than as justification for complacency and stagnation.

15

The National Council of Provinces:
A Unique Institution of Democracy

National Council of Provinces National Conference, Cape Town, 8 May 1998

GATHERED IN THIS ROOM is an important component part of the political leadership of our country, mandated by our people as a whole to see our country through its first transitional phase. We meet here today further to discharge our responsibilities with regard to that mandate.

The National Council of Provinces (NCOP), the product of the Constitution drafted by the elected Constitutional Assembly, is barely 15 months old. By any standards, it is a mere infant which, necessarily, must suffer from teething problems.

Despite the peculiar South African presumption that all problems, especially those that are intrinsically the most complex, can be solved overnight, I do not believe that anybody would accuse us of self-exculpation if we say that, naturally, the NCOP is afflicted by problems of infancy.

Accordingly, we meet here today to assist in the process of the growth of this important institution of our democratic life, the NCOP.

But I believe that as we deliberate among ourselves over the next two days, we must continue to be informed by the perspective which guided us as we drafted the Constitution which gave birth to the NCOP.

Two of the most important principles which were part of that perspective were participatory democracy and co-operative governance. We came to these positions not because we were particularly bright or inventive, but because we wanted to address the specific circumstances of our country, in a situation in which we had the possibility to draw on the accumulated wisdom and follies of the rest of humanity, and because we emerged out of our own definitive past.

The NCOP was conceived of as a critical vehicle for the achievement of these objectives. It must therefore succeed not because it exists as an

institution, but because the vision of which it is an expression is fundamental to the success of the new democracy which we sought to fashion.

Without seeking to be arrogant, we can say that the council has elements of uniqueness in the context of constitutional systems internationally. It may therefore have significance in a manner that transcends our
own national boundaries. The challenge to ensure its success, whatever
its complexity, therefore becomes that much greater.

This conference has been called at an important point in the life of our
new democracy. It is now a matter of months before we must once again
face the electorate in South Africa's second democratic elections. In the
nature of things, all of us will be called to account for work done or not
done since the historic elections of 1994.

The question on everybody's lips will be: What have you done to provide a better life for me and my children? The masses will seek to judge
us according to the contribution we shall have made, in the words of the
Constitution, 'to improve the quality of life of all citizens and free the
potential of each person'.

At this point, to plead institutional failure may not be of much help,
especially as institutions will be adjudged as not an end in themselves.

I say this to plead that what we do at this conference should not be
informed by the pressures of the need to secure electoral victories.
Rather, it must be driven by a common desire to ensure the permanent
entrenchment of a system of governance founded on the fundamental
concepts that, as South Africans, we share a common destiny and that the
people shall govern.

Put in more direct terms, the NCOP provides a mechanism for har-
monising the interests of national, provincial and local government.
Debates are aimed at achieving consensus on policy between the different spheres of government.

This point has been examined in close detail by the authors of a study
on the NCOP. I refer here to the study by Professor Christina Murray and
others, which was recently completed as part of the European Union
Parliamentary Support Programme.

Professor Murray outlines two competing views of the NCOP. It could
be seen exclusively as an institution through which provinces ensure that
national laws take their interests into account. This view would describe
the NCOP as a council of provinces.

Yet another view would see the NCOP exclusively as an institution through which national government ensures that provinces act in a manner consonant with the national objectives it sets.

But neither view is correct. To quote Professor Murray: 'The NCOP is not either a House of Provinces or an institution through which provinces are committed to national policy. It is both.'

Through the NCOP, national government is sensitised to provincial interests. Its own processes are accordingly enriched. But, equally, the NCOP engages provinces and provincial legislatures in the formulation of national policy, and demands that they do not become parochial.

By ensuring that national, provincial and local governments work together in partnership, we ensure that the concerns of people on the ground are brought into the spotlight when we develop policy. By involving provincial and local government in national processes, we bring government closer to the people.

And so how do we measure the success of the NCOP?

There has been a tendency to evaluate the NCOP on the basis of the number of amendments made to draft legislation submitted to it. What this amounts to is an impression that the NCOP is functional and effective only to the extent that it rejects legislation emanating from the executive and the National Assembly.

If the NCOP were to follow this approach, it would allow itself to be locked into a competitive mould that might be typical of other jurisdictions but which would constitute a departure from the vision and practice of co-operative governance to which the Constitution enjoins us.

There are more constructive criteria by which to judge the performance of the NCOP. Some of the questions we must ask are:

- Are provincial legislatures working to ensure that they engage their communities in evolving the important pieces of transformative legislation that has to be passed?
- To what extent are provinces evaluating legislative proposals emanating from the national executive against the conditions which prevail in their areas?
- Are provincial legislatures alerting national government to potential problems that may be encountered if particular policy proposals are pursued?

If the answers to these questions are in the affirmative, then we can say that the provinces are fulfilling their constitutional mandate.

There are other important questions that we need to pose and seek to answer. One of these is: How do we live up to the imperative of co-operative governance across narrow party lines, across provincial, regional and local boundaries? Are we capable of crossing our parochial boundaries and thus agree on the issues which would address the needs of our country and people and would constitute the substance of the matters which the institutions of co-operative governance would address?

Beyond this, there are other matters we will have to consider. One of these is whether the provinces are making full use of the opportunity to participate in national policy formulation. The experience of the NCOP over the past year would seem to indicate that provinces are failing to make use of the possibilities afforded them through the NCOP.

It would seem that most provincial legislatures have not yet fully taken on board the implications the NCOP has for their own institutions. These have not yet undergone the kind of wholesale reorganisation and reorientation required if they are to function effectively in the NCOP. Accordingly, it would appear that the NCOP is very often regarded as an 'add-on' function and not part of the core business of provincial legislatures.

Further, at the level of the executive, it would appear that in many, if not most provinces, there is minimal involvement by the provincial executive in debates at the level of the provincial standing committees, particularly when national legislation is discussed.

It would appear that the members of the executive councils (MECs) consider participation in MinMecs [meetings of ministers and MECs] as the sum total of their contribution to the development of policy and have failed to grasp the significance of the role of the NCOP in intergovernmental relations.

As a result, legislatures do not have at their disposal the experience and expertise of MECs and their departments when considering legislation that will impact directly on the lives of the people of the province. In most instances, provincial legislatures approve legislation in the NCOP without having fully examined the capacity of the province to implement such legislation. The final product that emerges from Parliament is impoverished, because the kind of co-operation amongst legislatures and executives demanded by the Constitution has not happened.

Understandably, because the NCOP is still relatively new, we experience these and many other problems we have to grapple with in the effort to improve our participation in the NCOP. These range from how to go about achieving proper mandates, co-ordination of work programmes with that of the NCOP, processing of information, to the lack of both human and material resources. The list might seem long. But we are convinced that no problems are insurmountable.

I am certain that we would all agree that it is important to weigh those problems against the achievements.

1997 was a busy year for the NCOP. It involved provinces in passing 108 bills. The majority of the bills that were amended by the NCOP were Section 76 bills[32], which affect provinces. This is a clear indication that provincial legislatures have decided to prioritise legislation that has a direct impact on the provinces.

But the real value the NCOP can add to the costly exercise of governance was evident in the last few weeks by the manner in which the NCOP dealt with the Eastern Cape intervention in the affairs of the Butterworth municipality.

Here was a situation where intervention was urgently needed to ensure that the people of Butterworth obtained basic services such as electricity and water, refuse removal and sanitation. It was also a situation in which, were it not for the NCOP's handling of the case, taxpayers' money and government funds would have gone instead to costly and lengthy court cases involving the provincial and local spheres of government.

The NCOP stepped in and fulfilled its constitutional obligations by ensuring that the intervention was able to proceed and that services were reinstated. At the same time, it ensured that the duly elected Butterworth Council was restored to its constitutional status.

The importance of the manner in which this was handled goes beyond the small town of Butterworth itself. Among other things, it clearly indicated the parameters of such future interventions. I am informed that one delegate who spoke in the plenary debate on the Butterworth intervention said that he was able to 'see for the first time what the NCOP is really about'.

The Butterworth intervention has also highlighted the important role that local government has to play in the NCOP. It is to the credit of the South African Local Government Association, who only joined the NCOP in February this year, that they so quickly grasped the importance of the Butterworth case and were able immediately to represent the interests of local government and play such a constructive role in reaching the final agreement of the amended terms of intervention.

The NCOP's handling of the Butterworth intervention has also brought to the fore the important oversight role the NCOP has to play in future.

If the NCOP is to fulfil its constitutional obligations with overseeing both provincial intervention in municipal affairs and national intervention in provincial affairs, it is obviously important that the NCOP works out a programme of monitoring the relations between the three spheres of government.

This is a role the NCOP has not yet begun to explore. I welcome the fact, however, that this conference will discuss the issue of legislatures and their oversight functions and trust that the matter will not end up as a mere agenda item for today.

The issue of the national legislative process itself needs to be addressed frankly and openly. As part of this, it must now be clear to all of us that the success of the NCOP is dependent to a very large degree on the extent to which both Houses of Parliament are able to forge a good working relationship. While progress has been made in this direction, much remains to be done to improve the relationship between the two Houses.

Much of what I have had to say in this address has highlighted shortcomings and weaknesses as we strive to build this institution called the NCOP. Yet we can also see how much has been achieved in so short a period of time. Clearly, we should not allow ourselves to be so overwhelmed by the difficulties we face that we do not see the possibilities that lie ahead of us and the greater capacity to move forward which experience gives us.

It would be a serious mistake if at this point I failed to recognise the contribution that the National Democratic Institute (NDI) has made in helping the NCOP along its path of development. The NDI was one of the first institutions to offer assistance to the NCOP after its launch. It has remained a faithful and generous partner over the past 18 months, as this conference demonstrates. Our country, and the NCOP in particular, looks forward to a continued good working relationship with the NDI.

In conclusion, I wish to commend the NCOP for the initiative in conceiving and organising such a conference. I believe it is this kind of initiative, and willingness to explore beyond the boundaries of the traditional, which the Constitution requires of us if the NCOP is to fulfil its mandate of providing a national forum for the discussion of issues of interest to all structures of governance.

True to its mandate, the NCOP has succeeded in placing on the agenda here today important matters relating both to the functioning of legislatures as well as some of the more topical policy debates of the day.

The fact that we have gathered such a representative group of individuals and representatives from national, provincial and local government is testimony to the durability of the spirit and principles of co-operative governance enshrined in our Constitution.

16

Equity within the Property Industry

Speech at the South African Property Owners' Association Convention, Durban, 24 May 1998

BEING INVITED TO this South African Property Owners' Association (SAPOA) convention on 'Property Countdown to the Millennium' gives us a window of opportunity to contribute to the agenda on the future of the property industry, so that we do not repeat the mistakes and reproduce the inequalities that derived from public and private policies and practices of the past. It affords us the opportunity to:

- reflect on the role of the commercial property industry within the South African economy and
- identify key issues and challenges for the future.

The critical role of the commercial property industry in our economy is highlighted by the 19 to 25 per cent of the country's total gross domestic fixed investment that has gone into new investment in residential and non-residential properties over the past eight years.

Investment in property on this scale significantly contributes to the creation of jobs, both during construction and in the management, maintenance and servicing of completed properties, as well as the impact on ancillary industries, such as brick making, cement production, furniture making, and so on.

Members of the South African Property Owners' Association (SAPOA) are responsible for a significant proportion of this impact on our economy, with their property asset base of more than R150 billion and their spending of approximately R5 billion per annum on building operating expenses, including the payment of municipal rates and taxes.

Given the scale of these operations, it becomes particularly important to address some key issues that we believe should be high on the agenda as our property industry prepares to enter the new millennium.

Our first comment on this agenda is the issue of economic empowerment.

We are all acutely aware of how, until very recently, apartheid's discriminatory policies and practices shaped our economy, and of their legacy in the present racially distorted ownership and employment patterns. These patterns are particularly evident in the property industry.

Our people have, through the adoption of our new Constitution, committed themselves actively to eradicate these historical imbalances.

The Bill of Rights contains a property clause, which both guarantees the rights of property owners but, among other things, also exhorts the state to 'take reasonable legislative and other measures, within its available resources, to foster conditions which enable citizens to gain access to land on an equitable basis'.

Our first democratically elected government is committed to these objectives. It will, in line with our country's Constitution, use the procurement and disposal of goods, services and property by organs of state as a powerful tool to facilitate the empowerment of previously disadvantaged individuals and firms, in the economy at large and, more specifically, in the property and construction industries. In the case of the property industry, policies of economic empowerment mean:

- altering the skewed ownership and control patterns of property;
- creating opportunities for and empowering previously disadvantaged individuals and firms – especially small, micro and medium enterprises – through outsourcing and subcontracting; and
- empowering employees by ensuring equitable recruitment practices, adequate and appropriate training, a systematic transfer of skills, and encouraging employee equity in property owning, management and services firms.

Even though the state, as legislator, consumer and investor, plays a very significant role in the property industry, it cannot on its own succeed in achieving those goals. The private sector also needs to play a role, by adopting, pioneering and championing policies aimed at redressing past inequalities.

Our second comment on the agenda for taking the property industry into the new millennium is the realignment of the historically distorted development and development patterns which characterise our physical landscape – in short, deracialising our cities, towns, villages and countryside.

Apartheid policy developed black townships in locations significantly distant from our towns and cities. They effectively became dormitory towns from where people commuted to their often distant places of work, while they lived in areas with an extremely limited or non-existent social and economic infrastructure.

Partnerships between the public and private sectors are required to create much-needed infrastructure in black townships, as well as in endeavours to link townships with city centres and other employment areas via development corridors. One such corridor includes Spoornet's Baralink and the Department of Public Works' NASREC [exhibition centre] development in a co-operative initiative to link Soweto with the Johannesburg city centre and the greater metropolitan area.

Businesses have in recent years fled from most of our city centres. Various reasons have been offered for this flight, ranging from increased levels of crime to international trends towards decentralisation and park-like work environments, and even to blatant racism and an inability on the part of business to adapt to the changing socio-economic and political environment.

Such movement threatens to leave us with under-utilised massive infrastructural investment in the buildings, roads, sewers and so forth that form the backbone of our city centres. We cannot afford to waste such resources or even to duplicate them elsewhere *ad infinitum*.

A clear vision for our city centres is required. Such a vision should not seek to romanticise and re-create the past glory associated with city centres. Instead, our African heritage, the competitive advantages which our city centres enjoy, current international trends in city centre renewal and the requirements associated with information age work and leisure environments should form the cornerstone of our vision for revitalising our city centres.

The key stakeholders in the property industry, both in the public and private sectors, must play a role in articulating the new vision, as well as in its realisation.

Government's Spatial Development Initiatives (such as Lubombo, the

Maputo Corridor, the West Coast initiative) also link disparate areas of Southern Africa and, by providing environments conducive to investment, as well as employment and wealth creation, help reverse the racial fragmentation of our society created by apartheid and promote the balanced development of the region of Southern Africa. These initiatives require vast investments in physical and social infrastructure from both the public and private sectors.

When democracy made it possible for South Africa to dismantle the apartheid economic laager and enter the competitive global economy, there were both risks and benefits. If our property industry is to remain competitive, we will have to conform with international best practice and, wherever we enjoy competitive advantages, set new standards for international best practice. This is our third contribution to the agenda for taking our property industry into the new millennium.

It is said that property investors and developers have always held their cards very close to their chest. While one cannot deny such investors and developers a competitive edge, a clear need exists for transparent, credible and freely available property industry benchmarks and statistics. This will ensure that our industry remains competitive internally and becomes more open to foreign direct investment.

The world now demands user-friendly, efficient and effective work environments which enhance productivity. The property industry will have to invest in the creation of such working environments if they, the occupants of properties and our country are to become globally competitive. This must include the very important issue of sensitivity to the needs of the disabled and the elderly.

Our fourth and, for the purposes of this address, final comment on the agenda of your industry is the question of public–private sector partnerships.

In accordance with its policies on reconstruction, development growth, employment and redistribution, government is constantly looking to create opportunities for the private sector to participate in the creation of the social and economic infrastructure. Examples include such initiatives as the involvement of the private sector in the design, building, financing and operating of prisons, as well as the Maputo Corridor toll road project.

Public–private sector partnerships, in line with international trends on fiscal restraint, good governance and efficient and effective delivery, will increasingly be used in the creation of social and physical infrastructure. In the South African context such partnerships can and will also be utilised by government as a tool for economic empowerment.

Such an agenda defines a set of challenges, to be met head-on by both the public and private sectors if we are going to build a property industry which can compete with the best in the world:

- Ownership, control, employment and opportunity patterns must be deracialised to ensure that new, previously excluded participants are drawn into the property industry on the basis of adding value to the sector.
- We must ensure the development of buildings as working environments which are environmentally sound, foster productive work and conform with international standards.
- Partnerships between the various tiers of government, as well as between the private and public sectors, must be forged to alter historically distorted development patterns, to revitalise our inner-city areas and to meet the infrastructure needs of the disadvantaged black majority.
- Apartheid cities and towns must be redeveloped so that they are economically viable, sustainable and can serve as internationally competitive locations for global business.
- Public–private sector relationships must be redefined to assume a more co-operative (as opposed to adversarial) nature.

These challenges are certainly daunting, but they are not insurmountable. The reason for our optimism is that the South African property industry today comprises men and women who have the ability to transcend our chequered past, and to place the industry at the centre of the global property map.

We look forward to a time when equity within the property industry will be achieved, so that we can move forward with a common national agenda. Until then, and even once there, we look forward to travelling with you, constantly in search of ways to enhance opportunities and improve the quality of life of all South Africans – a journey which, we believe, will also result in a renaissance within the property industry, not only in South Africa, but also in other parts of Africa.

I would also like to take this opportunity to express our appreciation for the co-operation that has and is taking place between SAPOA and the government. This has included such areas as land reform and redistribution, public works, the construction industry and local government. We stand ready further to deepen this co-operation in a mutually beneficial manner.

Let us begin the property countdown to the millennium by addressing the challenges and identifying the opportunities. Let us ensure that those opportunities are seized by individuals and firms in a manner that will result, among other things, in greater equity in ownership and control throughout the property industry.

PART FOUR

Reconstruction and Development

THIS SECTION BRINGS US to an important facet of Mbeki's thinking.

If democracy, from the point of view of values, could be described as a perennial trade-off between the values of liberty, equality, community and competence, then Mbeki's mission can be described as finding an acceptable and working trade-off between particularly the values of liberty and equality – which does however not mean the other two are left out of account.

'Liberty', the core value of a libertarian society, inspires the position of those who say that the state should not intervene in the economy. In its extreme form it propagates the idea that the 'market' should be allowed to sort things out.

'Equality' represents the core value of what is commonly called an egalitarian society. State intervention, for instance to foster socio-economic equity, effecting redistribution, is not regarded as unacceptable. In fact, it is seen as necessary.

Mbeki's views on macro-economic strategy and reconstruction and development do not represent any one of these positions. What he wants to do is to break out of the sterile ideological positions on 'liberty' and 'equality' as two contending and even mutually exclusive values.

In Mbeki's view, Growth Employment and Redistribution and the Reconstruction and Development Programme are not mutually exclusive. They form a holistic strategy, complementing each other. Economic growth and development should therefore be seen as going hand in hand – a position motivating Mbeki's emphasis on public sector–private sector partnerships.

17

Investment in Economic
and Social Infrastructure

Conference on Infrastructure Investment, Cape Town, 28 to 29 March 1996

TODAY WE MEET AS the leadership of government and the domestic investor community, together with representatives from labour and the civic sector, to agree on a framework for investment in much-needed economic and social infrastructure.

This is no easy task, as the funds we are discussing include major company assets and the accumulated life savings of our working populations. We are mindful of the sensitivity of these discussions and the concerns regarding risk and undue exposure of investments. We are also mindful of the crucial decisions facing the country as a whole – decisions which are necessary if we are to meet head-on the challenge of growth and development.

Only through linking our collective resources, and through maximising the synergy of our combined actions, will we be able to effect the socio-economic changes our society requires.

Inequality, unemployment and poverty will destroy the political gains we have made thus far unless they are addressed urgently. They are scourges that blight the enjoyment of freedom for a large majority of our people. They are therefore a weight on the conscience of every one of us here today. This underlines the urgency of our discussions and the importance of the decisions we will reach.

Soon after its establishment the Government of National Unity (GNU) adopted a Reconstruction and Development Programme (RDP). The vision of the RDP has since succeeded in fusing the fundamental principles of reconstruction and development throughout government. For instance, the expenditure priorities and programmes increasingly reflect our overall perspective as defined in the RDP policy.

Similarly as government charted a new way of governing and deciding on priorities, the private sector came out in support of the principles of the RDP, supported some of the RDP projects and made a strong commitment to supporting the RDP. Various industries have generously supported government's programmes through grants, technical support and even secondments of staff into crucial areas of expertise. This was an unprecedented move that we greatly applauded.

Since then discussions with the private sector have taken place on a broad range of issues – the Labour Relations Act, the tariff and trade strategy, restructuring of taxation, the formation of the National Economic Development and Labour Council (NEDLAC), the national training strategy, to name but a few.

But the central component of the relationship between government and the private sector has remained vague, ill defined – I am referring here to the way resources from government and resources from the private sector are combined to maximise both development and growth. How do we use our collective resources in ways which can deliver basic services to all our people, create jobs and grow the economy? These are the fundamental questions of the day, these are the matters with which you will be grappling at this conference.

The economists will talk to us about public sector spending 'crowding in' private sector investment, and of course will advise us against 'crowding out' private investment. These are important concerns for all of us.

What is clear is that there are simply not sufficient funds within the budget alone to deliver full services to everyone. Planners at central and provincial level have done detailed work on costing these programmes. For example, we know that to deliver municipal services to everyone within an urban local authority at an affordable level will cost us in the region of R61 billion over the next ten years. The combined resources of central and provincial government will not be able to cover much more than half these capital costs. For the remainder of these resources we must look to other sources: local authority budgets, community contributions, and the extensive investment portfolios of big business and the institutional investors.

What I am talking about is partnerships between major stakeholders on growth and development. One of the fundamental approaches of the GNU is to ensure that development takes place in a way that empowers people and communities and enables them to take control of their own development. We believe that this must be taken forward through a concrete set of partnerships around local projects in which local authorities, the private sector, the community and organised labour have a role to play.

For instance, the private sector has significant capacity in the field of project management and infrastructure maintenance – there are new ways of delivering and managing infrastructure more effectively, based on international best practice. We are working with local authorities and government parastatals to find new ways of organising projects, so that the private sector can have a role in the different stages of planning, implementation, financing and management.

At the same time, the workers involved in implementing and maintaining these projects have a major contribution to make – it is often the front-line workers who have the most acute insights into how a job can be done better. We believe in empowering front-line workers, because their skills and insights give them a leading role in restructuring public sector operations. It is also their contribution to improving productivity and creating a client-centred service that will assist the massive expansion in services that our people require.

Organised labour also has a crucial role to play in directing the resources of worker-controlled pension funds. We have been impressed by the success of these initiatives in broadening access for workers to the economy, and believe that government must support the extension of such programmes through a facilitatory framework. Unions therefore have a critical role to play in the infrastructure investment programme.

Communities must shape their own destinies through their democratic institutions of local governance. Government cannot create miracles. The process of democratisation imposes certain responsibilities on people and communities. It demands that ordinary citizens take part in stabilising communities, in driving out crime and violence, in maintaining proper community facilities, in getting all our children into decent schools, and in contributing towards municipal services. South Africa simply cannot afford to carry those who are not paying for services despite adequate incomes. Non-payment of service charges is unacceptable.

From the government side we have been working intensively with all line departments and tiers of government to create the basis for a major programme of investment by government infrastructure.

The rebuilding and reconstruction of community facilities, and the maintenance of services and their improvement will remain largely impaired unless communities contribute by paying for the services they receive and defending assets such as electricity cables within their areas.

Government is now putting the finishing touches to a growth and development strategy that provides the context and rationale for the infrastructure investment programme. Infrastructure is one of the pillars of this strategy – it provides the link between economic growth and meeting basic needs. It creates efficiency in urban areas by linking services and housing closer to work opportunities. Water, transport, electricity and communications are the supporting web for small and medium-scale enterprises, and job creation. And by meeting basic needs we are building our human resources for the national effort to rebuild our economy.

Let me take this opportunity to invite the private sector to join us in investing in the necessary infrastructure provision as one of the key pillars for meeting basic needs and economic growth. I would be very pleased if, at the end of this conference, we can come out with concrete commitments to actually go out there on the ground, roll up our sleeves, put our money where our mouths are, and put the nation to work.

I therefore urge you to use the unique moment this conference provides to the full. There is a window of opportunity for us to cement a relationship that will lead us on the path of prosperity. I am calling on you to meet us halfway. Let us invest in the future of this country, in the human resources that are the heart of the economy, in the technological development and innovations that are at the cutting edge of competitiveness.

Let us put our resources together to create an infrastructure development, and in the long term through building a competitive and more equitably owned economy. Let us use this conference to develop a vision for the country, and to chart the routes we must travel to attain that vision. Let us go forward together in the spirit of a new patriotism, to build and develop our people and economy.

18

Reconstruction, Development and Macro-economic Policy

Speech at the National Assembly, Cape Town, 14 June 1996

THE NATIONAL ASSEMBLY IS about to begin its debate on the budget of our minister of finance.

It had seemed right that before the honourable minister makes his remarks, we should say something about the broader framework which encompasses the important announcements he will make.

That broader framework is the Reconstruction and Development Programme (RDP). This remains the policy anchor on which all government programmes have been and will continue to be based.

As this House knows, the RDP is about the fundamental transformation of our society in all its aspects. It has to do with the construction of a truly democratic, non-racial, non-sexist, prosperous and stable South Africa, positioned within the rest of the world community not as the pariah of the past but as a responsible international citizen and an example of what a people-centred society should be.

The RDP is therefore not a conglomeration of particular projects, but an integrated and sustainable vision for the creation of the post-apartheid society for which so many of our people sacrificed everything, including their lives. Its abiding feature is revolutionary change. Its ethos is an all-pervasive optimism for a better life for all our people.

The vision it spelt out challenged all of us as South Africans, within government, the private and the non-governmental sectors, to address five critical areas, namely:

- meeting the basic needs of the people;
- developing our human resources;
- building the economy;

- democratising the state and society; and
- implementing programmes to achieve these objectives.

Members are aware that in February of this year, the Intergovernmental Forum, bringing together central and provincial governments and following its meeting in November 1995, met here in Cape Town to discuss a growth and development strategy for the accomplishment of the vision spelt out in the RDP. At that February meeting, this is what we said:

> The National Growth and Development Strategy will take the RDP forward by setting out concrete steps that will accelerate growth and development and hence reach our targets of reducing poverty, increasing employment and improving the quality of life of our people.

Earlier in the same speech we pointed out that 'The draft before (the forum) must also be viewed as an elaboration of the RDP base document and not its substitute.'

Among other things and to give concrete expression to the vision contained in the RDP, that draft spoke of a sustained annual growth rate of the gross domestic product of at least 6 per cent by the year 2000 and the creation, annually, of between 300 000 and 500 000 new employment opportunities by the end of this century. In addition, it identified other areas of focus, including:

- national crime prevention to secure life and property;
- a system of social security and social development;
- investment in the social and economic infrastructure;
- restructuring the public sector and the state; and
- investing in people for human resource development.

On the occasion of the assembly of the Intergovernmental Forum four months ago, we indicated that we would be reporting to the nation and government on work done at various times during the course of the year. The debate today provides an appropriate occasion for us to report on work done in the elaboration of the macro-economic framework that both provides the perimeters of all our future socio-economic work and will underpin the key pillars of our strategy.

Today, the minister of finance, having been mandated to lead our work on this element of our growth and development strategy for the implementation of the RDP, will present the government's macro-economic policy. This policy is the central compass which will guide all other sectoral growth and development programmes of the government aimed at achieving the objectives of the RDP.

As government, we are confident that the policy is right and that both this Parliament and our social partners will join us in its implementation.

We must also make the point that, while conscious of the impatience of many, including our own, for the government to pronounce itself on many economic questions, we have sought to make certain that what we would say would be scientifically substantiated, based on concrete reality and therefore realisable. We have therefore, and within the confines of reason and our national capabilities, chosen to make haste slowly rather than hasten to earn ephemeral accolades.

It is also important to point out to this House that since February government has further developed the other aspects of our Growth and Development Strategy on the same basis of objectivity in the detail and boldness in the determination.

We have worked and are working on the national infrastructure investment framework together with our partners in the private sector.

For the first time in our history, both the public and the private sectors have, within a structured and implementable framework, agreed to work together to plan, finance and undertake municipal and other infrastructure development in new ways. The report covering this area will be published soon.

One of the most concrete manifestations of this private–public partnership, which also impacts positively on Southern African co-operation, is the Maputo Development Corridor.

Similarly, we are convinced that we will make decisive progress in investment in the critical area of the telecommunications infrastructure.

As part of the strategy of growth and development for the implementation of the RDP, government has also approved and announced the National Crime Prevention Strategy aimed at the critically important objectives of combating and preventing crime, a matter which this House discussed extensively only yesterday during the Justice budget vote.

The Comprehensive Labour Market Commission, appointed by the president to investigate the crucial matter of labour market policy, also submitted its report to the president yesterday.

The findings of this commission and the policy decisions that will derive from its report will be another important element in our Growth and Development Strategy.

The report contains important policy recommendations, including matters such as the co-ordination of macro-economic and industrial policies with labour market policy as well as labour market reform. It places emphasis on economic growth and development with job creation – all of which are matters of central importance to the achievement of the objectives of the RDP.

The major policy guidelines for the restructuring of the public service have already been announced and detailed work in this regard is taking place under the leadership of the minister for the public service and administration.

The process of the restructuring of state assets is going ahead. In this regard, I must make it clear that government will not be stampeded to take precipitate action.

In conclusion, let me emphasise that the macro-economic framework that will soon be presented to the honourable members of the National Assembly and the country at large constitutes an important part of government policy.

It sets targets which will guide all government actions, including policy refinements, provides the mandate for the interaction of government with its social partners in the National Economic Development and Labour Council, adds an important segment to the Growth and Development Strategy for the implementation of the RDP, and firmly indicates the actual road we have to travel towards the goal of a better life for all.

I trust that all our people, both inside and outside this House, will use this occasion seriously and constructively to engage the issues raised in the macro-economic policy and to redefine their role and place in the reconstruction and development of our country, inspired by the challenge of the new patriotism which beckons.

19

Matters of Common Concern

Budget vote, National Assembly, Cape Town, 6 June 1995

THE GREAT SENSE OF joy which washed over our country last year, as we held our first democratic elections and installed our first democratic government, was based on the hope and popular conviction that 'now [was] the winter of our discontent made glorious summer...' by the ending of the system of apartheid.

Regardless of the ups and downs that we, as a country, might have had since then, the point needs to be made that indeed millions of our people who less than 18 months ago were disenfranchised and marginalised have now been empowered, as part of the making of that glorious summer, to participate in determining the destiny of their motherland.

Millions who had no basis to hope for a stable and better future and therefore could not be motivated to take up the cudgels for their own improvement are today driven by the great urge to acquire education, to enhance their skills, to improve their lot through their own application, to clean up their physical environment and to create a stable society.

The struggle of the young to enter the best schools that we have, their concern to ensure that we improve the quality of education and the elaboration of their own code of conduct to create the best possible conditions for the reinforcement of a culture of learning and teaching, are all symptomatic of the great resurgence of hope which has come with the end of the winter of discontent.

The manner in which the whole country has embraced our national rugby team, the improved and improving relations between our police and the people, the forceful manner in which our new national symbols, such as our flag, have captured the imagination of the people speak eloquently of how the glorious summer has begun to manifest itself in the new South Africa in which we are no longer forced into racial and ethnic compartments and in which the institutions of state are acquiring a new legitimacy.

In a survey carried out by the Human Sciences Research Council in March this year [1995], one of the questions posed is 'Have your personal life circumstances improved or deteriorated since the Government of National Unity came to power in May last year?'

Of those questioned, 11,3 per cent responded that their personal life circumstances had deteriorated a lot. On the other hand, 40,4 per cent responded that their personal life circumstances had improved or improved a lot.

Despite the pronouncements of the cynics and the Jeremiahs, who will insist that nothing good has happened since we all took our seats in this chamber, we must continue to recognise the positive and salute those in our society who, either as individuals or as members of institutions, have made a serious effort towards the achievement of the common goal of improving the conditions of life of all our people.

But in addition to this and without understating the difficulties ahead of us, we must all continue to be dissatisfied with what we have achieved. We must continue to be driven by a sense of urgency to create the better life for all to which, as we understand it, all the parties represented in this Parliament are committed.

In the struggle to give greater content and permanence to the glorious summer which it is the right of the people to enjoy, the principal challenge we face as a country is to improve radically the quality of life of all our people, in a manner that would also vigorously address the urgent question of making further progress towards the elimination of the race and gender discrimination which continues to characterise South Africa one year after its emancipation.

Clearly, we cannot say we have the kind of South Africa we all wish to see when we still have millions of people unemployed and while those who are employed are still subject to racial discrimination in the workplace.

We cannot say we have the kind of South Africa we all wish to have when great numbers of infants and children continue to perish as victims of diseases and poverty.

Neither can we be satisfied with what we have when so many are victims of the insecurity and the harm that derives from high levels of crime.

We cannot say we have achieved what we sought to achieve when millions are gravely disempowered by their inability to read or write.

Neither can we say that we have built a humane society when many of our mature citizens and the disabled are marginalised and discarded.

There is no shortage of statistics which indicate the size of the problem we face. Let me cite a few of these.

The income differential between whites and Africans in the country remains at about 8 to 1. In more graphic terms, this means that 60 per cent of the African majority lives in conditions of poverty. Of these, between 8 and 9 million are regarded as completely destitute. The majority of these will also be women.

Sitting as we do for many months of the year in the comfort of this House, it is critically important that we do not lose sight of what these statistics represent – a scale of human suffering and wretchedness which, by any standards, is impermissible.

To come back to the general plane, Africans constitute 95 per cent of those who fall below the 'minimum living level'. Whites constitute about 1 per cent of this group.

When we talk of improving the quality of life of all our people, we surely must mean this: that we will close this gap to end the situation in which poverty and wealth so easily translate into black and white, with special reference to black women.

How difficult the challenge is becomes obvious if we bear in mind that, to close this gap by moving the poor upwards without impacting negatively on the general standard of living, we have to increase the size of the economy a number of times over. Among other things, this requires that we develop a national consensus on economic policy.

Let us mention another statistic which bears directly on the pressing matter of safety and security – 86 per cent of all permanent police stations are located in the white areas of our country. To achieve a similar density in the present African, coloured and Indian areas, together with the human and material resources attached to each station, would once again require that we expend huge resources which are clearly not available.

In terms of the daily lives of many of our people, this means that they cannot access a police officer at the moment when they are in need of assistance. In many instances, it also signifies that even when contact has been established, the police are unable to reach where they need to, because they have no vehicles. What this describes is that even when there is the will, there is no way.

The terrible but actual reality which we have sought to describe poses an important question to all of us who sit in this House. It presents a challenge which requires an honest response from all of us who wish to present ourselves to the country and the world as genuine leaders and representatives of these masses, to whom the matter of the urgent and radical improvement of the quality of life is not a mere phrase in an election manifesto.

The question is: Do we as political leaders have the will to permit the fundamental national imperative of addressing the people's needs to take precedence over narrow partisan interests?

An answer to this question is important and urgent because it addresses in a very direct way the issue of the possibility of the creation of the climate of peace and stability which we need in order to begin to tackle in a significant and sustained manner the dire socio-economic situation which faces millions of our people.

It needs no repetition that, of course, both Parliament and the government are composed of different political formations which have different policies which they must pursue vigorously, as is their democratic right.

Even in the instance that we have all agreed to the broad framework provided by the Reconstruction and Development Programme, the reality is that naturally we will continue to differ about a variety of matters. Those who see themselves as opposition parties will and must continue to exercise their right to fulfil that function. None of this can be questioned and must indeed be accepted and encouraged as a healthy battle of ideas which is an inherent part of the democratic process. The issue we are raising has to do with the manner in which we exercise these democratic rights.

We believe it is not asking too much to say that, given the deep-seated problems which we face, none of us should engage the political battle in a manner which makes it more difficult or impossible to tackle what we understand to be matters of common concern, namely the upliftment of the deprived millions of our people, the closing of the racial and gender imbalances in our society which discriminate against Africans, coloureds and Indians, and the development of the youth on an urgent and sustained basis.

We believe that it is incorrect to continue to blame the past for our present. It is incorrect, in the pursuit of partisan interests, to pretend for instance that the high levels of crime in our country are the product of the transition to democracy or the wilful incompetence of the Government of National Unity and, in particular, its major component.

This argument is sometimes advanced in the context of the accepted right to oppose but is, in reality, intended to make the point that the majority party is inherently incapable of dealing with the problem of crime. Thus those who are further afield might be persuaded that what was alleged by some last year, that we are on the verge of chaos and anarchy, is indeed true and inevitable. We do not believe that it can be correct that, in the pursuit of partisan interests, we deliberately create an atmosphere of despair about the present and the future.

To ensure that I am not misunderstood, let me say this: that all of us, as well as the media, have every right to report and comment on crime as we deem fit. But the politicisation of this matter in a manner that distorts reality subtracts from what should be the common effort both to deal with the problem of crime vigorously and to create the climate in the country which will enable us to achieve the socio-economic advances which are the right of the people.

Some among us also seek to influence the present by pretending to be authoritative interpreters of the future. In this regard, a frightening picture is painted of an ANC that will be plunged into a deep crisis, with a terrible impact on the rest of the country and its future, as a result of some leadership struggle that will break out in future.

Those of us who are members of the ANC, who know the ANC and are familiar with its history, also know that this is a self-serving figment of imagination. For 83 years the ANC has handled the question of leadership in a democratic manner, without any instability arising as a consequence. Nothing has happened to suggest that, all of a sudden and for some inexplicable reason, the ANC will now lose the capacity to deal with this question in the manner that it has always dealt with it.

There is no leadership crisis in the ANC.

To incite and encourage uncertainty about the future on the basis of the pursuit of narrow partisan interests and on grounds that have no historical basis, communicating a message that all must wait until the future explosion has occurred, does little to contribute to the creation of the climate the country needs to deal with the urgent needs of the people with which we are all familiar.

The people of KwaZulu-Natal are among the poorest in the country. Millions of its residents cry out every day for development, to extricate them from the dehumanisation that results from poverty, which also leads to conflict as people are forced to compete against one another for scarce resources.

As we all know, this province is also victim to high levels of violence which continue to claim many lives. In this situation, development becomes impossible in a part of our country which patently is in dire need of such development.

It is the obligation of all the political formations in the province to take on board the understanding that they have a common responsibility to do everything in their power to create the conditions of peace, stability and co-operation among the people which are so necessary for development.

The pursuit of partisan objectives should not be allowed further to heighten tensions in the province, fed by an atmosphere of brinkmanship in the conduct of the political contest in the province.

None of us should behave in a manner which suggests that we could not care less about the obvious and urgent needs of the people for peace, safety and security, for jobs, food, land, water and shelter, and are prepared to sacrifice these on the altar of such political victories as anyone of us may seek to achieve.

Similar observations can be made with regard to the issue of the need to approach the question of the building of party constituencies, especially among the national minorities, in a manner which does not result in the further entrenchment of racial divisions and tensions in our society.

Here, once more, there lurks the danger that we could so conduct ourselves that, by presenting the interests of the various racial groups of our country as being opposed to one another, competing and in conflict, we can, in fact, provoke such conflict and make it impossible to achieve the fundamental objective of the creation of a non-racial society, a critical element of which is a fair and equitable distribution of resources and opportunities in the interest of all our people.

The fundamental and critical question we have been trying to address concerns a matter that is clearly on the national agenda – the question of the challenge of leadership during the present period.

It would seem obvious that for those of us who would claim to be faced with the obligation to lead both our parties and our people as a whole, we must address the question of what is primary and what is secondary, of what is necessary in the narrow political interest and what is imperative with regard to meeting the needs of the people.

None of us can pretend that we have all the answers to these questions. All of us are new to the democratic society which last year's elections brought into being. While international political experience is obviously useful and relevant in helping us to find the way, it is nevertheless also true that there is no experience anywhere in the world which we can merely copy.

However, there is no doubt that we must continuously address this question of the challenge of leadership, in the complex situation of a changing and dynamic reality which presents us with new scenarios on a daily basis.

Our country needs peace. It needs an end to the infamy represented by the continuing discrimination against people on the basis of race and gender. It urgently calls for an end to the blight of criminal violence which results in political assassinations, family murders, rape, child abuse and armed robberies.

Our people cry out for bread and peace. The entrenchment of democracy requires that we achieve development. Africa needs a stable and prosperous South Africa. The rest of the world remains committed to help us to sustain our success, convinced that that success would also contribute to the overall improvement of the situation in world politics and the world economy.

Those we claim to lead will respect and listen to us only to the extent that we address all these matters in a visible, sustained and successful manner.

Let us pose the question once again: Do we, as political leaders, have the will to permit the fundamental national imperative of addressing the people's needs to take precedence over narrow partisan interests?

What remains to be seen is whether we are ready and willing to live up to this challenge, to make a serious effort, which in a practical way can say to the people that when autumn is here, both spring and summer cannot be too far behind.

20
Immersed in a National Emergency

Speech at the Installation Banquet for Professor M. Ramashala, University of Durban-Westville, Durban, 9 May 1998

ALL OF US PRESENT here know the reality that our institutions of higher learning do need more and more resources to discharge their responsibilities properly.

This problem is compounded by the persisting apartheid disparities in this area. The following statistics graphically illustrate the depth of this problem.

The historically black universities are said to have 50 per cent more students above the capacity capable of being catered for by the existing physical infrastructure and equipment, while the historically white universities could accommodate 20 per cent more students than are actually enrolled.

The latter, with 35 per cent of the students, absorb 65 per cent of government funds allocated to universities while the former, with 30 per cent of the student population, receive 25 per cent of these funds.

The historically white universities better their black counterparts in terms of the staff–student ratio by a startling 50 per cent, in a situation where the relatively weaker pre-university preparation of the majority of the students at the black institutions would suggest that we need a higher concentration of educators relative to the student population.

Therefore there can be no doubt about the reality of the need to devote more resources to the task of redressing the apartheid imbalance.

The other reality, however, is that we are caught in the horns of a cruel dilemma. On the one hand there is a pressing need:

- to meet the increasing demand for access to higher education;
- to work urgently to increase the pool of properly qualified people in all areas of knowledge;

148

- to address the racial and gender imbalances among the strata of qualified people; and, therefore,
- to provide the necessary resources to ensure the accomplishment of these goals.

On the other hand, there is absolutely no social need in our country which is not both massive and pressing. And there is an expectation that each of these can and must be addressed immediately through adequate disbursements from the national budget.

Very few will pay any attention to the fact that, in real terms, the revenue flowing into the national public accounts are little changed from those collected into the revenue account during the years immediately preceding our transition to democracy.

The apartheid state poured resources into its racist project of upliftment of, at best, 15 per cent of our population. The democratic state has an obligation to spread virtually the same volume of resources among 100 per cent of our population.

And yet the expectation persists that the government will somehow find it within its power rapidly to bridge the yawning gulf between black and white by raising the standard of living of the former to equal that attained by the latter, and that in a short period of time. All logic points to the fact that however understandable this expectation, it cannot be realised, however intense our desire and fervent our prayers for this expectation to be met.

All I am trying to say is that the stark fact is that we are set on a long and difficult road to the goal of meeting our wish and commitment to ensuring a decent quality of life for all our citizens. The legitimate needs of the people cannot be met within the short time frames which those who are deprived are perfectly justified to dream of and plead for.

Without seeking to subtract from the joy of this particular moment, when we celebrate the accession of a black woman to a high post in an important institution such as the University of Durban-Westville (UDW), this we must say. The equally legitimate needs of especially the historically black institutions of higher learning cannot be met within the short time frames which all of us are perfectly justified to dream of and plead for.

At the same time and despite what we have said, the great historic project of rebuilding South Africa as a democratic, non-racial, non-sexist, peaceful, prosperous and advanced African country of joy, culture and individual fulfilment dare not fail.

Least of all should it fail because the poor and the wretched lose faith in the capacity of the democratic order to help them extricate themselves from the desperate condition of poverty, which the wealth of some in our society seems to mock every passing hour and towards whose alleviation the thieves and robbers offer a criminal solution of social disorder, anarchy, a descent into the dark world in which all are obliged to be a predator to ensure that they do not become prey to the predators.

Our situation demands of all of us that we accept the fact that the legacy of apartheid has left us with an entrenched social disaster of immense proportions. This is represented in particular by the millions who are poor, starving, unemployed. It finds expression among the victims of HIV/AIDS, of rape and physical abuse. It informs the behaviour of millions who lead lives without hope and will therefore kill easily or be killed easily, because life is without meaning and death bright with the prospect of rest and eternal peace.

This pervasive condition of a powerful social stench which infuses the entirety of our society cannot be wished away. It demands that we recognise the reality that whatever the outward glitter of any of our neighbourhoods, we are immersed in a long-term national emergency out of which we cannot escape unless we adopt emergency measures.

As South Africans we are called upon to perform new miracles.

The cynics sit everywhere in the theatre. Their voices are trained loudly to proclaim: No miracles are possible! Their minds are transformed into instruments to think up the best ways in which they can convince us that the rational response to the national emergency is to succumb to despair.

And yet, when all is said and done, and precisely because of the stridency of the voice of those whose daily preoccupation is to spread a doctrine of despondency, as South Africans we are called upon to perform new miracles.

The miracles I speak of have nothing to do with the world of mystics or the supernatural. They are about the need for us to draw on the resources which enabled us to maintain our humour and humanity during the brutal years of the apartheid tyranny. They are about the spirit which inspired us to be willing to sacrifice everything for the common good.

It would seem to me that the historic victory of 1994 has conveyed to many in our country that the struggle is over, that now is the time to harvest by means fair or foul the supposedly rich and limitless dividend of our sacrifices.

A new national mobilisation is required as a matter of urgency.

This new mobilisation has to produce a complex of related outcomes.

The first of these is that we must infuse it into the public consciousness that none of the great demands which relate to the achievement of the objective of a better life for all can be met in the short term or the intermediate future.

The second is that we must succeed to convince the masses of our people that the future of our country, as well as their own as individuals, is as dependent on what they themselves do to participate in the process of reconstruction and development as it is on the institutions of society, such as the democratic state and the corporate world.

The third is that we must mobilise the entire echelon of leadership, the so-called decision-makers in all sectors of social activity, to take this on board: that we are all faced with a national emergency. This emergency impacts negatively on all of us and remains the one factor which threatens the realisation of the national goal of a peaceful and prosperous society.

To overcome that emergency will require that each one of us in our sectors should think in fresh, bold and original ways, take flight from the concept of 'business as usual' and find ways in which we can contribute to the elimination of the national emergency imposed on the country by the legacy of apartheid.

Such are the new miracles that our country is called upon to realise.

I am convinced that all of us have an obligation properly to understand the actual reality of the situation in our country.

Further, we must abandon the notion that there is some other force, outside us, which has sole and exclusive responsibility to solve the problems that face us. We must each adopt the position that I, too, am responsible for the destiny of our country and will act in a manner that contributes positively to a good outcome.

To achieve these new miracles requires new mobilisation that will release the latent energies and talents that the millions of our people surely have among them.

The universities and technikons constitute a major resource for the generation of this new thinking. I believe, therefore, that a great responsibility rests on the shoulders of the leaders of these institutions, such as the new incumbent at the UDW, to rise to this challenge in a bold and determined manner.

One of the matters that will clearly have to be addressed is what we can do to respond practically to the disjuncture caused by the imbalance between the need for higher education and the resource constraint that limits the possibility to meet this need.

To take one example at random: Is there no possibility to use modern telecommunications to enable lecturers who might be based at one university or technikon to lecture simultaneously to students both at the institution where they are and, at the same time, communicate the same lecture to students at a different institution?

If this were to be done, it would obviously help to ease the shortage of teachers at the more disadvantaged institutions and ensure that the students who qualify at these institutions catch up with their colleagues in the better-placed centres of learning.

I am pleased that we have so many of our business leaders present here tonight. We depend on them to make a significant contribution towards meeting the goal of a better-resourced UDW.

I am certain that none of them needs to be lectured about the critical importance of human resource development to the building of the South Africa of all our dreams. This they know as well as I do – that the more we succeed in realising that dream, the greater the possibility for them to do more business.

The obverse is also true – that no business can truly succeed, however well managed and run, if all around it society is engulfed in flames born of the frustrations of the deprived.

We count on you to join in this partnership which will enable our universities and technikons to discharge their responsibilities to the nation. For its part, your government will continue to search for ways and means by which it can help these institutions to satisfy their material needs.

21

A New Patriotism:
What Have I Contributed?

Address at the University of the Transkei Fundraising Dinner, Johannes-burg, 30 April 1998

NONE OF US PRESENT HERE needs to be educated about the huge constraint on government fully to fund both universities and the students who seek university education.

Further, all of us are aware of the real need for financial support of especially black students, many of whom come from very poor families.

Surely we are all committed to the view that poverty, the heritage of our history, which will take a long time to address, should not turn into an insuperable obstacle, denying talented young people from poor families the possibility to access higher education.

We are also talking of the University of Transkei (UNITRA), whose catchment area is one of the most underdeveloped regions of our country, with very limited opportunities for income generation – a region which is therefore afflicted by levels of poverty which are above the national average.

Therefore no rational person can speak against the need for all of us – individuals, the public and private sectors – to join hands in addressing the all-important issue of education, training and human resource development.

Further, I am convinced that we are all of one mind in the view that education is central to the development both of the individual and our society. Without a society of educated people neither can we speak of the all-round development of the individual citizen nor of the reconstruction and development of our country and its placement among the countries of the world as a winning nation.

I am certain that we also think alike about the need radically to raise

153

the profile of the natural and economic sciences and engineering in terms of our intake into the universities.

This is not to question the importance of the arts, social sciences and the law but to correct the obvious imbalance that exists now, as in the past, and to respond to the dictates of contemporary society and economy which place a premium on high and modern skills levels.

When those responsible for the terrible genocide in Rwanda four years ago decided to carry out this criminal deed, among others they focused on that country's intelligentsia and sought to decimate this important sector of Rwandan society which, because of its education, had the possibility to question the imprisonment of its people by concepts of a permanent and irreconcilable hostility between the Hutu and Tutsi.

The government of Rwanda and others, even as far afield as Guinea-Bissau in West Africa, have requested our country to assist in the rebuilding of their national cadre of intellectuals, as part of their own imperative to develop their countries.

This process was further formalised at the recent African Continental Education Summit held in Durban. A Declaration of Intent was signed by 53 African education ministers at this conference as a consequence of which we committed ourselves to receive students from the rest of the continent who would be supported by the United Nations Educational, Scientific and Cultural Organisation (UNESCO).

Again, I would like to believe that none of us in this room would question the critical importance to ourselves and the rest of humanity of the project of the renewal of our continent and the need for us as a country and people to play our own part in ensuring the success of this historic project.

Having said all these things, I am also convinced that we seriously need to pose the question to ourselves as a country whether the national agreement that exists on the matter of the centrality of human resource development is merely rhetorical or whether it carries with it an actual commitment on the part of all of us to do everything that is necessary to achieve this objective.

This would include the allocation of funds, the restructuring of educational and training institutions, the elaboration of appropriate syllabi and training programmes, the improvement of the quality of our educators, counselling of students to enter the relevant fields of education and achieving success with regard to the national campaign to promote a culture of learning, teaching and service.

Each of the matters we have mentioned so far is obviously very important and has been part of the ongoing discussion in the country about the issue of education and training.

We could take advantage of this occasion to discuss any of these questions as they would all be relevant to UNITRA and education in general. However, given the fact that we knew that there could be no dispute among us about any of these issues, we thought it might be wisest to address other questions, perhaps of a broader nature.

During the apartheid years, the government and the state played a central role in ensuring the all-round upliftment of especially the Afrikaner people. Focusing on a minority of the population of our country, the possibility existed actually to use such resources and opportunities as were available to make a visible impact on the lives of that minority within a relatively short period of time.

It was natural that there would be an expectation among those who were the oppressed during those years that when a democratic government was formed, it would similarly use whatever resources and opportunities were available to make a visible impact with regard to providing a better life for the people, again within a relatively short period of time. As a consequence, the word 'delivery' seems to have assumed a particular place of eminence in the social and political language of change. And this word attaches in particular to the government.

The task of the government is to deliver – such is the notion that gets propagated every day.

The reason government exists is to deliver – again in many people's minds this constitutes the sum total of political science and wisdom.

Those in government feel greatly obliged every day to account to the people on how much they have succeeded in delivering. Indeed, in many instances, they join the chorus which reinforces the notion that government has legitimacy only to the extent that it delivers.

We have a place in society only because we have the miraculous power to deliver.

And what is this thing that must be delivered?

The goodies!

The cry goes out: Give us jobs!

Give us houses! Give us clean water! Give us land! Give us roads!

Feed the hungry! Heal the sick! Let those who are disabled arise and walk! Let the government proclaim – let there be light – and deliver light!

What remains is for us all to invest the government with the heavenly powers which would enable it to say: I am the Deliverer and none exists but I. Cursed are those who worship at the feet of idols, because it is I and only I, the democratic state, that will deliver you from your misery!

And so you and I can see these masses at the feet of the Deliverer, hands held out in supplication, incanting in unison: Deliverer, deliver!

Is it correct that we preach such a message of disempowerment of the people, predicated on the notion of a deliverer and a recipient?

When President Mandela has raised the question of the need for all of us to be driven by a new patriotism, perhaps many of us wondered what it is that this old man spoke of. After all, the doctrine of the political science of delivery teaches us that the only challenge that each one of us faces is to be first in the queue at the place where delivery will take place. Therefore, what does he speak of, except the requirement that I must wake up early enough to be first in the receiving line that waits for the democratic government to deliver?

There is an unquestioned responsibility for the government to address the many needs of all the people of South Africa, ranging from guaranteeing the safety and security of the citizens to caring for the children of indigent families. However, the question has to be posed: What is the responsibility of citizens to themselves and to the country, without whose progress the stable and permanent advancement of the individual is impossible?

When we who, for now anyway, occupy positions of political leadership speak only of a record of achievement illustrated by statistics of delivery, and do not address with the same vigour and consistency the issue of what each of our citizens is doing themselves to deliver to themselves and to society – are we not thereby also contributing to the demobilisation and disempowerment of the people and the inculcation among them of a frame of mind of dependence on a magnanimous Deliverer who has an exclusive obligation to see to the improvement of the conditions of life of the passive recipient whose only task is to say: Give me more! Give me more!

And so we see the consequences of this in our universities.

Many students, but fortunately not all, know it as a matter of fact that they are entitled to government funding. If they do not receive such funding, they have an obligation to be vexed, to be angry, to express that anger in any way they choose, to keep in their pockets the money they have to pay their fees or, better still, to spend it on the good things of life and to convey the message in its clearest terms: Deliverer, deliver!

You and I would agree that the young intellectuals of our country, among them the students at our universities, have a responsibility to ask the question: What do we do with the freedom we have gained to ensure that we build a better society and a country which every South African would be proud to call home?

As part of that process, these students, like their parents and communities, the teaching staff, the workers and the administration at universities, must participate in a process of the transformation of these institutions so that these contribute as best they can to the building of that better society.

Accordingly, they must ask themselves whether it is permissible for any student to stay at university for many years without making any progress in terms of meeting the expected academic requirements.

They must question whether the courses their institutions offer are suitable to the new world in which we live and will contribute to the achievement of the objective of a winning nation.

They must ask whether it is correct for a student who can afford to contribute to meeting the costs of his of her education to refuse to do so and thereby deny the possibility for a truly poor student to access the existing limited pool of funds.

As young intellectuals, should they not be the ones that should go out to the people to say to the people that we are a poor country? Should they not be out in the field educating the millions who expect the Deliverer to bring the goodies that, as young scientists, they have studied our reality and that out of that study they can say that the high-rise buildings of Johannesburg, Durban, Cape Town and Port Elizabeth tell half of the story of what South Africa is, that the comforts of Plettenberg Bay and the private game lodges on the edge of the Kruger Park only speak to an element of what South Africa is?

Should they not be out there saying to the people that you, who have sacrificed to ensure that we have power because we are educated, need to know that ours is a poor country, whose real possibilities are defined not by him or her who every year can spend their holidays in the South of France, but these millions who have no guarantee of any of their meals in all the days during which they have been blessed to be on this earth?

And so we come back to the notion of the new patriotism.

Surely it must be commitment to the success of the country. It must be about our abandonment of the concept of the Deliverer with its corollary of the Entitled Recipient. It must be about the joining of forces by the state and the citizen to address all these matters of common concern about which there are no differences.

In the context of all of this, perhaps the time has come that the government should make a number of points clear:

- that it is committed to addressing the matter of financial aid to students, but on the basis that they are needy, capable, disciplined and performing in terms of their academic obligations;
- that there shall be zero tolerance for flouting contractual obligations in our institutions of learning and teaching;
- that government policy will ensure that there will be maximum returns on its investment in the area of human resource development; and
- that where disputes arise and action is taken outside the agreed procedures, the principle of 'no work, no pay' will be applied strictly.

At the base of all of this must be the requirement that, as a country, we create the situation in which the citizen does not ask the question: What has the government done for me? but rather the question: What have I contributed to the solution of the problems that face me?

Hopefully, the students who will benefit from the scholarship fund about which we have gathered here tonight will themselves know that inasmuch as society contributed to the acquisition of their own skills and qualification, so must it be that they too address the issue of their contribution to the upliftment of the millions who have no possibility to enjoy the opportunity thus made available to them.

PART FIVE

The Information Revolution, Globalisation and Economic Development

THE FIVE SPEECHES IN this section represent and illustrate Mbeki's understanding of global economic and technological trends, and his conviction that South Africa is part of the global village.

Mbeki is not an isolationist. He fully understands the challenge to lead South Africa into the next century.

It is significant to note that Mbeki, in his reference to for instance the Asian Tigers, remains his own man. He does not commit South Africa to using the Asian Tigers as role model – as so many South Africans wanted him to do.

On the contrary, he says: '…we have been very keen to learn whatever we could' – implicitly signalling that South Africa, given her historical circumstances, will have to find her own way of dealing with challenges.

His speech on 'The Information Revolution' contains a reference to the need for media diversity, which caused some public debate. He made the point that 'the political tendency represented by the liberation movement is, by and large, not represented in our media', implying that the media world is in need of transformation.

In his speech to the NEDLAC Summit in June 1996, he again addressed the need for a national strategic vision by pleading for a partnership between government, labour and business. In fact, he stated it in no uncertain terms: '…we are condemned to live together and interact with one another, both the unwashed and the perfumed. Divorce is not possible.'

22

Building the Economy

Speech at the Asian Tigers and the African Lion business conference, Gallagher Estate, Midrand, 26 March 1996

THE POLITICAL RELATIONS between ourselves were formed and strengthened during the course of our common struggle for the emancipation of all our countries from colonial and apartheid domination.

We are privileged once more to express our appreciation to you for the fact that you stood with us during the difficult years as we fought against the system of apartheid, refusing to tire and to turn your backs on a struggle which to some might, at times, have seemed too long and possibly hopeless.

We are therefore particularly happy that you have been able to visit a free South Africa, to see the fruit of your labours and sacrifices and more, to discuss with us where we go from now, building on the firm political and economic foundation of co-operation that has already been set.

Almost two years after our historic first democratic elections, we can report to you that the democratic system in our country has taken root, thanks to the commitment of the overwhelming majority of our people to ensure that we should never again experience the oppression of one people by another and the denial of any individual of his or her right to participate in determining the future of our country.

The necessary democratic institutions have been and are being established. Popular participation in public life ensures that every day we entrench the practice of government by the people. As the political change brings about continuous improvement to the quality of life of all our people, so do the millions claim ownership of the new democratic order.

The unfounded fears that some had entertained that these masses would explode in anger if two days after liberation they had not acquired a new house or a job have failed to materialise, precisely because the ordinary people of our country see the new South Africa as their own, the product of the struggle they themselves waged, a young plant to be nurtured and cared for by themselves and with great delicacy.

This, in the end, is what guarantees stability – that inasmuch as the people were their own liberators, so will they be the architects of their own development and prosperity.

The miracle of our transition to democracy originates from these sentiments which led our people, both black and white, to conclude that they share a common destiny and that the only guarantee of a better life for each was not the segregation of one from another, but the joining of hands by all in a common effort to build a new society of democracy, non-racialism and non-sexism.

The majority shares a common resolve to overcome the legacy of our past and in a spirit of reconciliation, to effect the necessary transformation which will make South Africa, in the words of President Mandela, a winning nation.

A critical element of that transformation is the rebuilding of our economy. Fortunately, after many years of stagnation and decline, we have begun to record positive rates of growth. There is no reason why we should fail to continue this tendency. Indeed, we are determined to follow the example of our guests from the Association of South-East Asian Nations (ASEAN) by achieving high rates of growth on a sustained basis.

In this regard I must mention that we have been very keen to learn whatever we could of the factors that led to the ASEAN economic miracle. We greatly appreciate the willingness demonstrated by all the ASEAN countries to assist us in this regard and to open their doors to us so that, among other things, we could send our people to your countries for purposes of acquiring the skills which have been a central part of the miracle you have achieved.

The growth we are aiming at must also mean the development of our society so that we address the social ills that are the legacy of the past. These include unacceptably high levels of unemployment and pervasive poverty that afflicts millions of our citizens.

In addition to the political stability we have spoken of, our government has adopted policies which will ensure the achievement of the necessary macro-economic balances to ensure the creation of circumstances conducive to growth and development. Among other factors, this entails the management of public finances so that the public sector does not siphon off too much of the national wealth for purposes of meeting recurrent expenditures that are too high. Consequently, this has meant that we have committed ourselves not to increase the overall tax burden, but to stay on the road on which we have already embarked, of a continuous reduction of the dissaving by the public sector which resulted from the policies of the previous regime.

We are also committed to the removal of exchange controls over time and have already taken major steps in this regard, affecting especially the ability of foreign investors to move their capital freely in and out of the country.

Our president has already indicated that with regard to the remaining controls, the question is not whether these will be removed but merely when they will be ended. In this regard I would like to mention that we are fully conscious that we are part of the global economy and have a responsibility to ourselves to be as competitive in terms of investor-friendliness as any comparable country in the world, including the ASEAN countries.

Beyond this, we are also determined to ensure that we further open up our economy to greater and more varied trade exchanges with the rest of the world. This must include continuous change in the mix of products we export in favour of modern manufactured goods and services, with less reliance on our historic exports of precious minerals, raw materials and food products.

We are also committed to the implementation of the undertakings we made in the context of the Uruguay Round and the rules of the World Trade Organisation, in a manner that is sensitive to the central goal of job creation and the avoidance of policies that might result in further job losses.

The government is also working toward the finalisation of a comprehensive Growth and Development Strategy, which should also be agreed with our social partners, labour and the private sector.

That Growth and Development Strategy will, among other things, seek to identify the areas of our economy which are critical to such goals as job creation, the modernisation and enhancement of the international competitiveness of the economy, and the achievement of the sustainable high growth rates we have spoken of.

Among these must feature the major development of the infrastructure in both rural and urban areas; the growth of the hospitality industry and the necessary infrastructure; the restructuring of state assets among other things to attract foreign capital, to raise the levels of our performance to world standards and to provide affordable services to greater numbers of our people; the modernisation of various sectors of the manufacturing industry to enable it to provide goods both in the local and international markets at competitive prices; the implementation of a major housing programme; and human resource development.

We are also an integral part of the region of Southern Africa and a member of the Southern African Development Community (SADC). We are committed to the view that all of us in this region must work towards greater regional co-operation, towards our economic integration. This we must do in a manner that will contribute to balanced regional development in the interest of all our countries, including South Africa itself.

We are therefore speaking of a market of at least 100 million people, which is characterised by the need for reconstruction and development similar to our own.

In the end, what we have spoken of are the enormous business opportunities for trade and investment that the challenges of reconstruction and development in South Africa and in Southern Africa afford the enterprising and far-sighted business person.

Part of the critical importance of this conference is that it further enhances the interaction among ourselves, the countries of the South. It enables all of us to investigate and discover possibilities and opportunities that we may never have thought existed.

We are greatly encouraged by the fact that in the short period since our transition to democracy, the economic relations between ourselves and ASEAN countries have grown significantly.

I am informed, for instance, that our trade with Singapore is already over R1,5 billion, with Malaysia and Thailand following closely behind with R1 billion each. At the same time, we are experiencing encouraging inflows of investment, once again with Singapore leading, and an expectation of a further and significant increase in investments from Malaysia.

I am certain that all of us present in this room are conscious of the fact that all of this represents merely the beginning of an interaction that has great possibilities that would benefit all the players as we implement practically the shared vision of ever-increasing South–South co-operation.

That interaction will further be buttressed by the fact that friendly relations exist among our peoples and governments. Furthermore, the period since our transition to democracy has seen an important exchange of visits among ourselves, involving our governments, the private sector and tourists.

We are also all members of the Nonaligned Movement. All these factors point to a common resolve to build our relations on a comprehensive basis and with a view to lasting friendship among our peoples.

I am certain that this occasion will afford us the opportunity we both seek of enhancing the contact with one another across the Indian Ocean and discovering areas of mutually beneficial business co-operation.

It is also pleasing to see so many of our leading business people participating in this conference, as they are critical to the achievement of the common national objective of creating a better life for all our people and contributing to a world of shared prosperity.

On behalf of our government, I wish the conference success and commit our government to do all that is necessary and possible to support the positive results of your deliberations.

23

The Information Revolution

Budget vote, Senate, Cape Town, 11 June 1996

IT IS A REALITY OF OUR times that the modern world that we live in is one which is driven by information. Information has become so pivotal in the running of the day-to-day affairs of nations that its absence would render impossible the formulation of policies or the taking of decisions.

The revolution in modern technology has ensured that information is delivered at the next destination with a speed that defies imagination.

At the touch of a computer button, a businessman in Japan can access the markets of the United States, France, Germany, South Africa or any part of the world that he so chooses. He would be able to know what commodities are available in the world market as well as the competitive prices.

Within a very short space of time he would be having sufficient information at his disposal to make a decision as to where he wants to make his purchases and how and when the commodities would be transported to Japan.

Because of the speed with which information travels, the world is now referred to as the global village. Through the development of telecommunication and satellites we can speak to anyone anywhere in the world; we can also transport pictures and texts within seconds.

This has enabled leaders to be warned timeously about regional situations that have the potential to destabilise peace and to consult and take appropriate action to defuse the situation.

The developed countries of the West are cruising on the information superhighway and are daily bridging the gap of mistrust, suspicion and fear which are the products of ignorance.

It is a worrying phenomenon that the picture that we have painted above is not representative of humanity as a whole. The developing countries have been left behind. It would not be an exaggeration to say that as the West is cruising in automobiles on the information superhighway, we are still moving on horse-drawn carts in a dirt road in some small village.

We cannot even begin to speak about international communication while we have not improved interpersonal information or interprovincial and even intercontinental communication.

We need to jointly exercise our minds and to pool resources to overcome the ignorance and lack of information which is in part responsible for the high levels of poverty, disease and underdevelopment.

Because of the uneven development between the urban and the rural areas and between the provinces themselves, we need to give priority to the provision of telecommunication infrastructure to the disadvantaged because that is where the people need information like the fresh air that we breathe.

The people in these areas are fully conscious of the fact that they need to be empowered with information and knowledge to improve the conditions of their lives. A recent survey in the Northern Province conducted by the South African Communication Services indicates that over 90 per cent of that province's population wants to receive information and communication directly from the government. This is in addition to other sources of information, such as the privately owned media and the South African Broadcasting Corporation.

The need for the government to create the necessary mechanisms to provide people with information and to engage in a two-way dialogue with the citizenry becomes imperative because of the historical evolution of South African society. The majority of the people in South Africa have been excluded from the process of the acquisition of wealth and therefore ended up being marginalised from the economic as well as the political power centres that evolved.

In this context, it is pertinent to raise another larger and thorny question. This relates to the representation of different points of view in the media in general.

Historically, especially the African majority has been denied access to the mass media. Where it has established its own newspapers since the last century, many of these have failed to survive as independent entities because of the inability of this community, which is largely

169

poor, to dispose of sufficient incomes to sustain a substantial press. Where the political representatives of this community have deliberately sought to fill this void by issuing various publications, these became targets of repressive action with one journal after another being banned and closed down.

During the 1980s more effort was made to address this question through the establishment of what was described as the alternative media. I believe that every fair-minded person recognised the fact that, at that point, the commercial media and certainly the public broadcaster did not represent the views of the majority which apartheid society also excluded in many other ways.

In established democracies the general rule is that the major political tendencies are represented in the mass media to one extent or another. Consequently, newspapers openly support one political party or another as part of their editorial policy.

Clearly there is nothing wrong with this. It reflects the normal evolution of societies and is not determined by government decree. To the extent that it is also part of our own reality, it is again a matter that cannot and will not be addressed by government edict.

Because of the particular evolution of our own society, we find the remarkable situation that, because of the history we have already indicated, the political tendency represented by the liberation movement is by and large not represented in our media. The problem gets further compounded when that tendency becomes the government of the day because that lack of representation is then extended to the government.

It is for this reason that the issue of media diversity becomes very important because, quite frankly, the situation cannot be considered normal where a majority political school of thought finds no way of taking its place alongside other schools of thought in the mass media.

The issue is not to deny those who are well represented in the media the right and the possibility so to be represented. What is required is that we should work towards creating a more equitable situation such that all significant schools of thought, and not just some, are able to reach the people in their millions.

I believe that the public broadcaster has a role to play in this regard as well – not to act as the propaganda organ of any school of thought, but to ensure that it conveys news and views from all schools of thought in an equitable manner.

170

I also believe that in the disposal of some of its broadcasting assets to private owners, the public broadcaster and the Independent Broadcasting Authority (IBA) will also have to take example from some of the actions of existing businesses which are trying to diversify ownership to benefit those who have been disadvantaged, precisely to correct the gross imbalance in terms of access to the means for mass communication which we have inherited from the past.

Here we must address not merely the question of ownership, but the critical question of ensuring that as a true democracy no significant section of the population is denied the possibility to communicate.

I am aware of the fact that many of the issues we have raised are contentious. The situation is worsened by fears that arise from past government practices which result in relatively high levels of mistrust.

I believe that the core of the challenge confronting us is to create information resources and delivery systems dedicated to the principal information needs of citizens, especially in the provinces where the majority of our population resides.

In this endeavour, it is crucial that we discuss and debate the role of the public broadcaster. The Triple Inquiry Report of the IBA tabled in the National Assembly last year states that:

> Access to information is central to any democracy as a country can only be regarded as truly democratic when its citizens have a say that goes beyond the vote at national or local level.

As a result of apartheid, South Africa will take some time before this ideal of democracy is fully realised. Because of the high levels of illiteracy and disparities in development between rural and urban areas, as well as a communications infrastructure that is essentially underdeveloped, information dissemination is one of the greatest challenges that broadcasting faces.

If we are serious about building a genuinely participatory democracy, we cannot run away from the need to ensure that the public broadcaster carries out its responsibilities as defined by the IBA.

Since its inception, the Government of National Unity has been seized with the problem of correcting past injustices created by the policies of the apartheid system.

The experience that the government has gathered within the short space of time is that people are not informed about government activities. It was obvious that the government did not have the necessary infrastructure and capacity to fulfil this dire need.

In conclusion, I believe that it is in the interest of government as a whole to ensure that there is effective communication with the electorate and to create the necessary conditions which would enable the public to intervene in the process of governance in as effective a manner as possible.

24
Priorities for the Next Century

State of the World Forum, San Francisco, United States of America, 29 September 1995

IN HIS BOOK *The New World Order*, the English thinker H.G. Wells writes:

> There will be no day of days when a new world order comes into being. Step by step and here and there, it will arrive, and even as it comes into being, it will develop fresh perspectives, discover unsuspected problems and go on to new adventures. No man, no group of men, will ever be singled out as its father or founder. For its maker will not be this man nor that man nor any man but Man, that being who is in some measure in everyone of us. World order will be, like science, like most inventions, a social product, of an innumerable number of personalities who will have lived fine lives, pouring their best into the collective achievement.

I trust that you will excuse some of the language of this quotation, which bears the sexist stamp of the age in which the author lived and wrote.

But with regard to the subject we are supposed to address tonight, we should start by stating our view that it would either reflect the wisdom of a fool, intellectual arrogance or perhaps a manifestation of megalomania to seek to set 'priorities for the next century'.

To borrow from H.G. Wells, we shall therefore say that those priorities will be established step by step and here and there, and even as they are set, they will force everyone to develop new perspectives, confront unsuspected problems and push all who will be alive then, to enter into an unpredictable world of new adventures.

But what can one such as I, who emerges from our collective and finite cognitive past and present, say about what the next century – with its infinite possibilities – might set for itself as its priorities?

173

Nevertheless, having accepted the challenge, we must take the plunge. We must dare to peer through opaque surfaces to see what social product will emerge from the efforts of an innumerable number of personalities who will have lived fine – and not so fine – lives into the collective achievement.

Our speculative comments today will focus on the issue of the future of governance with regard both to form and content.

Let us make bold to say that the next century will face a process of the reformation of governance driven by the pull of two seemingly contending forces at either end of a magnet – the one being the globalisation of governance and the other the devolution of power to the citizen.

There can be no gainsaying the reality of the historical tendency towards a global village and a global neighbourhood. I believe that none can contest the view that this process is irreversible.

Spearheading this process is perhaps the globalisation of the economy, characterised by the transformation of our world into one marketplace as a result of the movement over all parts of our globe of capital, commodities, technology and economically active individuals.

No country in today's world can insulate itself from the impact of these processes, which result in the establishment of an intimate relationship between an institutional investor on Wall Street and a subsistence Zulu farmer in my own country, between the International Monetary Fund in Washington DC and a lowly civil servant in Bangladesh whose job is threatened by the institution of a structural adjustment programme.

Realisation has also grown of the epoch-making changes in international relations that attend the introduction of modern information and communication technology.

The worldwide reform in the telecommunications sector in recent years, leading to the privatisation of PTTs in many countries and therefore private sector investment in this sector, has further emphasised the global nature of this most modern sphere of economic activity.

This is a matter we shall come back to in the context of what we have described as the devolution of power to the citizen, as regards in particular the use of this information and communication technology to achieve two-way communication between the government and the governed.

Protection of the environment is yet another important matter we may cite which again emphasises the tendency towards the formation of a global neighbourhood.

Many of us present in this room can indicate a whole variety of examples which point to the same conclusion, including the life-threatening disease AIDS and other matters we have been discussing, such as the international narcotics crisis.

To come more precisely to the point we seek to make – the question must inevitably arise: How does humanity as a whole deal with this reality which clearly demands that there should be greater co-operation among the nations in a world which, daily, becomes ever more interdependent?

I believe that, in the light of this, it is inevitable that the century ahead of us will have to grapple with an accelerated process leading to the expansion of the system of global governance which, by definition, must result in the erosion of the spheres in the conduct of states and governments which are considered as falling within the inviolable area of domestic jurisdiction.

A number of immediate issues arise from this.

One of these, which is of particular relevance to the small and medium powers, is how that system of global governance should compensate them for the reduction of their sovereign powers.

Another is the process by which consensus will be arrived at on what the balance will be between international governance and the sovereignty of nations.

The gravity of this problem is exacerbated by the fact that in the real world in which we all live, the primary positive impulses towards the globalisation of human civilisation are seen as emanating from the wealthy nations that constitute the group, the 'major powers'.

The negative imperatives, such as the rapid spread of the AIDS epidemic, the production of narcotics, the demand for humanitarian assistance to refugees and the fight against poverty, become products of a developing world that is encircled by a fault-line that is structural in its nature.

The cold light of the exercise of power focuses on the banner headline: Can those whose contribution to the birth of the global neighbourhood consists in imposing on the global community the burden of aid and charity be equal co-determinants of what the world order of the new century should be?

Can the piper have equal influence on the choice of the tune he or she plays as she or he who pays the piper?

The current debate about the restructuring of the United Nations (UN)

175

must therefore be contextualised in a manner that extends beyond the mere fact of the expansion of the membership of the world body from 51 countries in 1945 to 184 in 1994. It must address more than the changes that have taken place in the last 50 years in the balance of economic power and the influence of major powers in world economics, politics and security.

It must address also the impact of the diminution of the powers of the small nations of the world which, if not properly handled, will lead to a new imperialism which, in its turn, will evoke the resistance of the new disenfranchised.

This is particularly so in the light of the fact that the expansion of the membership of the UN to which we have referred was accompanied by the prospect of and the actual or seeming empowerment of those who had previously been excluded from the international exercise of power. This led, for instance, to the emergence of tension between the UN General Assembly on the one hand and the Security Council on the other.

The same tension exists today between the UN Conference on Trade and Development (UNCTAD) and the World Trade Organisation.

It was at the heart of the Nuclear Non-Proliferation Treaty (NPT) negotiations earlier this year when it had to be decided whether the continued existence of the nuclear weapons stockpiles was to be determined exclusively by those who own these weapons.

The question that arose and still remains on the agenda is whether this matter of life and death should not be decided jointly by the nations of the world, on an equal basis – thus giving a preponderant vote on this issue to those who have no power to deploy these weapons of mass destruction but nevertheless represent the majority of human life in our universe.

The objective processes towards the birth of the global village dictate that to those that have power more power will be given.

On the other hand, the search for a stable world order demands that we institute a deliberate process to empower those who are thus disempowered. This has to be a conscious and deliberate act, predicated on the containment of the consequence of the powerful centripetal force that draws all of us towards a world centre dominated by the powerful, which, because of its concentration of power in particular hands, will inevitably produce a similarly powerful counter-active and centrifugal force.

This, surely, must be one of the priority items on the agenda of the new century!

But we have also spoken of the devolution of power to the citizen.

Surely, there can be no greater contradiction than this: that power should increasingly concentrate in the hands of an international consortium and, at the same time, begin to locate in the hands of the proverbial 'man in the street'!

Once more there can be no gainsaying the fact that, continuously, the citizenry is being activated to take charge of its destiny. Sometimes the assertion is made that this constitutes popular revulsion against the sterility of politics as a profession and the pursuit of personal interests by the politician as a professional. It is said that the perception of the electorate is that the delegate they elect is driven by the same impulses as any other professional, the impulses of self-advancement and the management of the constituency of such a professional in the self-interest of the latter. Furthermore, the elected delegate cannot but become hostage to the forces that lead the drive towards the concentration of power which result in the evolution towards the global governance which we have been discussing.

In the context of the subtraction or elimination of the revolutionary option in old, established democracies, peaceful struggle among representatives of different parties soon enough expresses itself as, at best, competition among interviewees for an advertised post or, at worst, a charade intended to mislead the innocent.

Matters are not improved by the situation in which the sovereignty of parliament is constrained by binding constitutions which thus give certainty to the citizens that the social framework in which they work and live will not fundamentally change, regardless of the party in power, and that if a serious effort is made radically to transform that framework, it is they, the citizens, who in any case will be asked or forced to decide the issue.

All change then becomes incremental, focused on the step.

Apart from anything else, this provides the means for the citizen to intervene in the determination of his or her destiny and to do so on an informed basis.

Thus we have a coincidence of the creation both of the political circumstances which enable popular participation and the means to take advantage of this opening.

And so, both theoretically and in actual practice, the issue of the role and place of civil society in governance is now firmly on the agenda.

The question that the next century will have to resolve is what the relationship should be between the three elements of the citizen and civil society, national government and the system of global governance.

But of this we can be certain: that having reclaimed its sovereign space, the citizenry is quite unlikely to slip back into a state of slumber, delegating its reclaimed powers to the governors.

At the same time, we are, of course, not speaking of a situation of anarchy, in which the citizen considers the democratic state to be an illegitimate institution, an entity superfluous to their needs and an expression of the limitation of their freedom and sovereignty. This is so because, in its own interests, the citizenry will, among other things, continue to delegate to the state the right to use force, to order relations both among the citizens and between nations.

But, at the same time, the citizens will seek to prescribe the limits and context of the use of that force, for example to protect the fundamental human rights of the individual, including the dignity of that individual, both within the nation and within the context of international relations.

Hence we speak here even of the intervention in matters of war and peace by the sovereign citizen, unencumbered by the sometimes self-fulfilling strategic game plans of army generals and grand geopolitical scenarios drawn up by politicians and their strategic advisers.

All this bears on the injection by civil society, into the conduct of human affairs, of the concept of a people-centred society. In such a society the process of governance is itself governed by an ethical framework which the people would seek to enforce. And the people will enforce it by the use of their sovereign mass power outside the specific framework prescribed by the party-political system which characterises conditions of democracy and, as an expression of the democracy, must make for the greater participation of the developing world in the system of global governance and therefore the rewriting of the international agenda.

The next century should therefore witness a process of governance that is more responsive to the concerns of all humanity and not only of those who occupy the areas of our globe which, today, have the power to dominate the process of the composition of that agenda.

Consequently, the issues which, at the end of this millennium, define the underdevelopment of the developing world will have to be part of the real content that fashions the priorities of the next century.

Central to those issues is, of course, the scourge of poverty which continues to afflict extremely large numbers of people on our own continent of Africa as well as other parts of the world. That seemingly endemic poverty stands in direct opposition to the process of the improvement of the human condition, which is an attendant part of the tendency towards the creation of the global neighbourhood.

Out of it are born the destructive conflicts to which my own continent has been prone, the political instability, the refugee populations and population migration, and the growing impoverishment, all of which have led to the growth of what has been described as afro-pessimism.

The point we seek to emphasise is that among the priorities of the next century, during which the welfare of one nation will increasingly become dependent on the welfare of another, must surely be the issue of radically improving the condition of the destitute masses of the world.

The growing system of global governance should itself be an important instrument to address this issue, given that it would precisely be poverty, strife and instability that would threaten the functioning of a universe characterised by interdependence.

What the new century will have to address in this regard is sustainable economic growth and development among the disadvantaged of the world, so that they too become part of the world market, contributing to the expansion of the process of globalisation rather than diminishing its reach or threatening its very actualisation.

This means that among the high priorities of the agenda of the new century will have to be included the issue of the shift of resources to the poor for purposes of sustainable development and an abandonment of the notion that the challenge of poverty can be addressed by means of dispensing aid and giving alms to the poor and deprived.

This would also address directly the important question of violent conflict within multicultural and multi-ethnic states, which, we are convinced, is fed by a scrabble for scarce resources. Where any group feels that it is politically disempowered and therefore discriminated against with regard to access to these resources, it is not difficult for leaders to agitate people on an ethnic basis, even to the point where the contending groups take up arms against one another.

Much of what we have said tonight is of direct relevance to our own experience and future as the new democratic Republic of South Africa. In that sense it is not speculative, but is a direct derivative of the new directions which we, as a democratic country, must take.

The birth of our new democracy at what is clearly a turning point in the evolution of human society has given us the exciting possibility, in a manner of speaking, to write on a clean slate.

It certainly would not do that in giving up our sovereign right we lose any capacity to influence the processes impacting on non-proliferation, disarmament, peaceful uses of nuclear energy and technology transfers. It was for these reasons that we intervened as vigorously as we could during the New York NPT negotiations earlier this year to ensure that these matters are in future addressed jointly by those who are armed and the rest of us who are unarmed and disarmed.

Within our own country, our new democracy defines itself in part by the manner in which it devolves power to the citizen. Consequently, we have had to alter the manner in which both the executive and the legislature take decisions, to ensure the greatest possible participation of the citizenry in the decision-making process. This we can say: that as a consequence ours is a citizenry in constant discussion of what its future should be.

This is not to question the legitimacy of the elected representatives and therefore the delegation of power to them by the electorate, but to respond to the tendency towards the empowerment of the citizen, which requires that the governed must have the possibility, in real terms, to determine their future.

As we draft our new Constitution, a process in which we are currently engaged, this is one of the major questions we have to answer: How should that Constitution be framed so that it gives power to the people in the new conditions of the exercise of that power, while maintaining the integrity of the overall system of national governance?

Let us conclude by beginning again: There will be no day of days when a new world order comes into being. Step by step and here and there, it will arrive, and even as it comes into being, it will develop fresh perspectives, discover unsuspected problems and go on to new adventures.

We make bold to say that some of those new adventures will consist in what we have sought to describe – the formation of a new system of governance marked by a dynamic interaction between an empowered citizenry, national government that will have been impacted upon by the erosion and diffusion of its powers, and the enhancement of global governance.

What it is that 'slouches towards Bethlehem to be born' remains to be seen.

25

South Africa and
the Information Superhighway

G7 Conference on the Information Society, Brussels, Belgium, 24 February 1995

WE BELIEVE THAT BY inviting me to address the opening session of this important conference, you sought to make the critical point that entry into the information society is not reserved for the G7 members and other developed countries – that the debate about the information society is of relevance to all humanity and therefore cannot ignore the position, the needs and role of the developing world.

The truth of this proposition is self-evident. We are sincerely moved that you, Mr President, by inviting me to address the opening session of this conference, began in a practical way to bring the developing world into the global debate on the information society.

With regard to information and communication, we are all witnesses to an extraordinary technological revolution which offers ever more powerful and astonishing capabilities affecting, primarily in the developed world, traditional patterns of work, public opinion, entertainment, education and so on.

These technological developments once more serve to highlight, emphasise and further enhance the disparities between the developed and the developing countries. All of us present in this room know, for instance, that access to basic telephony is far from being a reality in many parts of the world. More than half of humanity has never made a telephone call. There are more telephone lines in Manhattan than in all of sub-Saharan Africa.

We also see similar disparities within our own country – between the developed and the underdeveloped parts of our society. In the city of Durban, for instance, telephone penetration among white households stands at 75 per cent. In contrast, it stands at 2 per cent as far as the black house-holds are concerned.

Given these disparities, it is clear that bringing the developing world on the information superhighway constitutes a colossal challenge.

Nevertheless, we have to address this challenge if we are to promote economic growth and development world wide, consolidate democracy and human rights, increase the capacity of ordinary people to participate in governance, encourage resolution of conflicts by negotiation rather than war, and do what has to be done to enable all to gain access to the best in human civilisation within the common neighbourhood in which we all live.

In our own country, having recognised the critical importance and role of information and communication, we began, before our elections last year, to take an intensive look at this whole area, including the question of further building our information and communication infrastructure.

As a result of these early studies and discussions among the various stakeholders in our country, the construction of this infrastructure has been determined as one of the important policy objectives of our Recon-struction and Development Programme, which aims to achieve the fun-damental and all-round renewal of our society.

It is, of course, very true that the new democratic government has a whole range of pressing problems to attend to. These include such issues as job creation, housing, provision of clean water and adequate sanitation, education and health care.

It is, however, also clear that we need a vastly expanded and modern information and communication infrastructure to help us address these con-cerns, which helps to emphasise the urgency of attending to what at first glance might seem to be something to which we should give less priority.

Let me therefore state five principles which guide our own approach to these matters of communication and information which this conference is discussing.

First, the information infrastructure must serve as a means to support our goals of reconstruction and development. In this context we are con-vinced that information and communication technologies constitute an engine for economic development. As such, these technologies will, among other things, encourage growth within our boundaries and facili-tate the further insertion of our economy into the global economy.

The second principle I would like to mention concerns the region of Southern Africa. We strongly believe that any initiative which has as its purpose to build and modernise our information and communication infrastructure must be situated within the context of the needs of the Southern African region as a whole. Regional integration is the key to our approach and is an objective which all the peoples of our region have seized upon because it is both possible and necessary. This must also encompass the area of information and communication.

The third principle I would like to mention is that we must adopt a global approach. It seems clear to us that building our information and communication infrastructure is a multi-faceted proposition in the sense that it encompasses economic, financial, technological, social, cultural and moral aspects. Consequently, the solution to these problems must itself be global in nature, cutting across the traditional segments of the information and communication industry and bringing within its scope social and cultural concerns.

The fourth principle concerns the issue of content. Like all developing countries, we are very keen to acquire and grasp the technologies which enable people in institutions to access astronomical processing, storage, retrieval and delivery capacities. But we are also extremely interested to ensure that we are not mere importers and consumers of a predetermined content. Rather, we also want to be producers and exporters and therefore active and significant participants in the creation, production and formulation of content, including news, educational and cultural programmes, games, movies, songs and so forth.

To give an indication of what we mean by all this – we believe that the modern communication technology we are all talking about must help us educate our children, particularly in the rural and other underdeveloped areas of our country, teach our medical workers and parents how to care for babies, train our youth, and eliminate distance and infrastructure imbalances which act as a barrier in providing these social services.

The fifth principle we would like to mention concerns the issue of international co-operation. It is again quite clear that the building of our information and communication infrastructure offers a unique opportunity to enhance international co-operation. As we have said, we believe that this initiative must be global in nature and involve a great variety of actors, from investors, financiers and manufacturers to operators, educators, artists and so on, drawing into the global project both the domestic and the international, both South Africans and the peoples of the world, both ourselves and the participants at the conference.

Our late entry into the democratic world order has given us the opportunity to take on board exciting new concepts about governance. I refer here in particular to what is described as the participation of civil society in such governance.

As we draft our new Constitution and establish new institutions of government, our eyes are focused on the concept of what we have described as a people-centred society. This requires that the people themselves must be empowered to intervene in the decision-making process. For this to become a reality, the masses must be able to read, to write and to count, and be informed on a global basis, that is to say, not only about the plans of government but at the same time about the situation in their immediate neighbourhood. The people must not only be the recipients of communication from the rulers but should also be able to make their voices heard within the committees in which the rulers sit.

We believe that this radical expansion of the frontiers of democracy participation cannot but enhance the legitimacy of the democratic state, tap the initiative and intellect of millions of citizens, limit any tendency towards arbitrary rule and reinforce social stability and peace.

None of this can be achieved without recourse to the information and communication infrastructure we have been talking about – hence our keenness to move in practical ways towards joining the information superhighway.

Without in any way overestimating our own capabilities, and in the context of what we have said about the integration of the region of Southern Africa, we believe that South Africa can act as one of the bridging societies with regard to the realisation of the common objectives of bringing together, in a mutually beneficial way, the interests, the assets and the aspirations of the developing world and the technological and financial capacities that reside in the developed world.

In this context, I would like to say that our government is already considering various concrete proposals relating to the information and communication infrastructure. These proposals include the possibility to lay a fibre optic cable encompassing the whole continent of Africa, the extension of the telephone network to rural and underdeveloped areas of South

Africa, and a project sponsored by an international consortium which addresses our information and communication needs on a global, rather than piecemeal basis.

In all these instances, we would look forward to the participation, on the basis of partnership, of the private sector represented at this conference. At the same time, we would require that this critical international involvement should link up with our own domestic production and communication capabilities, while also encouraging and enabling the participation of small and medium business.

Undoubtedly, the concrete discussions that will flow from these initiatives will bring to the fore the important regulatory question which is one of the items of this conference. Among other things, adequate regulatory frameworks would have to address the all-important issue of ensuring that the developing world does not enter the information superhighway as a second-class road user. For instance, where the flow of information and cultural products on the information superhighway will originate mostly from the developed North, this naturally becomes a cause of concern to relatively less media-intensive cultures.

I strongly believe that censorship and control are not an appropriate way to deal with these worries.

The best insurance against the swamping of people's cultures is the reinvigoration of their creative spirit and universal appeal.

We in the developing world have much to contribute, and the superhighway should usher in an era where this contribution ultimately binds humankind closer together and enables all to shape our common destiny.

This leads me to the last point I would like to make. We believe that this initiative, which has brought us to Brussels, needs to be followed by another one, bringing together a cross-section of the developing world together with the G7 and the European Union (EU), in recognition of the global information and communication challenge, to exchange views on such questions as strategy, finance and international co-ordination.

We trust that the distinguished president of the EU, our host on this occasion, will find time to consider this proposal and perhaps agree to sponsor what we believe would be an important and necessary encounter.

I am certain that our own country, if called upon, would seriously consider the possibility of hosting such a conference.

26

The Inevitable Need
for a Culture of Co-operation

The National Economic Development and Labour Council Summit, Gallagher Estate, Midrand, 1 June 1996

THE HOLDING OF THE National Economic Development and Labour Council (NEDLAC) Summit gives all of us the possibility to assess our work since we were founded, to determine the extent to which we have discharged our mandate and to indicate where we go from here.

I trust that we will do all of this in an open and honest manner, aimed at enabling us to strengthen the capacity of this critically important institution to help our country to move with greater speed towards the accomplishment of our agreed goals of growth, equity and participation.

We are all conscious of the reality that in the more recent past some exchanges among the various partners in NEDLAC have raised questions about the very possibility of achieving the kind of effective and meaningful partnership and consensus in policy formation we all intended with the establishment of this body. It has seemed at times that perhaps the adversarial element in the relationship between and among ourselves was inherently so strong that on important questions it would of necessity always overshadow and overwhelm the factors that make for co-operation.

With your permission, I would like to make a few observations in this regard.

The first of these is that however divergent our interests might seem, we are condemned to live together and interact with one another, both the unwashed and the perfumed. Divorce is not possible.

Inevitably the actions of the one impact on the other, for better or for worse, with none in reality being capable of successfully pursuing their purposes without the co-operation of the other.

Being intelligent beings, we took the correct decision that we should find ways and means by which to govern this inevitable relationship for the good of all those who fall within the ambit of that relationship. Among others and important among them, NEDLAC is one of these ways and means and must therefore, in all our interests, actually work, with each one of its parts able to struggle for its interests while understanding that no partisan interest can be treated as supreme.

The second point I would like to make is that we have inherited a deeply divided society, burdened by a whole range of serious problems which will take some time to overcome.

At the centre of these are the continuing and frightful racial and gender disparities in the distribution in wealth, income and opportunity, the extent and depth of poverty, and the challenge to build an economy situated within the global economy and capable of giving us the means to address these problems.

Given these realities and the important factor of where we come from as a country, it had seemed right that to the extent that we can, we should seek to co-operate among ourselves to tackle these challenges rather than pursue a war of attrition against one another, which would feed and entrench the conflicts of the past, resulting in instability, stagnation and decline.

The transformation of our society will be a complex and protracted process, during which we cannot eliminate conflict. That transformation must take place, but we must also be on guard and seek to ensure that through our co-operation it is not drowned by the conflicts it will generate.

Among other things, such co-operation would enable us to identify the problems together, to understand the nature of those problems in the same way and, at least, to engage in a joint effort to define the optimal solutions to these problems. I believe that we are all of the same mind that each one of us as partners in NEDLAC has an interest in arriving at such a situation, in our self-interest first and foremost.

The third point I would like to make, which is of particular relevance to the process of governance, is that clearly human society in general is evolving towards the practice of greater inclusiveness in that process of governance.

This represents movement away from the notion that the governors are a specialised breed of people whose unique qualifications enable them to have access to the code that opens the door to heaven to enable the governed to enter.

Increases in levels of education, greater access to information and analysis, and the impact of new information and communication technology all work together to demystify the process of governance and empower society as a whole to participate in the process of determining its future.

By a twist of fate it may very well be that as South Africans we have the possibility to be among the leaders in the world with regard to a purposeful approach towards these issues that impact on governance and thus arrive at a situation in which we are not merely taken along by an historical tide but become makers of history.

I believe that NEDLAC, among others, provides us with such an opportunity.

The processes I have been describing necessarily imply that, in pursuit of their interests, each player in society must surely have the possibility to state their views, to promote and to canvass such views. In this regard, I am of the view that part of what has been happening in the recent past is that all of us have been tabling our views, especially about the economy and socio-economic matters, pending the discussion which must take place among ourselves about these issues.

It is both natural and necessary that, with regard to these, we must move beyond the general to the particular.

Earlier all of us needed to make speeches and circulate documents committing ourselves to the common goals of economic growth, participation in economic decision-making and social equity. This was a necessary part of the process of taking our country forward from a disastrous past to a brighter future, and not a meaningless exercise in building a fake consensus as the cynics would have us believe. But obviously the situation demands that we now engage one another about the specific steps we need to take to ensure the realisation of the broad goals we have set together.

In this regard, I believe that it is incorrect for any one of us to treat the tabling of a point of view for discussion as an act of hostility or a declaration of war, however much one may find that point of view offensive. Surely, this process of identifying agenda items cannot be approached as though it marks the end of the debate but the precise opposite, namely that it signifies the beginning of our detailed discussion, without which meaningful and substantive discussion would be impossible.

I would like to believe that the wider the seeming differences among ourselves, the more urgent the need becomes for us to engage one another in discussion. We should not treat those differences as though they were a summons to take to the barricades or act in a manner which indeed transforms them into a call to war.

The government occupies a special place among the NEDLAC partners. In principle it is mandated by the people as a whole and has an obligation to take into account all sectoral interests to an extent greater than can and should be expected of other institutions that draw their mandate from and are accountable to a narrower social base. The government therefore cannot abdicate its responsibilities to lead and to govern, while still striving to arrive at consensus with its social partners, in its own interest.

An understandable complaint has been made that government has lagged behind with regard to the elaboration of a comprehensive economic policy, which would go beyond merely stating global objectives and heartfelt wishes and desires and arrive at practical, realistic and implementable programmes.

Clearly, the government must and is addressing this issue with all due urgency. Having done what it has to do in terms of policy formation, it must then come back to this forum to ensure the necessary interaction with its social partners.

We trust that the combination of measures that the government will bring to NEDLAC as soon as possible, ranging from a macro-economic framework to sectoral proposals, will be both scientifically based and therefore realisable, as well as consistent with our common goals of growth, participation and equity.

The government must, by this means, play its role in answering the many policy questions that our situation demands.

This clearly does not remove the right and responsibility from the other NEDLAC partners themselves to elaborate their own positions on the policy matters so that they can make a representative and educated intervention in the decision-making process that will take place.

Whatever the seeming problems of the day, including the delay in the implementation of policies as a result of the need to engage many forces in meaningful discussion, there is no reason to despair.

PART SIX

South Africa, Africa and the World

MBEKI'S VISION GOES BEYOND the borders of South Africa, as illustrated by the eight speeches in this section. Special reference should be made to his views on the need for an African renaissance. Mbeki – visionary, strategist and African in bone and marrow – takes as his point of departure the following fundamental assumption: South Africa is intimately connected with the Southern African region and the continent as a whole.

He understands the forces of globalisation. He also understands the need for regionalism, the innovative development of interdependencies and the building of strong regional institutions such as the Southern African Development Community.

A number of important themes are developed in the present section: 'We have come home', 'Partnership in Africa', 'Bound by a common destiny', 'Europe and South Africa'.

All these themes express different facets of his vision of an African renaissance. This vision is not expounded in romantic and idealistic terms. Mbeki the visionary is also a realist. The African renaissance vision is rooted in four conditions:

- the history of Africa, which encompasses numerous achievements;
- the potential of Africa's peoples;
- the values of democracy and good governance; and
- the power of information and modern technologies.

27

We Have Come Home

Opening session of the Organisation of African Unity Conference of Ministers of Information, Sun City, 4 October 1995

FOR MANY OF US, the dawning of the realisation that we have, at last and in many practical ways, come back into Africa, evokes a strong sense of joy as it did that unrepeatable moment when Nelson Mandela was sworn in as the first democratically elected president of this country.

Your presence today, so soon after that moment, says to us as South Africans that we have truly come home.

But what was that struggle all about?

It was, we believe, about the recovery of the dignity of all black people everywhere. It was about closing a millennium which was, in part, defined by efforts to describe all who were not white as being less than human.

The peoples of our continent shed their blood, sacrificed their time and resources, and invested their pennies in an effort whose essential content was to demonstrate and establish in the reality the simple point that all persons are created as equal human beings, with none entitled to claim dominion over another on the basis of colour or race.

We trust that as you crossed the borders into South Africa to attend this important conference you saw and sensed that everybody in our country has accepted that you, like the black people of South Africa, are equal to any other human being in the world, and are entitled to be treated with the respect and dignity which are due to all human beings, regardless of their race, colour or gender.

Not long ago in Arusha, Tanzania, the leaders of our continent gathered to close down the Liberation Committee of the Organisation of African Unity (OAU). That moving and historic act, which said that the total liberation of our continent from classical colonial and racial domination had been achieved, also posed the question to Africa and the world: What next, whither Africa?

We are, in our own limited way, which is circumscribed by the dictates of our own history and our own contingencies, battling to address that question for ourselves.

We are committed to the building of a democratic, non-racial and non-sexist South Africa. Our transitional Constitution enshrines the principles of a democratic system which empowers the people to participate in their own governance and requires the government to be accountable to them for its decisions. What we visualise, therefore, is participatory, transparent and accountable government.

We are equally committed to the respect and protection of the fundamental human rights of all our people, regardless of race, colour or gender.

We have, however, also inherited the legacy of the apartheid system. The new order must therefore seriously address the problems of poverty, ignorance and disease which are a product of this system. The people have to use the political power that is in their hands to effect a profound transformation of our society so that it becomes truly non-racial and non-sexist.

It is for this reason that the country as a whole has adopted a Reconstruction and Development Programme which encapsulates that vision of transformation. I trust that while you are here you will have the opportunity to have sight of the programme.

The situation emphasises the importance of the involvement of the people in the process of governance. We could never afford the situation in which the government gets detached and becomes distant from the people. Rather, what we have to ensure is that the people themselves are exposed to and are conscious of the resource limitations imposed on the country by centuries of colonial and white minority domination. They must themselves participate in the decision-making processes and thereby share the responsibility with government of effecting the reconstruction and development of the country of which we have spoken.

We believe that information is pivotal to the achievement of these objectives. Such basic democratic freedoms as those of speech, association, assembly and the press are all constitutionally guaranteed.

We are determined that these freedoms should not merely be recognised as a matter of formality and rhetoric, but that the people must, in the actuality, exercise them.

We therefore see an independent press as being a vital component part in the process of communication from the government to the people and from the people to the government. To limit that freedom would not only be contrary to democratic precepts and the Constitution itself, but would also militate against the very objective of ensuring that the people are able, independently, to impact on the processes of governance.

Similarly, we are determined to ensure that the government's Communication Service, which is hosting you here today, should itself not become a propaganda arm of the government. Rather, it must be a channel for two-way communication between the government and the people, ensuring that the people are as fully informed as possible about the activities of the government, that the government is as fully informed as possible about the views of the people and that the people are empowered to make informed interventions in the process of determining their own destiny.

Once again, as my colleague Dr Pallo Jordan, minister of posts, telecommunication and broadcasting will tell you, the government has no intention whatsoever to exercise editorial control over the state-owned media, the South African Broadcasting Corporation.

We have also taken steps to ensure the adoption early next year of a Freedom of Information or an Open Governance Act. The purpose of the Act will be to give citizens access to information held by governmental institutions, as well as access to the proceedings of certain public bodies. Of necessity, the Act will also have to create effective mechanisms for the enforcement of the rights that it will spell out. Special attention will therefore have to be paid to the need to educate citizens to use the Act so that they do indeed obtain access to official information.

Much as we are concerned with the upliftment of our people and the improvement of their conditions of life, we are also fully conscious of the obligations we all share towards one another and towards the continent of Africa.

We view this important conference as part of the process of integrating the new South Africa in the process of sharing equal responsibility for the affairs of our continent with the member states of the OAU that you represent.

If it is correctly said that democracy, peace, security and stability are necessary prerequisites for socio-economic development, we have no hesitation in adding information and communication among those prerequisites.

I have come across an OAU document produced by this very conference in 1990 entitled 'The Common African Information and Communication Policy'. It impressed me because it did not only say what should be done, but also how it should be done, at what level and when.

Unfortunately it remained a document. We believe that this document has to be revisited as part of our continuing effort seriously to address the information and communications challenges which it poses.

In this regard, I would like to announce that the Republic of South Africa will adhere to the Pan-African News Agency Convention and that we are fully supportive of the decisions that have been taken to restructure and revitalise this news agency so that it becomes a viable and credible all-African medium of communication.

Within the broader plane, we would also like to reaffirm the commitment of this democratic republic to participate fully in the efforts of the OAU and our continent to confront the challenges that face us all.

We are enormously inspired by the fact that our continental organisation continues to grapple with such vital issues as democracy and stability, security and development, human rights and the socio-economic recovery of our continent. We are committed to full participation as an equal partner with other member states in the struggle to address all these matters.

We say 'an equal partner' because we are opposed to any efforts which might seek to project South Africa as some kind of superpower on our continent and deeply respect the right of all nations to independence as well as the precepts of solidarity and mutually advantageous co-operation.

We are, however, aware that in some instances some people place high hopes with regard to such positive contributions as South Africa may make to the socio-economic recovery of our continent.

We are indeed prepared to make a contribution. But it must be understood that in reality our own capacity is limited. Our fervent desire to help address Africa's concerns, which are also our own, are constrained by the fact of scarce resources.

We, however, proceed from the deeply held conviction that the people of Africa share a common destiny and must therefore, at all times, seek to address their challenges in a concerted manner, as a united force. For this reason, Africa stands at the centre of our foreign policy and is the focus of our attention with regard to the fundamental question of the creation of a new world order of democracy, peace and prosperity.

We are indeed deeply honoured that you chose our country as the venue of this important conference of the OAU and wish to pledge to you all that we will try our best not to disappoint your realistic expectations that our emancipation will contribute something, however small, to the rebirth of our continent.

Let me close by saying that the role of the OAU Secretariat, which worked in close co-operation with the staff of the South African Communication Service to organise this conference, deserves praise and appreciation.

28

Africa's Time Has Come

Address to the Corporate Council on Africa's Attracting Capital to Africa Summit, Chantilly, Virginia, United States of America, 19 to 22 April 1997

IT IS NOT GIVEN TO every generation that it should be present during and participate in the act of creation. I believe that ours is privileged to occupy such historic space.

Five years ago, many in this room would not have agreed that the people of Africa would have found it within themselves to end the system of apartheid peacefully, to queue one after the other, black and white mixed together, for hours on end under the African sun to decide on a government of their choice.

Many would have thought it insane that the thought would occur to these Africans, both black and white, that they should initiate and sustain a multiplicity of efforts to create a new South Africa, based on forgiveness, national reconciliation, non-racialism and national unity.

Indeed, the very notion of victory over white minority domination, resulting in the black oppressed majority participating in deciding the destiny of all the people of South Africa, was a thing which even the so-called experts on Africa seriously doubted.

All this has happened. Even I stand here today as a product of that process. The world has termed these extraordinary processes an unprecedented miracle.

As Africans, we are moved that the world concedes that miracles of this order can come out of Africa, an Africa which in the eyes of the same world is home to an unending spiral of anarchy and chaos, at whose unknown end is a dark pith of an utter, a complete and unfathomable human disaster.

Out of this same Africa a new star of hope has risen over that part of it which is described as Angola.

Only a few days ago, parties that had fought against each other for decades as deadly enemies came together to form a Government of Unity and National Reconciliation to serve the greater good of the millions of Angolans who have been victim to the pestilences of war, including disablement, displacement, degradation and death.

We are privileged to be witness to a gripping and epoch-making contest which assumes many forms and involves all layers among the people of Zaïre, to give a new birth to their country.

As Africans we have a vision, a hope, a prayer about what will come in the end. We see a new Zaïre, perhaps with a new name, a Zaïre which shall be democratic, peaceful, prosperous, a defender of human rights, an exemplar of what the new Africa should be, occupying the geographic space that it does at the heart of our Africa.

Much is now written about Zaïre. Daily events assume proportions of permanence. The confounding ebbs and flows of social conflict are seen defining moments. And yet, as Africans, we would like to believe that we know that, at the end, what all of us see, thanks to the wisdom of the people of Zaïre themselves, is not the heart of darkness, but the light of a new African star. Once more out of Africa, out of these towns which have joined the vocabulary of places that are part of our common knowledge – Goma, Kisangani, Lubumbashi and Kinshasa – a new miracle slouches towards its birth.

But still, outside our continent, the perception persists that Africa remains, as of old, torn by interminable conflict, unable to solve its problems, condemned to the netherworld.

Those who have eyes to see, let them see. The African renaissance is upon us. As we peer through the looking glass darkly, this may not be obvious. But it is upon us.

What we have been talking about is the establishment of genuine and stable democracies in Africa, in which the systems of governance will flourish because they derive their authority and legitimacy from the will of the people.

The point must be made that the new political order owes its existence to the African experience of many decades which teaches us, as Africans, that what we tried did not work, that the one-party states and the military governments will not work.

The way forward must be informed by what is, after all, common to all African traditions: that the people must govern!

Since 1990, more than 25 sub-Saharan countries have held democratic elections. This is what we mean when we talk of a process on our continent, perhaps seen through the looking glass darkly, which affirms an indigenous and sustained movement towards the elimination of the failed systems and violent conflicts which have served to define the continent in a particular way in the eyes of many in the world, including this country.

There exists within our continent a generation which has been victim to all the things which created this negative past. This generation remains African and carries with it an historic pride which compels it to seek a place for Africans equal to all the other peoples of our common universe.

It knows and is resolved that, to attain that objective, it must resist all tyranny, oppose all attempts to deny liberty by resort to demagogy, repulse the temptation to describe African life as the ability to live on charity, engage in the fight to secure the emancipation of the African woman, and reassert the fundamental concept that we are our own liberators from oppression, from underdevelopment and poverty, from the perpetuation of an experience from slavery, to colonisation, to apartheid, to dependence on alms.

It is this generation whose sense of rage guarantees Africa's advance towards its renaissance.

This is an Africa which is already confronting the enormous challenge of uprooting corruption in African life. The insistence on such notions as transparency and accountability addresses, in part, this vexed question.

On this, as on other questions on which the continent succeeded, however difficult they may have seemed, we are convinced that victory is certain.

The difficult period from which our continent is emerging imposed on Africa an enormous brain drain. Many among our best-prepared intellectuals left to seek better lives in countries such as the United States. As Africa achieves its rebirth, so will these, who have better possibilities to create something new on the continent of their origin, be encouraged and attracted to return to the challenging and satisfying life of the reconstruction and development of a motherland revisited.

The world investor community has understandably asked that as Africans we must establish the conditions to enable them to take rational business decisions to make long-term investments in Africa.

We are saying that many African countries, as you heard yesterday and will have heard today, are doing precisely that. And we are arguing that what we are witnessing is a sustained process of historic importance.

In addition to the social and political issues we have already addressed, sub-Saharan Africa and the rest of the continent have also embarked on a process of economic reform, which is necessary and vital if the continent is to succeed in attracting a growing slice of foreign investment.

We want to move beyond the current situation where Africa accounts for a small portion of all foreign capital that flows to the emerging markets. Already the success of recent reforms is apparent in the sub-region's accelerating growth in gross domestic product, which has reached an average of 4 per cent in 1995 compared to 1,4 per cent in 1991 to 1994. This is still way below what we would like to see. Given the challenge we have to address, none of us should be satisfied with an average growth rate of less that 10 per cent for the continent as a whole.

It is clear to all of us that we cannot achieve this sustained rate of development unless Africa succeeds to attract the necessary international private sector capital and directs such domestic capital as it can generate to productive uses.

With regard to economic reform, there are many issues which are of common concern, including the liberalisation of trade, the reform of financial, commodity and other markets, the functioning of multilateral institutions, development assistance and resource transfers from the developed to the developing world. We are interested that these matters be discussed in an atmosphere which recognises the legitimate interests of the poor.

In this context, we also recognise the importance of our own African business sector, which has a critical role in continuing the African renaissance into the twenty-first century, capable of both acting on its own and in partnership with international investors.

For instance, the exploitation of the continent's huge mineral resources, which is currently one of the most important growth sectors of the African economies, can no longer be the preserve of companies from outside the continent. Africa has been readying herself for growth and development, fuelled by her own efforts and the profitable and safe injection of international private capital.

Let us do what we have to do together to achieve the sustained development of Africa.

As all other peoples, ours demand a better life. This requires of our governments, the private sector and non-governmental organisations that they continue to work ceaselessly towards meeting people's basic needs in jobs, welfare, education, health, the alleviation of poverty and so on. Reforms that seek to undermine the continent's medium and longer-term ability to discharge its responsibility to its peoples in these areas, on a sustained basis, will lead to frustration and renewed social turmoil.

We are encouraged by and welcome the steps taken by members of the United States Congress to sponsor the Trade and Investment Initiative for Sub-Saharan Africa legislation that seeks to create a more coherent trade and investment policy between the United States and Africa. We are certain that this process will bear mutually beneficial results.

As we meet here today, the African continent is hard at work striving to convince the world that it is time that, for the first time, the Olympics are held on our continent. The bid by the City of Cape Town for the Olympics in 2004 is, in reality, an African bid. Apart from the fact that Cape Town can in fact successfully host the 2004 Olympics, we believe that the time has come for the rest of the world to demonstrate its commitment to the African renaissance by awarding the Games in the year 2004 to the African continent.

Africa's time has come.

We should no longer allow the situation where the world records growth and development, and Africa communicates a message of regression and further underdevelopment.

The new century must be an African century.

Africa needs your support to carry through the difficult and complex task of achieving her renaissance.

Africa awaits your arrival at the southernmost point of our continent to celebrate the prowess and excellence of athletic achievement which belongs, not least, to Africa's own youth.

29
Partnership Africa

Statement at the conference on Partnership Africa, Stockholm, Sweden, 25 June 1997

ALMOST A HUNDRED YEARS AGO, in the year 1900, the first Pan-African Congress was held in London, England.

One of the participants was the great African-American fighter for liberation, W.E.B. du Bois. In the closing speech of the congress, entitled 'To the Nations of the World', Du Bois said:

> In the metropolis of the modern world, in this closing year of the nineteenth century, there has been assembled a congress of men and women of African blood, to deliberate solemnly upon the present situation and outlook of the darker races of mankind... The problem of the twentieth century is the problem of the colour line, the question as to how far differences of race ... are going to be made, hereafter, the basis of denying to over half the world the right of sharing to their utmost ability the opportunities and privileges of modern civilisation. To be sure the darker races are today the least advanced in culture according to European standards. This has not, however, always been the case in the past, and certainly the world's history, both ancient and modern, has given many instances of no despicable ability and capacity among the blackest races of men. In any case, the modern world must needs remember that in this age ... the millions of black men in Africa, America, and the Islands of the Sea, not to speak of the brown and yellow myriads elsewhere, are bound to have great influence upon the world in the future, by reason of sheer numbers and physical contact... If, by reason of carelessness, prejudice, greed and injustice, the black world is to be exploited and ravished and degraded, the results must be deplorable, if not fatal, not simply to them, but to the high ideals of justice, freedom, and culture which a thousand years of Christian civilisation have held before Europe.

Needless to say, this quotation of course carries the sexist language of its time, despite the fact that in reality, and even at this early stage, Du Bois fought consciously for the emancipation of women.

The twenty-first century is already upon us. Time will answer the query whether another Pan-African Congress will be held in the closing year of the twentieth century, the year 2000, and at which metropolis.

The question that will face all of us then is whether it will be necessary and correct to say: The problem of the twenty-first century is the problem of the colour line.

Much has changed since W.E.B. du Bois spoke in the metropolis of the modern world. The millions of black men and the brown and yellow myriads for whom and in whose name he spoke have since achieved their political emancipation and much else besides.

We meet to discuss Africa, quintessentially the home of the black men and women whose cause the first Pan-African Congress was convened to champion. I do not know how we will conclude our discussions.

But these things we can say because they are true:

- that the peoples of Africa have achieved their political emancipation from colonial and white minority domination;
- that, in the aftermath of this historic victory, and everywhere on the continent, serious efforts were made to eradicate the cumulative consequences of the slave trade, colonialism and imperialism;
- that a good amount of what we have tried out, in a determined and well-intentioned attempt to achieve this objective, has failed;
- that what we have tried out with limited success includes:
  - the establishment of one-party states;
  - the resort to military rule;
  - the investiture of the state with the responsibility to be the principal owner of the means of production in the domestic economy; and
  - the dependence for our development on the charity of others wealthier than ourselves, counting on their altruism;
- that the peoples of Africa remain among the least advanced, within the world community of nations, in terms of their standard of living and quality of life;
- that, in many instances, three decades of independence and self-rule have left behind a trail of despoliation and regression;

- that, in this period, the disparity in income and wealth has worsened not only between ourselves and the developed world, but also within many of our countries, between those who had the possibility to use access to power to enrich themselves at the expense of the rest, who are the wretched of the earth;
- that this parasitic growth on the African body-politic is driven by its own internal dynamic which aims at self-preservation, uninterrupted reproduction and continued domination;
- that in a world characterised, in part, by the universal impact of the continuing revolution in science and technology, the globalisation of all economic activity and the further strengthening of the dominant positions of the dominant, the propulsion of much of Africa to the peripheral margin of the world community constitutes a present and imminent danger; and therefore,
- that the problem of the colour line will continue to pose itself as a problem of the twenty-first century.

However, the challenge we face cannot reside merely in the recognition and acknowledgement of what is wrong. Principally it consists in answering the question correctly: What must be done to ensure that the right thing is done?

I believe that, in this instance, our own experience is our most important teacher. That experience must say to us that we would be foolish to repeat our past mistakes. Accordingly, we must find within the contemporary African reality the inspiration, the forces, the means and the methods which will ensure that we do not act like fools, but that we build on the wisdom which we derive from our follies.

The first item that we must place on that new agenda is the centrality of the concept of a people-centred society, the affirmation and entrenchment in our politics of the view that the purpose of politics and policy is the promotion of the genuine all-round interests of the people rather than the acquisition of power by a social élite.

This, of course, immediately raises the question of accountable government and, therefore, the critical importance of the need to entrench democracy and human rights throughout our continent.

The appreciation of the very concept of the eradication of poverty and its proper and real integration into government policies depends, in a real way, not on familiarity with modern theories of development, but on the political commitment to the point of view that all governance is legitimate only to the extent that it both enjoys a popular mandate and serves the interests of the people.

We believe that these matters are fundamental to the rebirth of the African continent, this being a perspective which is underwritten by the very history of many countries of Africa – the history of failed experiments with alternative political systems.

As everybody present at this important conference is aware, our own country, South Africa, has been characterised by deep divisions and conflict. And it seemed to many that inevitably the exercise of power by one group had to be at the expense of the other, reflecting a situation in which the interests of the various groups were mutually exclusive. In these conditions it would be unavoidable that each group would have to eliminate the other in order to advance its own interests.

In the South African instance, we are dealing with a society which is divided in terms of race and colour, with all the consequences that derive from a long period of white minority domination.

The apartheid regime also made determined efforts to separate the people one from the other by seeking to build socio-economic systems based on ethnicity. The recognition of the inherently explosive nature of this situation led to the conclusion among many that the relatively peaceful transition of South Africa to a stable, non-racial democracy, constituted a miracle.

A critical contributory factor to the accomplishment of that miracle derived from the position sustained by the liberation movement over a long period of time that 'South Africa belongs to all who live in it, black and white'.

If this was the case, it was necessary that we all who live in it must find a mutually acceptable accommodation, without the domination of one group by another and without anyone feeling threatened by a social process which guaranteed the freedom of each individual and equality among the people.

Then we can say, without fear of contradiction, that in good measure we owe our miracle to an inclusive process which brought together the representatives of sections and layers of our society to define and agree on the question of what we wanted South Africa to be.

Informed by the global principles of democracy and equality, this process of the common definition of a common future was therefore characterised both by its inclusiveness and the willingness among all participants to enter into compromises, based on the understanding and acceptance of the reality that all of us shared a common destiny. It is true that all this did not come about as the result of some spectacularly inherent wisdom of the people of South Africa, but was the result of a set of historical circumstances which, in reality, left all of us with no choice but to find a commonly acceptable settlement.

Understanding the need continuously to sustain such a settlement, institutions have been or will be established further to make possible inclusive processes in the determination of national policy. I would like to mention only two institutions in this regard.

One of these, which is yet to be established, is provided for in our Constitution. This is the Commission for the Protection of Language, Cultural and Religious Rights. This was born out of the recognition that, indeed, the South African population is made up of different language, cultural and religious groups, and that normal democratic practice may not be sufficient to address the tensions that may arise out of the fact of such composition.

The second institution I would like to mention, and which is functioning already, is called the National Economic Development and Labour Council (NEDLAC). The council is made up of representatives of government, labour, business and non-governmental and community-based organisations. It therefore has a great possibility to ensure the accommodation of potentially conflicting interests within policies and programmes, which contribute to national cohesion and unity.

I have spoken of the South African experience because it is born of the common African resolve to overcome the problems of the past and to achieve its rebirth. Clearly, each one of our countries has its specific features and must find its own path to that rebirth. Experiences, including our own, cannot simply be transposed from one country to another. Nevertheless, it is true that certain commonalities among ourselves, as African countries, enable us to draw lessons from what has happened to each one of us.

And to that extent, I believe that the South African experience, like that of other countries, has relevance to the solution of problems that continue to afflict many of our countries, even in the broadest possible terms.

In this regard, again I believe it to be true that the construction and sustenance of a just and stable society in South Africa must continue to be based on the thesis that 'South Africa belongs to all who live in it'.

Without arrogantly assuming the right to prescribe to any other, we also believe it to be true that the creation and sustenance of a just and stable society in other countries on our continent, including Rwanda, Burundi, the Sudan, the Democratic Republic of Congo, Nigeria and so on, must be informed by the same notion that each of these belongs to all the people who live in it.

This of course carries with it the implications we have sought to describe, including inclusive processes of change and the ability and willingness to enter into compromises in a situation in which all share a common destiny.

If we take this route, thus shall we emerge from many years of instability and a seeming inability to meet the challenges of development and nation-building without drifting into situations of destabilising conflict.

I believe that the new African generations have learnt and are learning from the experiences of the past. I further believe that they are unwilling to continue to repeat the wrongs that have occurred. I believe also that they know that the situation cannot be sustained where everywhere else on the globe the peoples are making progress in improving their conditions of life.

It gives us great encouragement that Sweden, which stood side by side with us as we fought to end colonisation and apartheid, is now engaged in a serious effort to define what it can do as a developed country, in the interests of the expansion of human dignity everywhere, to lend weight to the success of the African renaissance.

Together we will win.

30

Bound by a Common Destiny

Statement at the Eleventh Conference of Heads of State of Governments of Nonaligned Countries, Cartagena de Indias, Colombia, 18 to 19 October 1995

WE ARE ESPECIALLY PLEASED to deliver this statement at this particular conference because of the critical role this movement and its members played in the struggle to defeat the evil system of apartheid and secure the liberation of all the people of our country.

We take this opportunity once more to thank you for that selfless and unwavering commitment to our emancipation and to the restoration of the dignity of all South Africans, both black and white.

We undertake that the new South Africa, which was born as a result of our common struggle, is one that will always remain loyal to the principle on which this movement was founded, true to the agenda which it has set itself over the years, and an active participant in the continuing struggle to address the concerns and aspirations of the millions of people who are citizens of our member states.

And yet, despite the many victories which the movement has scored during the four decades of its existence, as reflected in the important documents we will adopt here in Cartagena, many of the issues which were on our agenda when we first met in Bandung remain still on that agenda.

That clearly should not be cause for despair, but confirmation of the importance of those issues and a continuing indication of the need for us continuously to attend to the matter of strengthening our capacity to help find solutions to these challenges which confront all humanity.

We are certain that there are none among us who would contest the interconnectedness and mutual dependence of the values that this movement has always espoused – of freedom, democracy, human dignity, peace, stability, development and prosperity.

In the end, this message we seek to convey both to ourselves and to those who are not part of this great movement: that there must come into being a new world order for the citizens of all countries of freedom, democracy, human dignity, peace, stability, development and prosperity.

As our world grows ever more interdependent, it also becomes patently clear that no country can achieve these objectives on its own, in conditions of autarky. The objective processes of human evolution dictate that at last we recognise the fact that both the poor and the rich, the weak and the powerful, are all human beings who are bound by a common destiny.

That surely must bring to the fore the question: Who shall write the agenda and the programme of action that will move our universe continuously and steadily towards the new world order which we all visualise?

Individually and collectively, we are engaged in a protracted struggle to ensure that these become precisely the areas of genuine and sustained focus also for those in our common world who dispose of a disproportionate share of economic, political and other power.

We must surely ask ourselves the question whether we are succeeding or not! If the answer is in the negative, we must look for new ways and means whereby we can achieve that success. We cannot merely satisfy ourselves that we have met or largely decry our condition or simply be complacent because we have always met.

The issues we, as a movement, have placed on the world agenda stand at the centre of the great and historic project of a conscious and universal offensive to secure human advancement. These include the elimination of poverty in all its forms, as well as the consequent human conflict and degradation; achieving sustainable development universally leading to shared prosperity; ending war and violent conflict within and between countries and abolishing weapons of mass destruction; ensuring that both the individual and the nation have the possibility to be heard and their views and interests taken into account, thus militating against the resort to force and confrontation; and genuine respect both for the sovereignty of peoples and the fact of the growth of a common neighbourhood.

It may be that there are some who see these objectives as being nothing but the pious wish of the disempowered, a mere dream of the disadvantaged, which will for ever be confronted by the hard reality of the real world of the self-serving and cold exercise of power by those who have power. But we make bold to say that apart from these aims, there can be nothing else which can be said to constitute the heart of the great and historic project of a conscious and universal offensive to secure human advancement, to which we have referred. None will, in the end, be immune from the negative consequences of the failure to address them.

If we are convinced of the justice of our cause, as we are, and therefore moved to ensure that it advances because it bears directly on our very future as part of the common humanity, then we must closely examine the ways and means, the strategies and tactics by which we will achieve our common purpose.

It may be that there are particular matters on which we should concentrate our collective wisdom and strength in the period ahead of us actually to secure results in the same way that, in our short history, we used our collective wisdom and strength to secure the emancipation of millions of people from the curse of colonial and white minority domination.

I am certain that the distinguished leaders of the people of Africa who are present here would agree that our own continent has, among other things, taken the firm decision to focus on the great challenge to ensure that ours becomes a continent of peace, stability and good governance, free from intra- and interstate conflict and the heart-rending reality and sight of destroyed human settlements and millions of refugees and displaced persons.

Thus do we seek not only to enhance human dignity on our continent, but also to position ourselves so that we can attend to the urgent question of the continuous improvement of the conditions of life of our peoples. We count on the support of the rest of this movement in the difficult struggle to achieve these objectives.

South–South co-operation is, among us, correctly an article of faith. We believe that we also need further to enhance our capacity to encourage the expansion of this co-operation in our collective interest and thus concentrate on this important matter in a sustained and concerted way. Among ourselves this surely needs no justification.

In our documents we have correctly raised the issue of weapons of mass destruction with a particular focus on nuclear weapons. As we all know, negotiations are continuing to conclude a Comprehensive Nuclear Test Ban Treaty. The unacceptable tests that are and have been carried out by some of the nuclear weapons states emphasise the critical importance of our continued and vigorous intervention in this area, once more on a sustained basis, to ensure that the overall purpose agreed at the Nuclear Non-Proliferation Treaty Review and Extension Conference, including permanent and universal disarmament, is properly and effectively addressed.

The momentum towards peace in the sister republic of Angola, and the liberation of the people of Palestine and the establishment of a comprehensive, just and lasting peace in the Middle East should not be lost. None in this conference room needs any education about the critical importance of both these issues.

It is also self-evident that none of us needs to be taught anything about the need for our concerted support for and involvement in the struggle to end the war in Bosnia-Herzegovina, among other things, to put behind us the shameful history of ethnic cleansing which stands out as a terrible blight on all modern human civilisation.

The last matter we would like to raise is the restructuring and transformation of the United Nations.

We have given due and proper attention to this matter. Its consideration raises again the issue of creating the conditions which will ensure that we, who represent the millions of our globe who are disempowered, are able to play our role in the formation of the new world order that must be predicated on the general and all-encompassing improvement of the global human condition.

Thus must we act in a concerted and sustained manner to ensure that this matter is addressed properly, and thus must we place it, in practical terms, among those issues which occupy a strategic place on our common agenda.

Our success in this area may prove to be the one single factor which, for the foreseeable future, decides the issue whether we go on as before or the world as a whole accepts the implication of the growth of the common human village.

With regard to all the matters we have raised and others that will appear in our agreed documents, we take this opportunity to pledge the commitment of the new South Africa, which is a product of your struggle, to work as a true member of this movement, convinced that it is in the context of our principled solidarity that we can generate the strength to make a difference in the struggle for a better future for all humanity.

31

Europe and South Africa:
An Economic Perspective

Alpbach Forum, Austria, 30 August 1995

HISTORY HAS TIED THE TWO continents of Africa and Europe by an umbilical cord which cannot be severed.

Certainly many of the things that happen on this continent on which we meet today have a very direct impact on the continent from which we come. We, therefore, cannot but have a view about Europe and the Europeans, whether well founded or not and whether good, bad or indifferent.

We would like to believe that what happens on our continent also has an impact on the peoples of Europe. We know that you as Europeans definitely have a view about Africa and the Africans, both well founded and not, encompassing the good, the bad and the indifferent.

As Africans, we see the contradictory processes that are affecting the continent of Europe and recognise that we have to respond to these developments in a varied manner that acknowledges the opportunities and challenges presented by the interests and constraints on both sides.

Let me make some specific remarks on some of these issues, speaking as a South African.

We have been watching with great interest the evolution and growth of the European Union (EU), encouraged by the desire to see the steps leading to an actual progress towards European unity.

This audience will, of course, be aware that the peoples of our own continent are inspired by a similar desire to achieve African unity, which led to the foundation and defence of the Organisation of African Unity.

But of concern has been the possibility that the process of European unity might result in an exclusive concern for European interests.

This could lead to a turn inwards that would both draw the European peoples closer to one another, with the corollary result of drawing away

215

from other peoples. Accepted would be those with whom a united Europe would feel moved to relate to, in its own self-interest, narrowly defined.

Put crudely, there is a fear of the emergence of a fortress Europe which would set up its ramparts to exclude the 'surplus people' of the world, and specifically the Africans.

In part, that fear would arise because the Europe of the EU is South Africa's single largest economic partner. It is our largest trading partner. For example, in 1994 South Africa imported from Europe goods and services worth more than 104,5 billion Austrian shillings (R38 billion) and in turn exported more than 71,5 billion Austrian shillings (R26 billion) of goods and services to Europe.

It has contributed the largest share of foreign investment in our country. It has the largest influence in terms of our technological base and has been, together with Switzerland and the countries of Scandinavia, the major source of our loan capital and development assistance.

But we have also been observing with great concern the conflicts that have been taking place in the former Yugoslavia and Soviet Union, including Bosnia-Herzegovina and Chechnya.

We ourselves have experience of war and violent conflict and therefore share the fervent hope of the peoples of Europe that ways can be found of establishing new relations among these peoples without resort to arms.

Clearly these conflicts increase the pressure on countries of Western Europe, especially member states of the EU, to ensure the quickest possible recovery of the economies of Central and Eastern Europe, which in itself is a good thing that we, as Africans, would support. But again concern would arise if as a result of this the tendency was strengthened, especially within the developed part of Europe, to concentrate solely on the European economy to the exclusion of the struggling African economies.

Certainly, as South Africans, we would hope that European investors would not treat the issue of investment in Central and Eastern Europe as though it should be approached as a matter in opposition to investment in South Africa. We, of course, understand that we ourselves have an obligation to make our own country as attractive a place in which to invest and ensure that we market ourselves adequately and properly.

Since we are speaking of Europe, we must also mention the known fact that our country and Russia share a wide range of metals and minerals which they both mine and sell on the world market. Naturally, we therefore both share a common desire for stable commodity markets and sustained demand for the commodities we both produce. This provides yet another significant area of shared interest between an important region of Europe and ourselves which, handled properly and in a manner that serves the interest of both producers and consumers, would contribute positively to the further development of both Africa and Europe.

The burden of our argument is that as Europeans and as Africans we should indeed work consistently to widen our economic relations, basing ourselves on the felt need which the marketplace has already demonstrated exists.

Most certainly, from our point of view, these relations constitute a critical element in terms of our capacity to build an economy that is strong, modern, internationally competitive and capable of addressing the needs of our people.

We do believe that you too, as Europeans, have much to gain from a strong relationship with South Africa, which is also a gateway to a substantial part of Africa south of the Sahara.

At the broader strategic level, we believe that the point should be made that inasmuch as an economically depressed Central and Eastern Europe can never be in the interest of the rest of Europe, similarly an economically depressed Africa can never be in the medium and long-term interest of Europe.

Whatever the distance between our countries and continents, the reality will assert itself ever more strongly that we do indeed all belong to a common neighbourhood in which it is not possible to insulate one block from the other.

At this point we want to turn more specifically to our relations with the EU, whose political leaders, including those of our host country, are fortunately highly sensitised to the need to structure the relations between South Africa and the EU to create the best possible conditions for the growth of prosperity both in South Africa and the rest of our region.

As we have said, our country has a long-standing economic association with Europe. This relationship started more than 300 years ago.

Today we are shaping our economic relationships in a context that is defined by new developments within the world order.

First, they are taking place within a Europe characterised by the emergence of the Union, and of the new states in Central and Eastern Europe and the former Soviet Union.

Second, they are taking place within the context of the rapid globalisation of the world economy. This globalisation has, however, some peculiarities. On the one hand there is a process towards more integration as characterised by the Final Act of the Uruguay round of Multilateral Trade Negotiations (GATT) which culminated in the Marrakesh Agreement signed in April 1994 and the emergence of the World Trade Organisation (WTO). On the other hand there is a strengthening of regional trading blocs, as characterised by, for example, the EU and the North American Free Trade Agreement.

Third, they are taking place at a time when the world is witnessing an extraordinary technological revolution which is giving birth to what is often referred to as the information society.

Finally, from our perspective these relations are taking place within the context of a new democratic South Africa, which has embarked on a process to extricate itself from centuries of colonialism and racism. This democratisation process allows South Africa to enter into relations with the world as a respected partner and no longer as a racist outcast.

The establishment of a democratic government in South Africa gives us the opportunity to redefine and reshape our trading and economic relations in an environment free of economic sanctions and embargoes. It is in this context that we have initiated trade discussions between ourselves and the EU, which are aimed at improving and cementing our already very good economic ties. We in South Africa are very pleased that EU member states have given the Commission the mandate to begin negotiations with us, *inter alia*, on the basis of a qualified access to the Lomé Convention and an asymmetrical free trade agreement. We are very interested that these negotiations should proceed with deliberate speed so that we reach agreement without unnecessary delay.

One of the challenges we will face in these negotiations will be to ensure that our agreement with the EU does not negatively affect our partners in the Southern African Customs Union (SACU) and the Southern African Development Community (SADC).

While we are negotiating with the EU, we are, at the same time proceeding to liberalise our trade regime in line with our GATT and WTO obligations. We are seriously committed to opening our economy to ensure more effective trade with Europe and the rest of the world.

Outside of the EU, trade and general economic relations with other European countries are also beginning to expand. Historically there has been very little interaction between apartheid South Africa and countries of Central and Eastern Europe and the former Soviet Union. Our trade and economic relations with Northern European countries, especially Scandinavian states, have also taken off. Companies which disinvested from apartheid South Africa are gradually reinvesting and we are happy that some of these are doing so in partnership with emerging black business people.

In South Africa we have embarked on an ambitious but necessary process of reconstruction and development. At the heart of this process is the need to deracialise South Africa, to transform the lives of ordinary people, to free them from poverty and human degradation, and to set our economy on a sustainable high growth path. We recognise that the only way in which we can begin to address the inequalities we inherited from apartheid is through sustainable economic growth and development.

In our endeavour to ensure growth and development, we have been working very hard to create a situation in which domestic and international confidence in the management of our economy is firmly established.

We have also been working hard to rationalise investment incentives which we have inherited, and to develop new policies to attract foreign investment. Our investment policy is governed by the principle of national treatment. This means that all incentives generally available to South African firms are available to foreign firms, and that there should be no measures that prejudice foreign investors.

We are keen to increase the level of European investment within our economy, especially in the productive and traded goods sector. New investments in these sectors would create jobs, enabling us to reduce the high levels of unemployment while earning good returns for investors.

In our drive to attract European and other international investors, South Africa offers, among other things, the following:

- a very good and developed transport, physical and communication infrastructure;
- sophisticated financial institutions;

- a good legal framework;
- a favourable geostrategic position relative to the markets of Southeast and East Asia, and South America; and
- a market of over 40 million people locally and 125 million within Southern Africa.

Indications are that already we are attracting significant volumes of direct investment from Europe and other places. Since the April 1994 elections we have attracted new investments from, among others, the United Kingdom, Germany, Austria, Switzerland, Italy, France, the Netherlands, Sweden, Malaysia, Singapore, South Korea and Japan. As diversified as the range of investing countries is the range of projects. Projects from the United Kingdom, for example, include several investments in the media, in telecommunications, as well as in manufacturing and tourism. Those from Austria include investments in steel and micro-electronic systems. German companies have tended to invest in sectors they are already present in, such as the motor industry and synthetic fuels.

The opening up of the world to South Africa has also benefited our business community. Since the unbanning of the ANC, the abolition of economic sanctions and the establishment of the Government of National Unity, South African businesses have been very active in the international financial markets raising investment finance. They have also been active forming partnerships with and, in some instances, acquiring significant stakes in European companies.

These relationships between our respective businesses will surely benefit both South Africa and Europe. For us in South Africa they will enable us to gain access to the well-developed and tested technologies, management techniques, marketing and work practices which will no doubt have a positive impact, especially on the competitiveness of our industries.

Foreign investment is also critical in that it will provide access to new markets for South African businesses and will raise the competitive temperature within our economy.

We are keen to enter into economic relations with Europe in a new way. We want to enter into a partnership that transcends the traditional exchange of raw materials and semi-processed goods by South Africa for the supply of finished goods, capital equipment and services by Europe. For example, in 1994, 60 per cent of South Africa's exports to Europe consisted of mineral products, natural pearls, precious and semi-precious materials and base metals. In turn 66,5 per cent of our imports from Europe consisted of chemical products, machinery and mechanical appliances, vehicles, aircraft and transport equipment.

Our economic experience has shown us that it is difficult and risky to build and anchor our economy on potentially volatile commodity markets as we enter the twenty-first century. It will therefore be important that we enter into relations that assist us to escape the tyranny of continuously declining commodity prices and contribute to our endeavours to foster an economy that produces modern and sophisticated manufactured goods and services.

The new situation in our country opens great opportunities for co-operation with our small and medium businesses, especially black business in South Africa. Partnerships between these and their European counterparts will, I believe, be critical to the development of our own entrepreneurs, enabling them to hold their own in the competitive world of business.

We do indeed place great importance on the issue of black business development. We believe that if we are to succeed in deracialising ownership of the economy, we need to provide business know-how, access to capital, and marketing possibilities to help enable the emerging black business community to develop. The dream of a democratic, non-racial and non-sexist society will but remain a dream if we do not, among other things, succeed in broadening the economic ownership.

Democracy cannot be limited to merely a once-in-five-years voting ritual. It has to extend to the fundamental restructuring of economic power. At the moment more than 80 per cent of the economy is in the hands of white people who constitute only 13 per cent of the total population. Black business people control about 2 per cent of the quoted shares on the Johannesburg stock exchange.

Europe has a strong and vibrant small and medium-sized business sector. In the 1980s and the 1990s, when large companies were facing severe competitive pressures, small and medium enterprises showed robustness and flexibility which enabled them to survive the most difficult trading conditions. It is this robustness and flexibility which we hope can be transferred to our emerging black businesses as they set out to help change the structure of our economy which is dominated by a handful of conglomerates.

From the government side, the Department of Trade and Industry in

South Africa, together with the Competition Board, has embarked on a process to review and strengthen our competition laws to address the issue of uncompetitive behaviour in our economy. We hope that we will learn from some of the recent experiences of the EU, Russia and countries of Central Europe.

As we approach the twenty-first century, the world is experiencing a major information and communications revolution. Part of the challenge that confronts Europe, the rest of the developed world and the developing world is to act together in spreading the benefits of this revolution to everybody and in elaborating the regulatory framework which this revolution, with its global impact, makes necessary. Unless we pursue these objectives consciously, we face the danger of an ever widening gap between the developed and developing worlds.

South Africa would like to work together with Europe and other developed countries to place our country and the subcontinent on the information superhighway, with everything that this implies, including the provision of distance education, telemedicine, new business opportunities, universal access to information and the communication media, and better possibilities to act together to shape the global village.

In this regard we welcome the decision by the G7 at Halifax to organise a conference on this critical issue in South Africa next year. This conference will provide a platform for the developing and developed countries jointly to explore how this important development can benefit all humanity.

Let me conclude by saying that our government is ready to enter into dialogue, not only with the EU, but with the rest of Europe as to what is needed to ensure that we build strong and mutually beneficial socio-economic relations.

We believe Europe can benefit from the vast opportunities that exist in our country, to our advantage as well. We would like to see you continuing to play a key role in trade and investments and as front-line participants in the modernisation of our economy.

What in the end we are talking about is in some instances life itself and, more generally, the guarantee of the human dignity of millions of Africans in South and Southern Africa and the rest of Africa further to our north. Access to jobs and a growing prosperity among those who today belong among the wretched of the earth are what we need to address effectively.

Within South Africa, the democratic victory and progress towards the creation of a truly non-racial society need to be underwritten by an economy which can feed and clothe all our citizens.

To move away from dependence on aid and help Africa to overcome the disastrous consequences of her debt burden requires economic interventions that will result in the growth of the productive capacities of the African economies and an increase in her ability to participate profitably in world trade.

We are certain that as we continue to work together, as Europeans and Africans, we can ensure that the new century of the new millennium no longer carries the blight of the terrible picture of the African child who died because of shortage of food.

32

The African Renaissance:
Opportunities and Challenges for Asia

Address at a luncheon hosted by the Hong Kong Centre of the Asian Society and the South African Business Forum, Hong Kong, 17 April 1998

IT IS NOT SO LONG AGO when those of us who live far away from these shores knew of China, the ancient land of which Hong Kong is an important part, what those who had imposed themselves upon us as our masters wanted us to know.

And so in that peculiar world of unknowing, we knew of a China of opium dens and marauding warlords, of a people who had a particular fondness for a cuisine whose primary delicacy was the tender flesh of the African child, of an abstruse scholasticism, it was said, of a Confucian kind, which codified and legitimised a culture of fine and petrified barbarism.

In that imposed world of terrifying ignorance, terrifying because it translated in our minds as knowledge, we knew of a Japanese people far away whose only contribution to what might be soft and sweet and gentle and humane in all that constitutes human civilisation were what were called geisha girls, whose task was to create the illusion of tranquillity, to provide a short moment of rest and revitalisation for the barbarians.

As we sought to fathom a mysterious East, instructed to consider mysterious by those who had imported themselves into our lands as our lords, we came to know of a people who harvested pearls through the jaws of strange things that live in the seas. It was said that they survived by drawing rubber from the trees of impenetrable and menacing jungles.

They drank an exotic drink called tea, which only grew on their special native soil. They had nurtured an infant and sent him out into the world as an adult, an angel of death. It was said that he knew nothing of the concept of mercy. To him anything that was not of the East had intrinsic worth only because it was worthy of destruction, and whose name, which came to mean terror itself, was that of a distinguished son and product of the civilisations of the East, Genghis Khan.

You will ask me why I speak in these terms about yourselves and your neighbourhood. Why speak like this when the reality is of Asian civilisations that have produced great religions, scientific inventions, schools of philosophical thought, monuments of construction and architecture, the visual and performing arts and literature, delicate cuisine and the capacity for original thought in the comprehension of our universe?

My answer to that question, which you may feel obliged not to ask because of politeness to a visitor, is that we have a task to repair a breach and refuse to tolerate a chasm between Africa and East Asia which emerged, not because either you, as Asians, or we, as Africans, sought to manufacture it. This chasm came to define our interaction because time and space, history and others other than ourselves intervened as a force that stood between us, creating the circumstance in which it became inevitable that as continents and as peoples we drifted apart.

As we grew up and graduated from a state of unknowing, we came to know that as Africans we were in contact with the Asian East, which our oppressors told us was barbaric, long before we succumbed to the fateful impact of the colonising spirit of the countries of the European West, which historical episode they described as a civilising mission.

What I speak of you are familiar with. I refer to the extraordinary fact of the landing of the Chinese fleet on the east coast of Africa by Admiral Cheng Ho during his voyage of 1421 to 1424 and as a result of which official relations were established between the Ming court and the rulers of Mogadishu, Malindi, Mombassa, Zanzibar, Dar es Salaam and Kilwa.

I speak of the fact of the arrival in China in 1415 of a gift of a giraffe shipped by an African king, probably from the East African town of Malindi, sent to an emperor of China of the Ming Dynasty. It is said that 'A contemporary painting on silk shows the giraffe with halter and lead-rope standing calmly beside its Chinese handler; and the painting's inscription congratulates the emperor on the arrival of such an auspicious beast.'

A Chinese ship, capable of traversing the great distance between the Pacific and the western edge of the Indian Ocean, had ferried this extraordinary gift.

And if you asked why the gentle giraffe rather than an animal obviously representing the prowess and invincibility of the African kingdoms, as would be represented by the elephant, the lion or the leopard, I would answer that the kings of Africa sent a giraffe to the Forbidden City in Beijing to pay tribute to a ruler who could see into the distance, watching to ensure that his kingdom and its people came to no harm.

In our own native languages, the giraffe is known descriptively as *indlulamthi* – the animal that towers above the trees. And so this special animal arrived at the court of the Ming Dynasty as a tribute to the fact that the people of the East had managed to grow beyond the trees of their forests. As a result, they had espied the coast of Africa to which they had brought a message of co-operation, mutual respect and trade in commodities, which would have an impact in improving the lives of the peoples of both Asia and Africa.

Despite that historic message of six centuries ago, if I asked for your impressions of Africa today, I believe that some of these may be no different in quality from our own state of unknowing about the Asian East which we mistook for knowledge. They would describe a barbaric people of Africa whose continent is characterised by political turmoil, social unrest, dictatorships, military coups, genocide, disease, massive displacement of people, an unquenchable thirst for misappropriation of public wealth by those who have installed themselves as rulers over the people, and cultural backwardness.

To make matters worse, it would not be possible to dismiss these impressions as being mere products of a jaundiced mind of a prejudiced observer.

This would be so because the modern means of mass communication would have brought into your rooms and mine scenes of the barbarity that was represented by the apartheid system, the gruesome massacres that took place in Rwanda, and the incongruous splendours of a basilica of shining marble and golden domes in the middle of the African jungle in the former Zaïre, beyond whose trees the ordinary citizens lead miserable lives of grinding poverty.

That mass media would correctly tell a story of those who are dying today as a result of conflicts that are taking place in Algeria, the Sudan, Rwanda and Burundi.

And yet the Africa of today is an Africa of hope, a continent that has resumed its journey out of the period of despair.

It is for this reason that we have spoken of an African renaissance, of the rebirth of an entire continent.

Ghana and Mali in the west, which have had their fair share of military dictatorships, are today ruled by democratically elected governments whose policies have resulted in the recovery of the economies of these countries of hope.

Though Somalia in the east disintegrated and ceased to exist as a nation state, strangely, the guns have fallen silent and the contending clans are engaged in a search for a new path to a new Somalia of peace.

Hardly four years after the appalling genocide of Rwanda, the peasants of this country of Central Africa are reaching out to one another in an unprecedented drive to achieve national reconciliation, to forgive one another, to rebuild lives of hope out of a shattering experience of inexcusable barbarity.

After their continuous and deadly chatter for over three decades, the guns have also been silenced in Angola in the south-west. Those who had been at war one against the other sit together as the government of this sister country which is blessed with extraordinary natural wealth.

So too, in the south, has the apartheid blight on the human landscape been overtaken by a new order of democracy and peace, and the combined efforts of all our people to reconstruct and develop South Africa in a spirit of national reconciliation.

All these represent our determined efforts as Africans to take charge of our lives so that life for every citizen becomes better. They may not be susceptible to the dramatic presentation of the slaughter of the innocents, but contain the drama of rebirth which asserts the beauty of a new life.

The will of the peoples of Africa to liberate themselves from corrupt, unaccountable and undemocratic regimes is demonstrated by the fact that during the present decade more than 25 sub-Saharan countries have established multiparty democracies. All of them held democratic elections to enable the people to decide on governments of their choice.

The departure from the African political stage of personalities such as General Mobutu Sese Seko of the former Zaïre symbolises the end of a debilitating era of neocolonialism in Africa and the resumption of movement forward which had been interrupted.

A new indigenous and energised African movement for the liberation of the continent has surely emerged. It is set to change the face of the politics and governance, and the economy of Africa.

In an article in its edition of 4 April this year, the magazine *The Econ-*

omist says: 'In 1996 and 1997, for the first time in many years, the economies of sub-Saharan Africa grew faster than its population. A handful of countries did even better: last year 11 of them had growth rates of more than 6%.'

Another report in the January 1998 issue of *Business Africa* says that: 'In 1992 only 17 of the 47 sub-Saharan economies grew by more than 3 per cent, but by 1995 the number had increased to 29 and is thought to have risen again to 35 in 1997.'

These economic changes are indeed remarkable if seen against the backdrop of a history of the actual decline in standards of living in many parts of Africa. They are directly traceable to the political changes of which we have spoken which, among other things, have resulted in the wholesale review of economic policies of the past.

That review has resulted in the abandonment of the perspective which saw the state as the principal owner of the productive economy, which led to the birth of an extensive system of malfunctioning state corporations.

As a consequence of this, many countries across the continent have embarked on programmes to privatise these assets, thus giving primacy to the domestic and foreign private sector in the struggle to achieve economic growth and development.

Furthermore, more prudent approaches have been adopted with regard to the management of the public finances, sometimes as a result of painful structural adjustment programmes designed by the International Monetary Fund (IMF) as a condition for extending assistance to countries that had fallen on hard times.

The process of recovery has also been driven by better exploitation and management of the natural and agricultural resources of the continent, which, as you know, is richly endowed and therefore can provide products which the economies of the world need, from gold, platinum and diamonds, to cobalt, copper, aluminium, iron and steel; from oil and natural gas to cocoa, coffee, timber and cotton.

Similarly, the further expansion and modernisation of the infrastructure, as well as the growth of tourism to this continent, which can be described as grossly under-visited, have also contributed to the gradual process of economic recovery whose signs are visible in many parts of Africa.

Of course, as this process gains pace, so do the domestic markets expand, creating opportunities for further growth.

It is true that despite all we have said, we cannot speak as though no problems exist. Many of our countries continue to suffer from a high level of foreign indebtedness as well as small inflows of foreign capital.

But what is possible is reflected in the little-known story of the Republic of Botswana, our neighbour to the west, which is told in the same issue of *The Economist* to which we have referred. Correctly, the magazine reports: 'Between 1975 and 1990, this land-locked southern African state was the world's fastest-growing economy. Multiparty democracy is entrenched, state welfare is more developed than in any other sub-Saharan country, and external debt is negligible. Foreign reserves are close to $5 billion, so that, far from depending on aid, Botswana lends hard currency to the IMF.'

Clearly, the addition of South Africa to the free nations of Africa will also contribute further to reinforce the movement towards the radical improvement of the economic fortunes of our continent.

A first requirement we too have had to address has been the need to adopt new policies which, among other things, would end the period of an economy under siege and integrate our country within the rapidly globalising world economy, ensuring higher levels of growth and employment, increasing the international competitiveness of the economy and maintaining healthy macro-economic balances. I am pleased to report that progress is being achieved in all these areas.

I must also mention the important fact that South Africa belongs to the regional interstate organisation, the Southern African Development Community (SADC), whose combined population is 140 million people. SADC is the instrument through which the peoples of our region, understanding the importance of large markets as well as the reality of their interdependence, seek to achieve balanced and mutually beneficial economic growth and development. In pursuit of this goal, the member countries of SADC are involved in negotiations to transform the subcontinent into a free trade area which would further enhance the attractiveness of the countries of the region as an investment destination and a base from which to reach into the larger African market.

229

Hong Kong is an important centre of the world economy. As its global role increases, we believe it would make no sense to define the world in which it would make its presence felt as the universe minus Africa.

We are greatly encouraged by the fact that the Hong Kong Trade Development Council opened an office in South Africa, as well as the existence in Hong Kong of the South African Business Forum.

As the government of South Africa, we are keenly interested to co-operate with these bodies to look for and exploit all ways and means by which we can increase our economic co-operation.

As you know, you will find in South Africa a developed infrastructure of modern communications and energy, a sound banking system and legislative framework, as well as stable and transparent policies spelt out in such documents as our Reconstruction and Development Programme, the Growth Employment and Redistribution programme for a stable macro-economy and the Medium-term Expenditure Framework.

Yesterday, one of the South African business dailies reported that 'Foreign investors flocked to South Africa's bond and equity markets yesterday, taking the government benchmark bond to its best level in four years and driving shares on the Johannesburg Stock Exchange to fresh highs.' The paper attributes the positive sentiment which led to these results, among other things, to 'a favourable inflationary environment' and 'a steady rand'.

You will find in this South Africa of great promise a bridge to access much of the rest of the African continent.

The leaders and members of the Asia Society are better placed than we are to speak on what seems to us to be an evolving identity of and cohesion within the region of East Asia. As this region defines its own place in world politics and the economy, we believe that it should see itself as a partner of the Africa of the African renaissance, a partnership from which it would benefit as much as we.

History tells us that during these days many centuries ago, neither of us considered the other barbarians. Rather, sovereign efforts by peoples separated by great geographical distances reflected a view which indicated a willingness to act in a manner which celebrated a common humanity based on the fundamental notion that the successful existence of one was dependent on the equally successful existence of the other. Accordingly, the Chinese fleets of the fifteenth and sixteenth centuries brought

230

to the East African ports not the destruction and despair of the Arabian and European slave trade and European colonialism, but mutually beneficial co-operation which the ancient rulers of our continent acknowledged by sending the tall, graceful and gentle giraffe as their messenger to the peoples of the East.

Once again, we are present in the East, in this vibrant place called Hong Kong, perhaps not so tall that we can tower above the trees, as graceful and gentle as the gentleman or gentlewoman of the wilds, the giraffe, but bearers nevertheless of the same message of old: that as Asians and Africans we must reach across the great geographical divide, to build a partnership worthy of the sentiment which drove the ancient rulers to exchange gifts which spoke of mutual respect and mutually beneficial co-operation.

We believe that Africa's renewal through her native-born renaissance presents an opportunity to Asia to benefit from Africa's enormous economic potential and for us to gain from your ingenuity and initiative, for Asia to acquire a reliable political partner in a world of globalisation which demands that each reinforces its sovereignty by combining efforts with the other.

Our times demand that we do not wait for another day to build on a partnership which is 600 years old.

33

Great Expectations: From
Global Village to Global Neighbourhood

The United Nations at 50, University of Melbourne, Australia, 28 April 1995

FIFTY YEARS AGO, with the fall of Berlin and the surrender of the Fascist allies across the European theatre of war, the guns in the battlefields of Europe fell silent.

Still to be written as the last chapter of this conflict were the atomic bombs that fell on Hiroshima and Nagasaki, an epilogue which was at the same time a prologue to a new and continuing discussion on the great issues of war and peace.

Quite correctly, as peace descended on Europe, the cities, towns and villages of this continent and other parts of the world erupted in a festival of triumph and celebration. But as that joyful sound wafted across the face of the globe, it did so over a world darkened by the terrible consequences that emanated from the destructive fury of the Second World War.

The European, Asian and African continents had acquired new historical monuments in the forms of mass graves of those who were martyred by the armed conflict. Europe was also home to other mass graves, these containing Jews, Slavs and others who had been slaughtered as a result of a demented racism which resorted to genocide and ethnic cleansing as a matter of policy.

Millions of those who had survived the destruction, the refugees and displaced persons, tramped the earth, tormented by their wounds, by disease and by hunger, searching for solace and comfort among the ruins of the homes, the factories, the farms, the hospitals and the schools, which wanton destruction was the heritage of the titanic battle that had just been concluded.

As all humanity surveyed the spectre of death and misery, those who had the time to reflect on the past could not but remark the failure of the

League of Nations which had been unable to prevent the genocide, the war and the destruction imposed on the peoples by Nazi tyranny.

Then a new sun dawned to give hope to the peoples of the world: the United Nations (UN) was born. It was created to succeed where the League of Nations had failed.

And so those who could, set about to establish a new world of freedom, peace and prosperity.

Those important documents, the UN Charter and the Declaration of Human Rights, were adopted, as was the Statute of the International Court of Justice, to give meaning to a law-governed world.

The eminent leaders of the day went on to establish the Bretton Woods Institutions as instruments to repair the destruction of the war, create wealth and attend to the improvement of the quality of life of humankind. Significant among these was the appropriately named International Bank for Reconstruction and Development, the World Bank.

Great expectations had indeed been created.

South Africa's involvement with the UN goes back to the inception of this body. The then prime minister of South Africa, Field-Marshal J.C. Smuts, helped to draft the Preamble of the Charter to the UN. In the Preamble, many lofty ideas were expressed, among which the following objective is stated:

> ... to reaffirm faith in fundamental human rights, in the dignity and worth of the human person, in the equal rights of men and women and of nations large and small.

It is ironic that the then South African government was party to such a noble vision, while in South Africa itself the dispossession and oppression of the vast majority of our people was ruthlessly intensified. This indeed was the experience of many countries in Africa, Asia and Latin America.

This, in part, and the so far limited capacity of the UN in practical terms 'to reaffirm faith in fundamental human rights, in the dignity and worth of the human person, in the equal rights of men and women and of nations large and small', might explain why, even as we speak here tonight, 50 years later, the world is still seeking answers to issues of war and peace, arms proliferation, gross violations of human rights, lack of democracy, discrimination against women, intolerance, ethnic cleansing, racism and mass poverty.

233

The question remains: Why have we not been able to create a mechanism, as was originally intended, that would rejuvenate the world and free it from the human tragedy we witness today? What went wrong and how do we correct it?

The observance of the fiftieth anniversary of the UN demands that we seek answers to these questions and make the necessary transformations required for the realisation of the noble vision of the founders of the UN.

During his opening speech at the World Cultural Diversity Conference earlier this week, Prime Minister Paul Keating correctly observed that: '...despite the complications and the setbacks of the following half-century, the UN managed to notch up substantial achievements, not enough of them, ... but many more than some of its critics allow.' He went on to say: 'But fifty years on, the Cold War is over and there has never been a better time to ask ourselves if the UN we now have is what we now need. And what we will need in the twenty-first century.'

In order to answer this question, we need to determine the objectives of the UN today.

We believe that the principal objective of the UN remains the maintenance of international peace and security.

While a third world war has been prevented, we are confronted by the reality that many wars have been fought in the Third World. Even now we continue to experience violent conflicts in various parts of the world, the vast majority of which are not interstate but intrastate.

On a daily basis, we are exposed to the stark reminders of horrific events in places such as Angola, Burundi, Rwanda, Somalia, Afghanistan, the former Yugoslavia and Soviet Union.

The challenge to us is to address the root causes of this. Among these, all of us surely agree, are underdevelopment, poverty and hunger, lack of democracy, injustice, religious extremism and ignorance.

Originally, the UN mechanisms were created to deal with interstate, but not intrastate, conflicts. It would therefore seem obvious that a reassessment of these mechanisms must be urgently undertaken, taking into account the practical experience of half a century. Today an important objective of the UN must be preventive diplomacy, peace-making, peace-keeping and peace-building. The secretary-general's Agenda for Peace and the Agenda for Development are an attempt to deal with this challenge.

All of us have the serious responsibility to consider these and other initiatives to enable us to ensure that the UN organisation lives up to the great expectations that its founding inspired. We are also of the view that regional organisations must play a greater role to enable the UN to achieve this objective. The recent creation by the Organisation of African Unity (OAU) of the Mechanism for Conflict Prevention, Management and Resolution is Africa's initial step in this direction.

Our continent is unfortunately the recipient of the majority of the UN peace operations. Preventive action will be increasingly necessary to address the burning question of conflict. As a member of the OAU, South Africa is actively playing a role in the Central Organ of the OAU Mechanism for Conflict Prevention, Management and Resolution. In the sub-region of Southern Africa plans are well advanced for the formation of the Association of Southern African States. The purpose of this association will be to respond rapidly and effectively to any threat to peace, security and democracy in the Southern African region.

The UN review initiatives must take these new developments into consideration. It would seem obvious to us that, in this context, the issue of national sovereignty has to be revisited. Is it possible, for instance, to speak of preventive diplomacy while subscribing to a doctrine of the absolute sovereignty of nations? Are the interventionist positions spelt out in Chapter VII of the UN Charter sufficient to cope with what the last 50 years have taught us about the prevention of conflict?

And yet, it is equally true that this matter cannot be addressed outside of the consideration of the similarly important issue of the democratisation of the system of international relations. Another important objective, which the UN must surely pursue, is the abolition of weapons of mass destruction and the restrictions in the growth and proliferation of conventional weapons. As you are aware, South Africa is the only country in the world that voluntarily destroyed its nuclear weapons capacity. South Africa has become a state party to the Non-Proliferation Treaty (NPT) and is actively involved in the development of an African Nuclear-Free-Zone Treaty.

However, there are still countries intent on obtaining weapons of mass destruction. We must not only take steps to stop this, but we must also ensure that those countries that possess weapons of mass destruction move decisively towards complete disarmament. It is for these reasons that we favour the indefinite extension of the NPT. However, we must also state this very firmly, that the five nations that acknowledge having nuclear weapons have to adhere to disarmament and security principles as well as a review process that would meet the concerns of many countries without such weapons,

Pivotal to all the efforts of the international community to maintain peace and stability is the fundamental prerequisite to promote and consolidate democracy throughout the world.

President Mandela has correctly said: 'Our common humanity transcends the oceans and all national boundaries. It binds us together in a common cause against tyranny, to act together in defence of our very humanity. Let it never be asked of any one of us: What did we do when we knew that another was oppressed?'

This underscores our view that the UN should become the instrument for the democratisation of societies throughout the world. This will also necessitate continued support for societies undergoing the difficult process which accompanies democratisation.

As we said at the important Sydney Conference on Global Cultural Diversity, our own experience shows that we can no longer describe democracy merely in terms of regular, multiparty elections. As we said, we believe that it is impossible to bring peace and stability to divided societies unless conditions are created for democratic, open and meaningful participation by all role players, however small, in the determination of the destiny of the country.

We ourselves have evolved towards the view that we must exploit the opportunity we have to establish a new democracy, to construct our democratic system in such a manner that it entrenches popular participation in the decision-making processes and thus bring us closer to the realisation of the concept that 'the people shall govern'.

The success we seek with regard to our own country depends not only on the opening of democratic space. It rests also on our ability to create a situation in which there is an equitable access to material resources both for the individual and the community, to address any sense of grievance that some are discriminated against, and to work towards the situation in which the inalienable dignity of the individual is not compromised by poverty and deprivation.

I believe that what is applicable to us in South Africa has relevance internationally, without in any way suggesting we can transpose our experience to other countries.

We merely speak as we have to underscore the reality that the new world order of democracy, human rights, peace, stability and prosperity cannot be achieved in a world in which a handful of countries (20 per cent) are rich while the vast majority of countries (80 per cent) are fighting to achieve sustainable economic growth, and where the masses of people live in abject poverty and deprivation.

In these circumstances, it is surely appropriate that we all take another look at the Bretton Woods Institutions to seek an answer to the questions that Prime Minister Keating posed – whether what we have is what we need and what we shall need in the twenty-first century.

Development and environmental protection should go hand in hand in order to ensure that forthcoming generations are not condemned to an environmental wasteland created by the relentless search for economic success.

The Rio Conference on the Environment was an important development in getting international consensus on the vexed issue of the environment. Many important decisions were taken and resolutions adopted. It is necessary for us to determine how many of the decisions that were taken have in fact been implemented.

Similarly, we must assess the International Conference on Population and Development held in Cairo, the recent World Summit on Social Development held in Copenhagen, as well as the Conference on Gender Equality.

On the basis of our assessment we must then consider whether the existing UN mechanisms are in fact adequate to implement the decisions taken.

The challenges that we face, as outlined above, necessitate that we vigorously pursue the debate that has already started at the UN about the reform of that body and its specialised agencies.

In this respect let me briefly comment on two aspects. Firstly, it is necessary to work for the revitalisation of the Economic and Social Council, especially with regard to its role as programme co-ordinator. Some progress has been made in the fields of economic and social development, human rights and the environment, but more needs to be done to bring the strands together for maximum effectiveness.

Secondly, with regard to the reform of the Security Council, our own position is that the institutionalisation of the balance of power at the end of the Second World War in the composition of the Security Council should be addressed.

Modern developments have led to a situation where outdated 'realpolitik' should be replaced with an inclusive international consensus reflecting the further democratisation of international relations. This, we believe, could be more readily obtained through a more representative and democratic Security Council. This should include the enlargement of the Security Council to meet the principles of more equitable geographical representation and transparency.

Today we live in a global village, characterised by economic and political blocs and the increasing trend towards a global market; an information revolution that transcends borders; the universal impact of environmental degradation; the necessity to establish early warning systems to enable the international community to deal effectively with conflict prevention, management and resolution; and the necessity for international intervention where gross violations of human rights and genocide occur.

These developments bring into sharp focus the need to revisit long-established notions of the sovereignty of nations and non-interference in the internal affairs of states.

I sincerely hope that our continuing deliberations on these issues will help all of us to reach a new consensus on the way forward.

The global village must transform itself into a global neighbourhood.

34

The African Renaissance,
South Africa and the World

Address at the United Nations University, Tokyo, Japan, 9 April 1998

WE MUST ASSUME THAT the Roman Pliny the Elder was familiar with the Latin saying, *Ex Africa semper aliquid novi!* – Something new always comes out of Africa.

Writing during the first century of the present millennium, Pliny gave his fellow Romans some startlingly interesting and supposedly new information about Africans. He wrote:

> Of the Ethiopians there are diverse forms and kinds of men. Some there are toward the east that have neither nose nor nostrils, but the face all full. Others have no upper lip, they are without tongues, and they speak by signs, and they have but a little hole to take their breath at, by the which they drink with an oaten straw... In a part of Africa be people called Pteomphane, for their king they have a dog, at whose fancy they are governed... And the people called Anthropomphagi, which we call cannibals, live with human flesh. The Cinamolgi, their heads are almost like to heads of dogs... Blemmy is a people so called, they have no heads, but have their mouth and their eyes in their breasts.[33]

These images must have frightened many a Roman child to scurry to bed whenever their parents said: The Africans are coming! The strange creatures out of Africa are coming!

Happily, 15 centuries later, Europe had a somewhat different view of the Africans. At the beginning of the sixteenth century, Leo Africanus, a Spaniard resident in Morocco, visited West Africa and wrote the following about the royal court in Timbuktu, Mali:

> The rich king of Timbuktu ... keeps a magnificent and well-furnished court... Here are great store of doctors, judges, priests, and other learned men, that are bountifully maintained at the king's cost and charges. And hither are brought diverse manuscripts or written books out of Barbarie, which are sold for more money than any other merchandise.[34]

Clearly, this was not the Dog King of which Pliny had written at the beginning of the millennium, but a being as human as any other and more cultured and educated than most in the world of his day.

And yet, at the close of our millennium, we read in a book published last year:

> I am an American, but a black man, a descendant of slaves brought from Africa... If things had been different, I might have been one of them [the Africans] – or might have met some ... anonymous fate in one of the countless ongoing civil wars or tribal clashes on this brutal continent. And so I thank God my ancestor survived that voyage [to slavery]... Talk to me about Africa and my black roots and my kinship with my African brothers and I'll throw it back into your face, and then I'll rub your nose in the images of the rotting flesh [of the victims of the genocide of the Tutsis of Rwanda]... Sorry, but I've been there. I've had an AK-47 [automatic rifle] rammed up my nose, I've talked to machete-wielding Hutu militiamen with the blood of their latest victims splattered across their T-shirts. I've seen a cholera epidemic in Zaïre, a famine in Somalia, a civil war in Liberia. I've seen cities bombed to near rubble, and other cities reduced to rubble, because their leaders let them rot and decay while they spirited away billions of dollars – yes, billions – into overseas bank accounts... Thank God my ancestor got out, because, now, I am not one of them.[35]

And this time, in the place of the Roman child, it is the American child who will not hesitate to go to bed when he or she is told: The Africans are coming! The barbarians are coming!

In a few paragraphs, quoted from books that others have written, we have traversed a millennium. But the truth is that we have not travelled very far with regard to the projection of frightening images of savagery that attend the continent of Africa.

And so it may come about that some, who harbour the view that as

Africans we are a peculiar species of humanity, pose the challenge: How dare they speak of an African renaissance!

After all, in the context of the evolution of the European peoples, when we speak of the Renaissance, we speak of advances in science and technology, voyages of discovery across the oceans, a revolution in printing and an attendant spread, development and flowering of knowledge and a blossoming of the arts.

And so the question must arise about how we – who in a millennium only managed to advance from cannibalism to a 'blood-dimmed tide' of savages, who still slaughter countless innocents with machetes, and on whom another, as black as I, has turned his back, grateful that his ancestors were slaves – how do we hope to emulate the great human achievements of the earlier Renaissance of the Europe of the fifteenth and sixteenth centuries?

One of our answers to this question is that, as Africans, we recall the fact that as the European Renaissance burst into history in the fifteenth and sixteenth centuries, there was a royal court in the African city of Timbuktu which, in the same centuries, was as learned as its European counterparts.

What this tells me is that my people are not a peculiar species of humanity!

I say this here today because it is true, but also because I know that you, the citizens of this ancient land, will understand its true significance.

And as we speak of an African renaissance, we project into both the past and the future.

I speak here of a glorious past of the emergence of *Homo sapiens* on the African continent.

I speak of African works of art in South Africa that are a thousand years old. I speak of the continuum in the fine arts that encompasses the varied artistic creations of the Nubians and the Egyptians, the Benin bronzes of Nigeria and the intricate sculptures of the Makonde of Tanzania and Mozambique.

I speak of the centuries-old contributions to the evolution of religious thought made by the Christians of Ethiopia and the Muslims of Nigeria.

I refer also to the architectural monuments represented by the giant sculptured stones of Aksum in Ethiopia, the Egyptian sphinxes and pyramids, the Tunisian city of Carthage and the Zimbabwe Ruins, as well as the legacy of the ancient universities of Alexandria of Egypt, Fez of Morocco and, once more, Timbuktu of Mali.

When I survey all this and much more besides, I find nothing to sustain the long-held dogma of African exceptionalism, according to which the colour black becomes a symbol of fear, evil and death.

I speak of this long-held dogma, because it continues still to weigh down the African mind and spirit, like the ton of lead that the African slave carries on her own shoulders, producing in her and the rest a condition which, in itself, contests any assertion that she is capable of initiative, creativity, individuality and entrepreneurship.

Its weight dictates that she will never straighten her back and thus discover that she is as tall as the slavemaster who carries the whip. Neither will she have the opportunity to question why the master has legal title both to the commodity she transports on her back and the labour she must make available to ensure that the burden on her shoulders translates into dollars and yen.

An essential and necessary element of the African renaissance is that we all must take it as our task to encourage her, who carries this leaden weight, to rebel, to assert the principality of her humanity – the fact that she, in the first instance, is not a beast of burden, but a human and African being.

But in our own voyage of discovery, we have come to Japan and discovered that a mere 130 years ago, the Meiji Restoration occurred, which enabled your own forebears to project both into their past and their future.

And as we seek to draw lessons and inspiration from what you have done for yourselves, and integrate the Meiji Restoration into these universal things that make us dare speak of an African renaissance, we too see an African continent which is not 'wandering between two worlds, one dead, the other unable to be born'.

But whence and whither this confidence?

I would dare say that that confidence, in part, derives from a rediscovery of ourselves, from the fact that, perforce, as one would who is critical of oneself, we have had to undertake a voyage of discovery into our own antecedents, our own past as Africans.

And when archaeology presents daily evidence of an African primacy in the historical evolution to the emergence of the human person described in science as *Homo sapiens* – how can we be but confident that we are capable of effecting Africa's rebirth?

When the world of fine arts speaks to us of the creativity of the Nubians of Sudan and its decisive impact on the revered and everlasting imaginative creations of the African land of the pharaohs – how can we but be confident that we will succeed to be the midwives of our continent's rebirth?

And when we recall that African armies at Omduraman in the Sudan and Isandhlwana in South Africa out-generalled, out-soldiered and defeated the mighty armies of the powerful and arrogant British Empire in the '70s of the last century – how can we but be confident that, through our efforts, Africa will regain her place among the continents of our universe?

And in the end, an entire epoch in human history, the epoch of colonialism and white foreign rule, progressed to its ultimate historical burial grounds because, from Morocco and Algeria to Guinea-Bissau and Senegal, from Ghana to Nigeria to Tanzania and Kenya, from the Congo and Angola to Zimbabwe and South Africa, the Africans dared to stand up to say the new must be born, whatever the sacrifice we have to make – Africa must be free!

We are convinced that such a people has a legitimate right to expect of itself that it has the capacity to set itself free from the oppressive historical legacy of poverty, hunger, backwardness and marginalisation in the struggle to order world affairs, so that all human civilisation puts, as the principal objective of its existence, the humane existence of all that is human!

And again we come back to the point that we, who are our own liberators from imperial domination, cannot but be confident that our project to ensure the restoration not of empires, but the other conditions in the sixteenth century described by Leo Africanus – of peace, stability, prosperity and intellectual creativity – will and must succeed!

The simple phrase – we are our own liberators! – is the epitaph on the gravestone of every African who dared to carry the vision in his or her heart of Africa reborn.

The conviction, therefore, that our past tells us that the time for Africa's renaissance has come, is fundamental to the very conceptualisation of this renaissance and the answer to the question: Whence this confidence?

Unless we are able to answer the question: Who were we? we will not be able to answer the question: What shall we be?

This complex exercise, which can be stated in simple terms, links the past to the future and speaks to the interconnection between an empowering process of restoration and the consequences of the response to the acquisition of that newly restored power to create something new.

If, at this point, you asked me whether I was making a reference to the Meiji Restoration and its impact on the history and evolution of this country, my answer would be: Yes!

However, I would also plead that you should not question me too closely on this matter, to avoid me exposing my ignorance.

But this I would like you to know, that in the depth of my ignorance, I am moved by the conviction that this particular period in the evolution of Japan, to the point, today, when her economic problems are those of a surfeit rather that the poverty of resources, has a multiplicity of lessons for us as Africans, which we cannot afford to ignore or, worse still, not to know.

And if we, as students, are badly informed, you have a responsibility to be our teachers. We are ready to learn and to become our own teachers as a result.

We would also like you to know that our determination to learn is exemplified by the willingness we have demonstrated to learn on our own from our experiences.

I refer here in particular to the period since the independence of many of our countries. Among many Africans this has been referred to as the neocolonial period.

This constitutes an honest admission of the fact that an important feature of African independence at that stage was that the development of these independent states was determined by the reality that the fundamental, structural relationship between the independent states and the former colonial powers did not change.

As a consequence of the acquisition of independence, new state symbols have been adopted and were displayed daily. New state institutions were created. Political and other decision-making processes commenced, which represented and signified the formation of new nation states. At last Africans were governing themselves.

However, reality, including purposes of the Cold War, dictated that the former colonial powers continued to hold in their hands the power to determine what would happen to the African people over whom, in terms of international and municipal law, they no longer had any jurisdiction.

The mere recognition that this signified a neocolonial relationship rather than genuine independence affirmed the point that the peoples of our continent had not abandoned the determination to be their own liberators!

Much of what you see reported in your own media today, represented, for instance, by the exit from the African stage of a personality such as General Mobutu Sese Seko of the former Zaïre, represents the death of neocolonialism on our continent.

And so we must return to the question: Whence the confidence that we, as Africans, can speak of an African renaissance?

What we have said so far is that both our ancient and modern history as well as our own practical and conscious deeds convey the same message: that genuine liberation, in the context of the modern world, is what drives the Africans of today as they seek to confront the problems which for them constitute a daily challenge.

The question must therefore arise: What is it which makes up that genuine liberation?

The first of these is that we must bring to an end the practices as a result of which many throughout the world have the view that as Africans we are incapable of establishing and maintaining systems of good governance.

Our own practical experience tells us that military governments do not represent the system of good governance which we seek. Accordingly, the continent has made the point clear that it is opposed to military coups and has taken practical steps, as exemplified by the restoration to power of the elected government of Sierra Leone, to demonstrate its intent to meet this challenge when it arises.

Similarly, many governments throughout the continent, including our continental organisation, the Organisation of African Unity (OAU), have sought to encourage the Nigerian government and people to return as speedily as possible to a democratic system of government.

Furthermore, our experience has taught us that one-party states also do not represent the correct route to take towards the objective of a stable system of governance which serves the interests of the people.

One of the principal demands on our liberation struggle, as we sought to end the system of apartheid, was – the people shall govern!

It is this same vision which has inspired the African peoples so that, during the present decade, we have seen at least 25 countries establish multiparty democracies and hold elections so that the people can decide on governments of their choice. The new South Africa is itself an expression and part of this African movement towards the transfer of power to the people.

At the same time, we are conscious of the fact that each country has its particular characteristics to which it must respond as it establishes its democratic system of government. Accordingly, none of us seeks to impose any supposedly standard models of democracy on any country, but wants to see systems of government in which the people are empowered to determine their destiny and to resolve any disputes among themselves by peaceful political means.

In our own country, conscious of the need to handle the contradictions and conflicts that might arise among different ethnic and national groups properly, aware also of the fact that such conflicts have been an important element of instability on the continent, we have made it a constitutional requirement to establish a Commission for the Promotion of Cultural, Language and Religious Rights.

In this context, we must also mention two initiatives which the continent as a whole has taken through the agency of the OAU.

We refer here to the establishment of the interstate Central Organ for the Prevention and Resolution of Conflicts, which is empowered to intervene to resolve conflicts on the continent and which is currently working on the design of an instrument for peace-keeping to increase our collective capacity to intervene quickly to ensure that we have no more Rwandas, Liberias or Somalias.

The second initiative to which we refer is the adoption of the African Charter of Human and Peoples' Rights, which sets norms according to which we ourselves can judge both ourselves and our sister countries as to whether we are conducting ourselves in a manner consistent with the defence and promotion of human and peoples' rights.

Like others throughout the world, we too are engaged in the struggle to give real meaning to such concepts as transparency and accountability in governance, as part of the offensive directed against corruption and the abuse of power.

What we are arguing, therefore, is that in the political sphere the African renaissance has begun. Our history demands that we do everything in our power to defend the gains that have already been achieved, to encourage all other countries on our continent to move in the same direction, according to which the people shall govern, and to enhance the capacity of the OAU to act as an effective instrument for peace and the promotion of human and peoples' rights, to which it is committed.

Such are the political imperatives of the African renaissance, which are inspired both by our painful history of recent decades and the recognition of the fact that none of our countries is an island which can isolate itself from the rest and that none of us can truly succeed if the rest fail.

The second of the elements of what we have described as the genuine liberation of the peoples of Africa is, of course, an end to the tragic sight of the emaciated child who dies because of hunger or is ravaged by curable diseases because his or her malnourished body does not have the strength to resist any illness.

What we have spoken of before, of the restoration of the dignity of the peoples of Africa, itself demands that we deal as decisively and as quickly as possible with the perception that, as a continent, we are condemned for ever to depend on the merciful charity which those who are kind are ready to put into our begging bowls.

Accordingly, and again driven by our painful experience, many on our continent have introduced new economic policies which seek to create conditions that are attractive to both domestic and foreign investors, encourage the growth of the private sector, reduce the participation of the state in the ownership of the economy and, in other ways, seek to build modern economies.

Simultaneously, we are also working to overcome the disadvantages created by small markets represented by the relatively small numbers of people in many of our nation states. Regional economic associations have therefore been formed aimed at achieving regional economic integration, which in many instances would provide the necessary condition for any significant and sustained economic growth and development to take place.

In our own region, we have the Southern African Development Community, which brings together a population of well over 100 million people. The Community has already taken the decision to work towards transforming itself into a free trade area and is currently involved in detailed discussions about such issues as the timetable for the reduction of tariffs, to encourage trade among the member states and thus to take the necessary steps leading to the creation of the free trade area to which we have referred.

We are also engaged in other initiatives aimed at the development of infrastructure throughout the region, both as an expression of development and to create the basis for further development and therefore a sustained improvement in the standard of living of the people.

As part of the determined offensive to achieve integrated and mutually beneficial regional development, we have taken other initiatives to deal with common regional problems, going beyond the directly economic. I refer here to the establishment of a regional instrument to address questions of regional security, peace and stability, including the building of regional peace-making and peace-keeping capacity. I refer also to the development of a regional system of co-operation to combat crime, including trade in narcotics and illegal firearms, as well as the evolution of common programmes and legislative frameworks to deal with such challenges as violence against women and children.

We are therefore determined to ensure that we end the situation according to which, for many years, Africa recorded the slowest rates of economic growth and, in many instances, actually experienced economic decline.

Already a significant number of countries have shown relatively high rates of growth as a direct consequence of changes in economic policy and, of course, the achievement of stability within our countries, as a result of the establishment of democratic systems of government.

These economic objectives, which must result in the elimination of poverty, the establishment of modern multi-sector economies and the growth of Africa's share of world economic activity, are an essential part of the African renaissance. We are certain that the movement towards their achievement will also be sustained precisely because this movement represents an indigenous impulse which derives from our knowledge of the mistakes we have made in the past and our determination to put those mistakes behind us.

I say this to emphasise the point that necessarily the African renaissance, in all its parts, can only succeed if its aims and objectives are defined by the Africans themselves, if its programmes are designed by ourselves and if we take responsibility for the success or failure of our policies.

As South Africans, we owe our emancipation from apartheid in no small measure to the support and solidarity extended to us by all the peoples of Africa. In that sense our victory over the system of white minority domination is an African victory.

248

This, I believe, imposes an obligation on us to use this gift of freedom, which is itself an important contribution to Africa's renaissance, to advance the cause of the peoples of our continent.

The first thing we must do, clearly, is to succeed.

We must succeed to strengthen and further entrench democracy in our country and inculcate a culture of human rights among all our people, which is indeed happening.

We must succeed to rebuild and reconstruct our economies, achieve high and sustained rates of growth, reduce unemployment and provide a better life for the people, a path on which we have embarked.

We must succeed to meet the needs of the people so as to end poverty and improve the quality of life by ensuring access to good education, adequate health care, decent homes, clean water and modern sanitation and so on, again a process on which we have embarked.

We must take decisive steps to challenge the spread of HIV/AIDS, of which Africa accounts for two-thirds of the world total of those infected. Our government has taken the necessary decisions directed at launching and sustaining a big campaign to confront this scourge.

We must discharge our responsibilities to ourselves, future generations and the world with regard to the protection of the environment, cooperating with all nations to meet what is, after all, a common challenge.

We must rise to the critical challenge of creating a non-racial and non-sexist society, both of which objectives are also contained within our Constitution.

I believe that we, who were exposed to the most pernicious racism represented by the system of apartheid, have the historic possibility and responsibility indeed to create a non-racial society, both in our own interest and as our contribution to the continuing struggle throughout the world to fight racism, which remains an unfortunate feature of many societies.

Similarly, we have a real possibility to make advances in the struggle for the genuine and all-round emancipation of women and have, with this objective in mind, established a Constitutional Commission for Gender Equality, which will help our society as a whole to measure the progress we are making to secure gender equality.

Many African peoples throughout Southern Africa sacrificed their lives to help us secure our freedom. Others further afield ignored the fact of their own poverty to contribute resources to guarantee our emancipation. I am convinced that this immense contribution was made not only so that we end the apartheid crime against humanity, but also so that we build a society of which all Africa would be proud because it would address also the wrong and negative view of an Africa that is historically destined to fail.

Similarly, the peoples of Africa entertain the legitimate expectation that the new South Africa which they helped to bring into being will not only be an expression of the African renaissance by the manner in which it conducts its affairs, but will also be an active participant with other Africans in the struggle for the victory of that renaissance throughout our continent.

Necessarily, therefore, we are engaged and will continue to be engaged in Africa's efforts to guarantee peace for her children, to feed and clothe them, to educate them and to bring them up as human beings as human as any other in the world, their dignity restored and their equal worth recognised and valued throughout our universe.

We would like you to join us in the noble struggle to achieve these objectives.

The process of globalisation emphasises the fact that no person is an island, sufficient to himself or herself. Rather, all humanity is an interdependent whole in which none can be truly free unless all are free, in which none can be truly prosperous unless none elsewhere in the world goes hungry, and in which none of us can be guaranteed a good quality of life unless we act together to protect the environment.

By so saying, we are trying to convey the message that African underdevelopment must be a matter of concern to everybody else in the world, that the victory of the African renaissance addresses not only the improvement of the conditions of life of the peoples of Africa but also the extension of the frontiers of human dignity to all humanity.

Accordingly, we believe that it is important that the international community should agree that Africa constitutes the principal development challenge in the world. Having made this determination, we believe that we should then all join forces to ensure that we elaborate and implement practical programmes of action to respond to this principal development challenge.

Urgent steps are required to bring about debt relief to the many countries on our continent which suffer from an unsustainable debt burden.

Measures must be taken to encourage larger inflows of capital into the continent, taking advantage of the fact of changed economic policies and improved political circumstances which have brought many of our countries into the mainstream of world developments with regard to the creation of circumstances which make for high and sustained economic growth.

The developed world has to follow more generous trade policies which should ensure easier access of African products into their markets.

Further, we still require substantial flows of well-directed development assistance. Accordingly, we believe that steps should be taken to reverse the decline in such assistance which has occurred in many countries of the developed world.

Similarly, as the process of globalisation develops apace, enhancing the need for a multilateral process of decision-making affecting both governments and the non-governmental sector, it is necessary that, acting together, we ensure that Africa, like other regions of the developing world, occupies her due place within the councils of the world, including the various organs of the United Nations.

It is our hope and conviction that this important member of the world community of nations, Japan, will see itself as our partner in the practical promotion of the vision of an African renaissance.

By acting on the variety of matters we have mentioned and others besides, we trust that Japan will continue to place herself among the front ranks of those who are driven to act not only within the context of a narrowly defined national interest, but with the generosity of spirit which recognises the fact that our own humanity is enriched by identifying ourselves especially with those who suffer.

When, once more, the saying is recalled: *Ex Africa semper aliquid novi!* – Something new always comes out of Africa! – this must be so because out of Africa reborn must come modern products of human economic activity, significant contributions to the world of knowledge, in the arts, science and technology, new images of an Africa of peace and prosperity.

Thus shall we, together and at last, by bringing about the African renaissance, depart from a centuries-old past which sought to perpetuate the notion of an Africa condemned to remain a curiosity slowly grinding to a halt on the periphery of the world.

Surely those who are the offspring of the good that sprang from the Meiji Restoration would not want to stay away from the accomplishment of so historic a human victory!

PART SEVEN

General

EIGHT SPEECHES ARE ASSEMBLED in this section. The first three illustrate Mbeki's broad interests and wide-ranging commitments.

Mbeki the politician is also a man of culture, as shown by his speech at the launch of Business Arts South Africa. Here he defends the thesis that culture constitutes the barrier that prevents mankind from regressing to beastly ways.

The speech on the emancipation of women reiterates his commitment to the Constitution and the Bill of Rights. The same goes for his speech on the disabled and the moral obligation resting on society to create space for them.

In these speeches his own deeply held conviction and commitment to fight and fight again and again for the emancipation of women and human rights for the disabled comes through very strongly. A recurrent theme of his thinking and commitment to socio-economic justice is touched upon in his speech 'Our Duty to End Poverty', delivered at the opening of the Ministerial Meeting of the Nonaligned Movement. While emphasising the challenge facing poor countries to develop their societies by implementing the right policies, Mbeki also makes it clear that it is in the interest of the rich countries of the world to help fight poverty.

The book concludes with another speech on the African renaissance, delivered at a function of the South African Broadcasting Corporation. On the podium we meet Mbeki the visionary. But also Mbeki the realist who does not whitewash the ills of Africa, but challenges us to rebel against everybody and everything demeaning our continent and ourselves.

35

Culture: The Barrier which Blocks Regress to Beastly Ways

Launch of Business Arts South Africa (BASA), Pretoria, 3 February 1997

I WOULD LIKE TO WELCOME and thank our friends from Great Britain who helped us to get to the point where, today, we participate in the launch of Business Arts South Africa (BASA).

I would also like to say this to them: that when the British Queen Elizabeth II came to our country recently, the people received her with great warmth and enthusiasm. When her son, the Prince of Wales, visits us, we will again receive him with the respect and warmth that is his due. I say all this in part because, later, I will quote some rude things which some of our poets said in the past.

If you will permit this, let me start by citing some words from the Bible: 'For what shall it benefit a man if he should gain the whole world and lose his soul?'

To which Pieter Dirk-Uys might remark that we must therefore proceed to set up a ministry with the appropriate name of the Ministry for the Protection of the Soul, with himself as the minister – naturally!

After all, we do have the ministers entrusted with the task of ensuring that we do indeed gain the whole world, through the creation of jobs, building houses, supplying clean water, increasing investor confidence, acquiring corvettes for the Navy as well as judges to ensure that the deputy president gets a higher salary!

In 'Sailing to Byzantium', the Irish poet W.B. Yeats writes:

> An aged man is but a paltry thing
> A tattered coat upon a stick, unless
> Soul clap its hands and sing, and louder sing
> For every tatter in its mortal dress[36]

257

I think the Bible meant the same thing that Yeats celebrates in these lines – or rather, and to avoid the charge of sacrilege – Yeats understood what the Bible meant when it spoke of us standing in danger of losing our souls.

To extend Yeats's imagery, we may perhaps say that we are all of us 'a paltry thing' unless our souls sing and louder sing to give meaning, dignity and the elevation of humanity to the bodies which are us, but are after all mere matter which, as much for golden lads and lasses as for chimney-sweepers, will at the end turn to dust.

The arts belong to that form of human and social existence which both the Bible and William Butler Yeats describe as the soul – the spiritual as opposed to the material, the spiritual which cannot exist without the corporeal, the capacity for noble thought which gives the human world the special dignity which separates the human from the rest of the animal world.

Painting, sculpture and the crafts, music and dance, literature both written and contained in folklore, decorative dress, cuisine, the ornamentation of the human body – all these, and perhaps more, constitute a message of humanity to itself that there are such things as beauty, elevating thought, a variety of emotions, the capacity to create a mode of behaviour which is concerned with much more than a mere response to the impulses and imperatives of the material body.

They are part of the phenomenon of human existence described as culture, which constitutes the barrier which blocks your path and mine towards regress to the ways of the beastly world. Their practice is not a luxury reserved for the idle rich, but an affirmation that our humanity presents a call to individuals and societies to a form of behaviour which must respect the individuality of each person and the humanity of all.

Dumile Feni died in distressful conditions in New York, far away from his motherland, because our erstwhile white masters could see that his anguished figures, in painting and in sculpture, were a pained cry for the recognition of the humanity of others who were different in colour.

In Mozambique, to save himself from imprisonment and torture, the painter Valente Malangatana had to explain to the Portuguese secret police that his painted images of the sick and extended bellies of the young constituted a tribute to Portuguese colonialism for the way it fed those whom it despised and oppressed.

And so some trooped into jail and into exile because in their different creative ways they sought to affirm the dignity of all and the immorality of all actions that sought to demean and degrade.

And because some decided neither to see nor to hear, we can today hear the stories told at the Truth and Reconciliation Commission which speak of a level and extent of human depravity of those who could never have heard the meaning nor been moved by the poetry of the words *umntu, ngumntu ngabantu!*

As we decry the violent crimes that afflict our society and which take away innocent lives, impose the foulest of dehumanising crimes on women and children, signify a search for material gain which takes precedence over everything which entitles us to call ourselves human – so must we recognise that over the years, we created a society which removed the boundaries which demarcated what is human from what is merely and brutally animal.

And further, as each group went its separate ways, acting in accordance with the enforceable and enforced decrees of the apartheid system, we lost the possibility to hear one another.

Whereas my mother told us allegorical fairy tales to teach us to hate laziness, many among the Afrikaners and others besides said this as a matter of fact: *Die kaffer is lui!*

Where by chance I came across the statement attributed to Beethoven that 'humanity may perish, but the Ninth will live for ever!', what meaning could I attach to this, when the powers that be presented Beethoven's powerful Ninth Symphony, with its incomparable choral 'Ode to Joy' by Schiller, as but part of the things which made them, who described themselves as Europeans, entitled to oppress and exploit?

Neither could others among my compatriots hear the Xhosa poet Mqhayi, when he recited his praise poem to the British King George VI, and described him, who represented the British people who had betrayed us in 1910, as distinguished by a funnelled mouth fit to emit foul air?

The political order that tore our country apart is now no more. Yet it gave us a bitter heritage which we must strive to overcome.

Above all else we must create the situation in which the soul can sing and louder sing to restore a social morality which says the pursuit of material gain at all costs is not and cannot be what distinguishes us as South Africans, a patriotism which is imbued by love and respect for the fellow citizen, regardless of race, colour, gender or age and a recognition of our common humanity which says to all that we are after all, one nation, bonded together by the variety of cultures, with none superior or inferior to the other. A nation cannot be, if any of these cultures is absent – inasmuch as the ancient poet of Georgia, Shota Rustaveli, said the sun cannot be without each one of these, because each is a particle of it.

Let the formation of a new nation that has a soul be an inalienable part of our rebirth. The business people who are here daily pursue the legitimate task of making profit. In pursuit of that task they create jobs, help provide goods and services to serve the corporeal beings that we are, and help create the wealth without which human existence and progress are impossible. But even they exist not as mere automatons to do all these things. They exist as human beings who laugh and cry, who love and hate, who are kind and cruel, who are human and animal.

I am deeply moved that we are able to meet today – the elected representatives of our people, the cultural workers, the profit-makers, those who serve as they only stand and wait, to say together: We shall each do what we have to do, to contribute to the common effort to ensure that ours is a people that has recovered not only its freedom but its soul, also.

Let BASA do what it has to do so that, increasingly, life in its living, inspired by the noble feelings of genuine individual and social creative activity, becomes, even for the most lowly in our society, an ode to joy.

At midnight today, our Interim Constitution will cease to be the law of our country. The new Constitution will come into force. The BASA that is born today is born into and of the new world.

To celebrate its coming, simultaneous with the new constitutional order, we must repeat after the minister of constitutional affairs, Mohammed Valli Moosa:

> Ring in the new,
> Ring out the old,
> Ring in a thousand years of peace!

36

The Emancipation of Women

National Conference on Women Abuse and Domestic Violence, Cape Town, 23 November 1995

THE PROGRESS WE MAKE towards the attainment of a democratic society can only have full and deeper meaning if it is accompanied by significant progress in the struggle for the emancipation of women.

I believe that we should accept the proposition that we must measure the success of progress towards social transformation by advances we make in the struggle for a non-sexist society. Indeed, we should measure the progress towards a democratic transformation by the progress we record in the struggle for gender equality.

The road we still have to traverse towards the attainment of a democratic and fully non-sexist society can be measured by the frightening scale of woman abuse and domestic violence. Statistics which quantify this scale of human anguish and suffering is, by any standard, impermissible.

It is estimated that roughly 30 per cent of all the cases of violence reported to the South African Police Service (SAPS) are domestic in nature. One out of every four women is either physically, emotionally or sexually abused by her male partner. An average of 15 000 cases of child abuse is reported to the Child Protection Unit of the SAPS every year.

This scale of violence and abuse against women and children demands that we give full appreciation to the fact that this form of oppression is a human cancer which affects all sectors and all levels of society. As a result, the struggle against woman oppression and child abuse should be situated within the broader struggle for political, constitutional, social, cultural and economic emancipation.

In order to fully exorcise the body of society of this cancer, it is important to address political, constitutional, social, cultural and economic conditions which give rise to this disease. Surely we shall not have done enough if we were to limit our effort to the symptoms and effects of this cancer.

The people of South Africa have already placed the issue of women's rights firmly on the constitutional and political agenda of transformation. South African women, in their organisational formations and as individuals, have played an indispensable role in that regard.

Never again shall the chambers of the Legislative Assembly, as corresponding structures in the provinces and localities, be the preserve of the male voice. The growing voice of women in those chambers continues to enrich the substance of political and constitutional debates.

The establishment of several structures, for example the Human Rights and the Gender commissions, is one of the ways in which the new Constitution aims to go an extra mile in order to provide against gender discrimination.

The government is also wholly committed to upholding and adhering to the United Nations Convention on the Rights of the Child.

The Women's Charter for Effective Equality, adopted by many women's organisations at their National Convention in February 1994, is an important milestone in providing a national policy framework within which the struggle for the emancipation of women should be pursued. It sets the agenda for the attainment of gender equality in all spheres of public and private life.

Economic discrimination against women is one of the important conditions which give rise to woman oppression and woman abuse. The condition where the woman is institutionally placed in the situation of economic subordination and the man is perceived as the sole provider of family livelihood perpetuates the situation of economic and social oppression of women.

Our Interim Constitution as well as the draft of the new Constitution go a long way in an attempt to remove institutionalised economic discrimination against women. Legislative provisions which relate to economic issues like taxation, land restitution, equal pay for equal work and property ownership reflect a strong commitment to a non-sexist society. The plight of rural illiterate women, the most downtrodden of all women, can now receive priority attention.

Our progress in the struggle against violence and abuse of women and children also depends on the progress we make in establishing a democracy characterised by political and social stability, personal security and the promotion of peace. In communities which are afflicted with political and criminal violence, it is women and children who bear the brunt of the culture of violent conflict which is nourished by such conditions.

The intensity of violence, poverty and general want leads to large-scale disruption of family and personal life and creates fertile conditions for the spread of social ills like rape, violence against women and child abuse, and the spread of diseases like AIDS.

One of the greatest challenges facing our democracy is the need to cultivate a civil society imbued with and capable of promoting a social ethos which places human interest at the centre of its outlook. Our society needs a democratic culture which is dynamic, always ready to insulate itself from social degeneracy whilst learning and assimilating the best out of human achievement and civilisation.

The integratedness of the world today and the ascendancy of the information superhighway with its little regard for territorial boundaries makes the challenge of cultivating such a civil society formidable. Television, audiovisual cassette, magazine and paperback have all brought the worst and the best of human achievement right into the living room.

The positive morality of the society we seek to build shall depend on the strength of organisations of civil society to set a people-centred agenda for transformation.

Our ability to set such an agenda also depends on our ability to forge and consolidate a social and cultural partnership between government and organisations of civil society. We see the establishment of the National Interim Committee against Women Abuse and Domestic Violence clearly as an effort towards the attainment of this goal.

We need to set in place mechanisms and programmes which are designed to mount an ongoing campaign to educate the whole of society about the immensity of the problem of domestic violence, as well as ways and means in which it can be combated.

We need to increase the capacity or organs of safety and security to do their work. There is also a dire need for institutions designated to assist victims of domestic violence to reconstruct their life psychologically, socially and materially.

37

Space for the Dignity of the Disabled

Disabled People of South Africa National Congress, Bloemfontein, 18 October 1997

IN THE YEAR 1988, deadly apartheid assassins exploded a car bomb in a street of Maputo. It was a huge explosion which reverberated throughout the city. It threw up a cloud of black and white smoke which ended in the air and, for a moment, hung up there as though uncertain of what had happened. A distance away, pieces of hot metal clattered, strewn on the cobbled street.

Albie Sachs was dragged out of the rubble; his blood splattered on the pavement, his limbs broken.

A few years after that horrific experience, and indeed several years before the birth of our democracy in 1994, Albie put down in one of his books the following philosophical truth:

> All revolutions are impossible until they happen; then they become inevitable. South Africa has for long been trembling between the impossible and the inevitable, and it is in this singularly unstable situation that the question of human rights and the basis of government in post-Apartheid society demands attention.

Certainly, Albie Sachs's limbs had been broken on that fateful day. But his soul, his heart, his integrity as a member of the human race, and more important, his belief as a fighter for justice and everything which sets us apart from and above the animal kingdom had not been broken. If anything, it had been tempered in that experience.

In these words, Albie was talking of human rights in the universal sense. But certainly he was also speaking for many who might have been disabled in the cause of the struggle for liberation both inside and outside the country. He was speaking on behalf of those who have been physically and mentally challenged through lack of adequate nutrition and access to medical attention. Those who are victims of road accidents, of inadequate safety in the mine and on the shop floor. Those who met their challenged condition in the cause of the pursuit of sporting excellence have also not escaped his consideration.

His words were both philosophical and prophetic. He was addressing himself to the inevitability of a thorough discussion and a clear policy formulation by the democratic government on the question of human rights.

In the same book, Albie Sachs goes further to attest that 'No one gives us rights, we win them in struggle. They exist in our hearts before they exist on paper.'

This statement underscores what is more intrinsic in our political philosophy than the existence of a document called the Constitution and the Bill of Rights.

Our political philosophy, regardless of our past and indeed because of it, commits us to the continuous and sustained material, spiritual and moral upliftment and fulfilment of all the individual persons who constitute our society regardless of race, ethnicity, gender, creed and disability.

We are not shy in stating that all of us as South Africans need an ongoing programme of education, mobilisation and organisation in order to appreciate the significance of the position which the disabled occupy in our society. We still need to appreciate the extent of the potential which resides in the condition of those who are challenged.

We need to commit our society to the creation of an ever-expanding frontier of the dignity of the disabled. The achievement of that dignity for this section of our society should be predicated on the freedom of the individual to determine his or her destiny.

It is estimated that South Africa has a population of six million disabled people. That is roughly six times the population of Swaziland. This stark statistic is an indication of how much of our human resource can be unleashed for the betterment of our country if we can succeed to help the disabled of our country to empower themselves.

The progress we make in the betterment of the condition of life of the people finds a sterner judgement when evaluated against the progress we make in improving the condition of those who move from the starting point of greater disadvantage. It is they who deserve our unqualified attention.

We have also committed ourselves to be signatories to those international conventions which seek to prevent the infliction of disabilities to the innocent. For example, we recently spearheaded the treaty for the abolition of the production and distribution of anti-personnel land mines in the world with great success. We also suffer the burden of pain, of shame and of guilt when we behold on our television screen the African landscape peopled by multitudes, young and old, who carry torn bodies and broken limbs.

Our quest and our effort to bring about an African continent characterised by peace, stability and prosperity is motivated by the same principles, which underpin our struggle to empower the disabled.

We are about to table the White Paper before Cabinet. This paper attempts to lay down the policy and strategy which will guide the actions of the government and the state on the question of the disabled. This paper has put paid to the old notion of disability as a medical problem, the problem of those who are ill, weak and requiring of our pity in abundance. This is not the challenge facing departments of welfare alone.

The challenges and experiences of the disabled are the challenges and experiences of society as a whole. All of us must rise up and face our weaknesses because it is precisely here that the real disability is located. To that extent the White Paper sets out a programme of action for all government departments which will encompass not a separate disability programme, but the incorporation of a disability programme and related rights into the entire function of government and the state.

We assume this position speaks to what we mean when we speak of a people-centred society – that the criterion we wish to be used to judge the success or the failure of our actions is the extent to which these actions result in the betterment or the worsening of the condition of us all.

Certainly we cannot claim that we are liberated if we do not assume the struggle of the disabled as our own. This is a clear endorsement of the conviction that we are all part of a greater nation, a nation whose very strength lies in its diversity, whose greatest resource is located in a destiny towards which we are all moving together.

Another significant thing about the White Paper is that an attempt has been made to make sure that it is the product of wide consultation, especially among those whose contributions in the struggle for the empowerment of the disabled cannot be doubted. It has also, where appropriate, drawn from the experience of people in other parts of the world.

The Office of the Status of Disabled People already exists in the Presidency in Pretoria. The location of this office in the Presidency signifies our conviction that the struggle for the empowerment of the disabled should be driven and be co-ordinated at the highest level in government. It is a task which cannot be left to the care of individual line departments.

In 1995 I felt greatly honoured when I was asked by some of you to assume the patronship of the disabled people of South Africa. I acceded to the honour because I believe that the attainment of human dignity cannot be reduced merely to the attainment of civil and political rights.

I sincerely believe that our human dignity also derives from our preparedness to confront the greatest challenges which face all of us as members of a common humanity.

But I have often said that, having accepted the challenge and the honour presented to me by you, you need to go further and formulate an agenda programme which the patron of the disabled in South Africa should promote. I certainly take no comfort nor satisfaction in being a patron who, all that he can do, is to pronounce his existence. I sincerely believe that something more purposeful can be done to promote this noble task.

Our political liberation in 1994 marked the end of the revolution of one kind and the beginning of another. It marked the beginning of the revolution for the transformation of our country. If this second revolution was impossible before 1994, it has now become inevitable.

There is an unstoppable fountain of desire in our hearts. The White Paper we have been talking about is simply an expression of this unstoppable fountain. As Albie Sachs said, this unstoppable desire exists in our hearts before it exists on paper. It is a human essence of life. It is not merely the White Paper that will promote our rights but a continuous struggle to uphold our dignity and our humanity.

We would like to draw your conference's attention to the fact that the White Paper is extensive and comprehensive. It is not possible for the government and the state to implement everything contained in the White Paper all at once. Apart from the fact of the limitation imposed by the scarcity of the resources available to all of us, the Paper envisages a revolutionary overhaul in our approach and our programme of action.

It is for that reason that we propose that we help the government to work out priorities on what needs to be done. We don't believe that this is an exclusive right we should abrogate to ourselves. We need guidance in drawing up the programme of priorities.

38

The Need for a Culture
of Learning and Teaching

Address at the launch of the Culture of Learning and Teaching Campaign, Fort Hare University, Alice, 28 February 1997

'IT SOMETIMES SEEMS to me that our days are poisoned with too many words. Words said not meant. Words said and meant. Words divorced from feeling. Wounding words. Words that conceal. Words that reduce. Dead words.'

These are opening lines of an essay by one of the great contemporary writers of Africa, Ben Okri. I thought I should begin with these words for two reasons.

Firstly because I thought I would gain respect among all the learned men and women present here today when they realise that I can also quote a few lines. Secondly I thought I should acknowledge from the beginning that what I am going to say are words, and should be seen in the same manner as Okri describes words in general. But most importantly, I thought that this is the most appropriate way of describing the reason why we are gathered here today.

Our country's higher education sector is currently characterised by too many words. The different stakeholders are exchanging accusations against one another. Students against management, management against staff and workers, students against students, students against the ministry of education and the government as a whole, leaders of institutions against the minister of education and his department – the list is endless. Just this last week we have witnessed scenes of confrontation between some students and management in more than five of our institutions. We are also told that students will be marching to various centres of government in the coming weeks.

And in everyone of these situations, without exception, people exchange words, 'wounding words, words that reduce'. More than just words, they even exchange other objects, like stones, knives, sticks, dustbins, golf sticks, baseball and cricket bats, and even gunfire. It is because of all these exchanges of words and the other objects that accompany them that we have decided to gather here today.

We have to say that it is now time for us to reduce these words because, as Ben Okri says, they are now too many.

But how can we say we want to reduce words when the whole business of higher education is the production of knowledge, whose main tools are words? Are we not coming to negate the very mission of the higher education sector, which is to produce knowledge through an exchange of ideas?

Allow me to respond to these questions, which I am sure you are all beginning to ask, by using Ben Okri again. Okri says:

> The greatest art was probably born from a profound and terrible silence out of which the deepest enigmas of our lives cry: Why are we here? What is the point of it all? How can we know peace and live joy? Why be born in order to die? Why this difficult one way journey between the two mysteries?
>
> Out of the wonder and agony of being come these cries and questions and the endless stream of words with which to order human life and quieten the human heart in the midst of our living and our distress.

This is what I believe we are here to call for in our higher education sector. The culture of learning and teaching in higher education means a culture of silent reflection, of deep thought, of curiosity and questioning, of exploration and examination, of thought, search for more questions and more answers, of investigation, of more search and research. Only words that emerge out of these silent activities begin to bring us nearer to an understanding of the matters that we are grappling with as a human species. It is these activities that combine knowledge, new knowledge and the unknown, to produce the understanding and the programmes of action that will enable us to address the miseries of the people and help to make their lives better.

Yet even as we engage in this quiet reflection, this silent activity, we must allow our own history and past experiences to inform our decisions as to the correct path that we must follow for us to overcome the inherited legacy of ignorance and the poverty of the spirit; we must begin by understanding our own history, where we come from and where we are going. A people that do not understand their own history are unable to comprehend the present, let alone engage in strategic thinking for the future.

On 16 June 1976, almost 21 years ago, this country experienced an uprising which shook the pillars of the apartheid system to the core and precipitated the birth of the miracle that we refer to as the new democratic South Africa.

This uprising, which was led by students, was the continuation of a tradition of struggle that stretches back to our colonial past. The significance of the June 16 uprising is that our youth and students confronted what was perceived as a formidable enemy, hundreds of our best youth and students laid down their lives, and thousands of others left the borders of this country and joined the liberation movement.

They engaged in struggle so that future generations may breathe the purified air of freedom, so that the youth of today could participate in the process of improving themselves and developing their country. The youth and students of that time responded to the call they heard – the cries of anguish emanating from a nation trampled under the jackboot of apartheid tyranny.

We can justifiably be proud of that generation because it understood its calling and rose to the challenge of the times.

In our moment of silent reflection, one moment of deep thought and exploration, have we determined what are the lessons of the June 16 uprising? This is a question directed more at our youth and students today, many of whom were mere toddlers at the time. This is not intended to single them out as a particular group in society but it is in recognition of the fact that they are our future leaders and the future belongs to them.

The question that begs for an answer with a growing sense of urgency is whether we have achieved the ideals for which so many of our best youth and students sacrificed their lives. During the moments of deep thought and reflection we must come up with answers to the vexing questions of the day.

We cannot do that through the usage of dead words, words said without meaning and words without content. We cannot do that through the trashing of our institutions and the destruction of valuable property. This is tantamount to the betrayal of the memory of the generation of 1976 and many more who came before them.

The country cries out for salvation. It is yearning for development, for progress and the upliftment of our people who have been dehumanised for all these years.

It is only through the acquisition of knowledge, the production of engineers, scientists, doctors and teachers that we shall be able to conquer the scourge of poverty, disease and underdevelopment, which is the lot of our people today.

We are therefore here to call upon all stakeholders in education to begin working together with the government and the country as a whole to ensure that the culture of learning and teaching is developed in our institutions. It is time we began to transform our higher education institutions into centres of knowledge production second to none in Africa and the world.

The task of developing the culture of learning and teaching in our institutions is indeed a very urgent one. Our institutions need to produce the human resources that are so crucial for the Reconstruction and Development Programme to succeed. We cannot meet the basic needs of our people if we are unable to produce the necessary knowledge and skills to help us develop mechanisms for doing so. We have the potential, but we need to direct our energies to the national task at hand, and bring all our forces together to face the challenge of addressing the backlogs facing our country in skills and knowledge.

What is it that we need to do in order to meet these challenges? Firstly we need to go back to basics, and ensure that all our institutions are engaged primarily in the business of learning and teaching. We must see all our institutions showing characteristics of serious pursuance of academic excellence in all their activities. Students must attend lectures, write their assignments, do their projects, read, read and read. Academic work needs a lot of discipline. We cannot afford to have students who can hardly sit and concentrate on reading for more than two hours.

Our lecturers should also commit themselves to teaching. In this regard I must say that to me teaching means being able to communicate with all students regardless of who they are. We are all aware that many of our students come from disadvantaged education backgrounds and therefore come to universities and technikons underprepared. We have a responsibility as institutions to teach these students and to enable them to succeed. Lecturers therefore need to take seriously the task of developing innovative and relevant methods of teaching. This will be their contribution to the culture of learning and teaching.

We would not have achieved anything in our campaign to develop this culture if we do not develop the culture of research, especially among black students. The level of research among blacks is far from satisfactory. We therefore have a challenge to produce black researchers for the country as a matter of urgency.

Let me hasten to say that I do not believe that when I talk about teaching and research I am talking about activities that should be done by some institutions and not others. I believe that excellent research will grow out of excellent teaching. Therefore all institutions should become teaching institutions. Similarly, all of them should become research institutions.

All these we can achieve if we begin to engage differently with one another, and not in the same old ways. All of us, the government, the leaders of institutions, the students and the workers must commit ourselves to new ways of engagement, ones that reflect our commitment to the culture of learning and teaching.

I therefore want to challenge our student movements to commit themselves to a new approach to words. I believe that there are many words that are now being bandied around the student movements. The big question is whether these words are a product of careful consideration and reflection. One of these words is 'transformation'. It is our task as students to rescue this word from becoming a dead word, a word that has no substance, by ensuring that we liberate it from misuse and give it its proper content based on meaningful debate and careful interrogation. The students have to take the lead in subjecting their notions and transformation to rigorous intellectual scrutiny and constant debate.

To the management of institutions, I believe it is high time we also gave serious consideration to our commitment to transformation and to a culture of management through participation.

Higher education institutions are supposed to be bastions of dialogue and debate. This needs to be reflected even in their management styles. Only a participatory style of management can contribute meaningfully to the culture of learning and teaching.

I therefore have pleasure to launch this campaign and to call upon all the stakeholders in the higher education sector to make our institutions work for us. Let me give the last word to Okri once again: 'To poison a nation, poison its stories.'

Let us rescue our stories from poison, so that we may tell good stories, for 'when we have made experience of chaos into a story we have transformed it, made sense of it, transmuted experience, domesticated the chaos'.

39

Our Duty to End Poverty

Opening of the Ministerial Meeting of the Twelfth Summit Meeting of Heads of State and Government of the Nonaligned Movement, Durban, 1 September 1998

OVER THE LAST FEW YEARS, a number of words and phrases have entered into the vocabulary of international discourse.

Among these are globalisation, liberalisation, deregulation and the information society or information superhighway.

Stripped of the sophistication attached to these terms and processes, these represent the international context in which all of us have to work to eliminate poverty in our countries, to improve the quality of life of the millions of our people, to close the gap between the rich and the poor – both internally and universally – and to attain sustainable rates of economic growth and development.

The fact of the matter, however, is that all these processes originate from the developed countries of the North, reflect the imperatives of the economies and the levels of development of these countries and, therefore, naturally serve the purposes of our rich global neighbours.

At the same time, the very fact of the process of globalisation, in all its forms, means that our own success as developing countries in terms of the upliftment of our peoples cannot be achieved in conditions of autarky or self-contained development within our national boundaries or regions.

It cannot be achieved through opting out of the world economy and therefore extricating ourselves from the process of globalisation.

Accordingly, the question that arises is: What intervention can the developing countries make to ensure that a process which, by its nature, will favour the rich, addresses also what are clearly the more urgent needs of our peoples, millions of whom lack the most basic things that a human being needs?

It is clear that we, as the developing world, cannot make that intervention by autonomously affecting capital or trade flows or unilaterally altering any of the variables which make up the totality of the world economy.

The stark reality is that the power to influence the markets lies exclusively in the hands of those who dominate these markets, which we, even collectively, do not.

A few figures here will amply demonstrate this point.

Much is made of the increased flow of direct foreign investment into the developing world in the recent past, and the fact that in aggregate these flows have significantly surpassed overseas development assistance. The reality, however, is that the bulk of this investment still flows among the developed countries, with the developing countries attracting a mere 30 per cent of foreign direct investment in 1996. We must also take into account the fact that by 1994, China accounted for about 40 per cent of the total for developing countries.

Similarly, with regard to trade in merchandise, World Bank provisional figures for 1995, excluding China, show the developing countries as accounting for only 22,5 per cent of total world trade.

In its 1998 annual report, the Bank for International Settlements (BIS) makes some startling revelations which emphasise the extraordinary imbalance in the control of economic resources as between the North and the South:

> A hypothetical shift of just 1 per cent of equity holdings by institutional investors in the G7 countries away from domestic equities would represent slightly more than a 1 per cent share of total market capitalisation in 1995. The same funds would be equivalent to a 27 per cent share of market capitalisation in emerging Asian economies, and a share of over 66 per cent of Latin American equity markets.

Understandably, the BIS does not bother to place Africa on this comparative ladder.

Reflecting on these figures, the Bank makes this correct, yet ominous observation:

> An aspect of the international diversification of institutional investor portfolios ... is the asymmetry between the investor and the recipient perspectives, especially in the case of emerging economies.
> The high concentration of institutional assets in some of the most financially developed countries contrasts with the relatively small

size of many recipient markets. This asymmetry, coupled with the ebbs and flows that have historically characterised portfolio investment in emerging economies, highlights the potential for instability, as a marginal portfolio adjustment by the investor can easily amount to a first order event for the recipient.

A marginal portfolio adjustment by the investor can easily amount to a first order event for the recipient! A slight turn by the sleeping elephant, to make itself more comfortable, can result in the complete annihilation of the entire universe of a colony of ants!

The scale of what we are talking about is also starkly demonstrated by the fact that, according to the same report of the BIS:

> The volume of financial assets under management [of the institutional investors] in North America, Japan and Western Europe ... exceeds that of aggregate GDP for the [18] industrial countries concerned.

The question that arises is: What must we do? Others would ask: In any case, given the power of the powerful, is there anything we can do?

I believe that our answer has to be a resounding yes!

The first consideration on which we must base that answer must start with the realisation of the fact that the process of globalisation ineluctably results in the reduction of the sovereignty of states, with the weakest, being ourselves, being the biggest losers – those who, already the worst off, suffer losses of the first order as a result of a marginal adjustment by another, who is already the best placed and which adjustment is intended for his or her own further comfort.

If what we have said is true, it must follow that for us to be able to influence the process of globalisation so that it also favours the interests of the poor, to be able to do something, we must ensure that ours becomes an important voice at the place to which we are losing some of our sovereignty.

The second consideration on which we must base our answer to the question, Is there anything we can do? is that for the first time ever, humanity is faced with the extraordinary reality that the world economy has generated and is generating volumes of resources which make it possible to end poverty everywhere.

Again, if what we have just said is true, and we believe it is, were ours to become an important voice at the place to which we are losing some of our sovereignty, then clearly we would say that the world economy should be managed in a way that ensures the transfer of resources from those who have them to those that do not, so that both can end poverty among their peoples and achieve or maintain sustainable rates of growth and development.

In this context, we must make the fairly obvious point that the untapped markets in the world economy are those of the developing world, represented by us, members of the Nonaligned Movement.

Clearly, therefore, the further, qualitatively new expansion of the world economy must derive from the expansion of these markets or, in other words, the development of our economies such that we outgrow our designations both as developing countries and emerging economies.

There is no logical reason to assume that this would not also benefit the countries of the developed North. Indeed the opposite is true, as is being demonstrated even as we meet here at the Twelfth Summit Meeting of the Nonaligned Movement, that the poverty of some may very well become a threat to those who are well off.

This point was made by a writer in the London *Financial Times* in June this year when he said:

> At present the West, in general, and the US, in particular, seem blessed even by the dire misfortunes of others. But the stability of this world of divided fates is doubtful – economically and ultimately politically. Either sustained prosperity in the West will help bring stability and renewed growth to Asia and elsewhere, or the spreading crisis is all too likely to export instability to the West. Today's Western complacency could tomorrow look mere vainglory.[37]

The questions we must all ask and seek to answer is whether a stable world of divided fates is possible, but more important, whether such a world, even if it were possible, is desirable. And, in this instance, my all includes the developed countries of the North.

Is it possible for some to maintain and expand their prosperity while billions of others are victim to dire misfortunes?

Our own answer to that question is: No!

Clearly, something must be done.

That doing requires that the political leaders of our contemporary world should face up to the question as to whether universal human values have any place at all in the ordering of human affairs.

How can it be permissible that some die of hunger and curable diseases and exposure to the elements because of poverty and perish in civil wars driven by competition for virtually non-existent resources, when the volumes of wealth concentrated in some parts of our globe are themselves becoming something of a destructive force?

In this regard, the same report of the BIS to which we have referred observes that:

> Inflows of international capital [into the emerging markets], in large part in the form of short-term bank credit, rose from virtually zero in 1989 to a peak of almost $170-billion in 1996, to be followed most recently by major outflows. Coping with these swings has been enormously difficult, as they have generally fuelled existing spending booms on the way in and precipitated crisis on the way back out.

Enlightened self-interest should inform those who have, that where the manner of the reproduction of wealth begins to precipitate crisis, our graduation out of the condition described as 'developing' is, in reality, in their interest as well and is human as well.

If that 1 per cent of the equity holdings of the institutional investors of the G7 countries of which we have spoken, and which amounts to more than two-thirds of Latin American equity markets, flowed into our countries and stayed as a productive resource, it is not difficult to imagine its impact with regard to the eradication of poverty and backwardness.

But to borrow a phrase, we, the poor, must now become our own liberators! We have to lead the global offensive according to which all humanity should take advantage of the fact of the emergence of the possibility to end poverty in the world, and devise ways and means by which this can be achieved.

What we speak of is not the expansion of a system of charity and aid, important though these are, but resource transfers which would ensure that those who are on the margins of the world economy themselves arrive at the point where they can achieve their own sustainable development.

The market, so called, has no inherent mechanisms, intrinsic to itself, as a result of whose functioning this objective will be achieved. The new god of our world, the market, is not informed by a tablet of commandments on which is inscribed: Thou shalt banish poverty in the world!

Mortals must address this challenge, consciously and purposefully.

And therein lies the challenge to the Nonaligned Movement!

Inasmuch as the slave cannot ask the slavemaster to provide the strategy and tactics for a successful uprising of the slaves, so must we, who are hungry and treated as minors in a world of adults, also take upon ourselves the task of defining the new world order of prosperity and development for all and equality among the nations of the world.

For the weak to challenge the strong has never been easy. Neither will it be easy to challenge powerful vested interests on the current and entrenched orthodoxies about the modern world economy.

We must therefore organise ourselves to mount that challenge of historic importance to the evolution of human civilisation.

Clearly, any among us who is preoccupied with denying his or her people their democratic and human rights, who is fixated on waging wars against others, who is too busy looting the public coffers or who thinks that he or she must bow in supplication for charity to those whose wealth sets them aside as the mighty, will not have the time to participate in meeting this historic challenge.

That is why all of us also see the Nonaligned Movement as the repository of democracy, human rights, good governance and the sovereign voice of the poor.

But we must see our movement also as a serious instrument for the transformation of a world driven by the process of globalisation, so that we meet the objectives of the upliftment of our peoples of which we have spoken.

The institutions of global governance are central to the achievement of this objective. We are therefore correct to be focused on the matter of the restructuring of the United Nations system so that it pursues an agenda truly determined by the united nations of the world.

Further, it would seem to us that as a movement we must radically review the manner in which we make our interventions into such important organisations as the World Trade Organisation, the International Monetary Fund and the World Bank.

I speak here of a review which will influence these organisations to address the issue we have raised of setting a new agenda focused on the sustained and sustainable development of our countries.

We will also have to look at ourselves, to see whether the way we are organised and the way we work as a movement, the way we co-operate and work with one another as members of this movement, whether all these are such that we will be able to live up to what to us seem to be obvious challenges and opportunities of our age.

In this context, we must set rational objectives, however challenging they might be to the established order, about such critical matters as the international system of governance affecting politics, the economy and security, global capital markets, world trade, human resource development, the emancipation of women, technology transfers, the information society, intellectual property, the environment and poverty eradication, and seek to speak with one voice on these matters.

I am convinced that on all these matters, and others besides, you will be able to provide the advice to our heads of state and governments which will enable them to take the important and seminal decisions they have to adopt.

I am honoured and pleased to welcome you to the new South Africa, towards whose birth this movement and its individual members contributed so much. Our indebtedness to you all knows no qualification.

You will pardon us if you suffer any inconvenience while you are in our country due to our negligence or failings. It is, after all, given to the young to make pardonable mistakes.

I am also honoured to welcome the Summit Meeting of the movement back to the African continent. Whatever the problems we may be experiencing anywhere on the continent, as Africans we are convinced that our continent is set on the road towards its renaissance and that we, the children of this land, have it within us to bring about that rebirth.

We trust that this movement, which stood firmly with us as we fought for the end of colonial and apartheid rule, will walk with us in a firm and meaningful South–South partnership, a critical element of whose agenda must be the achievement of an African renaissance.

We welcome you to the City of Durban, which is located not far from the burial place of a great hero among our people, King Shaka of the Zulu, and trust that this example of courage, vision and fearlessness will characterise our movement as it prepares to lead us into the new millennium.

40

The Struggle Continues

Speech at the launch of the ANC Archives, University of Fort Hare, Alice, 17 March 1996

FIRST OF ALL, I WOULD LIKE to extend the sincere apologies and regret of our president, Nelson Mandela, that he is unable to be with us today.

I am also honoured to convey to this gathering his best wishes and his confidence that, thanks to the work that has been done by the dedicated people who have been engaged in establishing this archive, these opening ceremonies will be most successful.

I believe that we also owe him our thanks because it is by virtue of the Agreement of Deposit which he signed in 1992 that the University of Fort Hare became the official repository of the ANC archive.

This is a place of learning and research which occupies a preeminent place in the history of the struggle of the peoples of Southern and East Africa for national emancipation and the birth of the new African civilisation.

During the 80 years of its existence, it has seen a significant part of the African intelligentsia from as far afield as Uganda pass through its portals. Each brought to this eminently African place their particular experience, the special aspirations of their people and their views as to what needed to be done at that particular moment and in the future to actualise the African dream.

And from Uganda to South Africa, many came here as members of liberation movements that shared one name that had originated from this country: the African National Congress. Such indeed was the nature of the liberation organisations of the various peoples of Africa: national congresses of the African nation, parliaments of the people.

Ultimately it was to fall on the shoulders of the peoples of Southern and East Africa themselves to extend their solidarity to us, as a critical and decisive contribution to the victory of the peoples of the world over the apartheid crime against humanity.

The record of that struggle, in which the South African section of the African National Congress has been engaged for 84 years, has come to stay at what is incontestably its natural home, the alma mater of many to whose leadership we owe the emancipation of many of the peoples of our continent.

It is with great pleasure that I welcome our distinguished guests from our sister African countries who have honoured us with their presence here today. Your presence, dear friends and comrades, has given both weight and joy to this occasion and an opportunity for us, once again, to reaffirm our commitment to the strengthening of our ties of solidarity and friendship for the mutual benefit of all our peoples.

It is also a matter of great inspiration to see, gathered in this hall, representatives of many generations of our own struggle for freedom, all of them makers of the glorious history of struggle recorded in the items that have been and will be collected in this important archive.

I am also pleased to extend our welcome to the other outstanding personalities drawn from all walks of life, who have sacrificed some of their time to be present here, among them leaders of our broad democratic movement, vice-chancellors of our universities, academics, students and members of the community of Alice.

I would also like to take this opportunity to extend our sincere thanks to the donors who so generously helped to make the establishment of this archive possible. We are pleased that some of them are with us today to have sight of what we have done with their selfless contributions and to be exposed to all of us as we gather here to express our appreciation that our country has gained a resource as invaluable as this one.

We would also like to take this opportunity to appeal to all our people who might have personal papers relevant to this archive to consider donating them as their contribution to this important national initiative.

As work started to build this archive, the late president of our movement, Oliver Tambo, said it would reflect 'authentic and real experiences of the past'. Those authentic and real experiences of the past have to do with the struggle the ANC has waged for eight-and-a-half decades to bury the demon of tribalism, but which, to this day, some seek to resurrect and nurture in

283

pursuit of goals which have nothing to do with the unity of our nation, the genuine emancipation of our people, and their liberation from the want and suffering imposed on them by centuries of colonialism and apartheid.

By the demon of tribalism I refer to the attempt to set any of our ethnic groups against another on the basis of a canard that any of these groups can be presented as a cohesive political entity, with political, economic and social aspirations which are unique to itself and which therefore set it apart from the rest of our people.

The authentic and real experiences of the past which Oliver Tambo spoke about include the struggle the movement for national liberation waged – not only to secure the unity of the African people, but also to ensure the birth of one South African nation, made up of a people inspired by a common patriotism, despite their variety, which is as multiple as the colours of the rainbow.

The victory the past generations sought in this regard and the successes we continue to sue for are based, as a *sine qua non*, on the emancipation of those who were oppressed, the elimination of the socio-economic disparities based on race, colour and gender, and therefore the realisation of the goals of equality among all our national groups and between the genders.

That experience also includes a sustained effort never to allow ourselves to fall prey to the destructive forces of blind bigotry and intolerant fanaticism.

It is a result of that determined struggle that, as the oppressed, we never succumbed to the temptation to respond to white racism with black racism, that we never sought to meet apartheid terrorism with our own campaign of terror or to glorify the use of force in the ordering of human relations, that we battled and continue to battle for national reconciliation rather than vengeance, that today, in a spirit of forgiveness, we sit together with those who only yesterday considered and treated us as less than human, determined to work jointly with them to fashion a future of justice and happiness for all our people.

Sometimes, when some of us witness the continued manifestation of arrogance and experience resistance to fundamental change, all deriving from the conscious and subconscious habits that come of half a millennium of white racism, we wonder whether these, who considered themselves as destined to be our masters, understand and will ever comprehend the depth of the spiritual sacrifice that the millions made when they chose to forgive and to bury their pain in the poetic words: *akwehlanga lungehlanga* – let bygones be bygones!

The authentic and real experience which Oliver Tambo spoke about includes unwavering respect for the masses of the people as the true makers of history, the real motive force of all meaningful progressive change, whose sustained and all-round betterment must lie at the centre of the purpose and actions of all those who wish to describe themselves as fighters for the true liberation of the people.

That experience therefore tells a tale of how the masses of the people dared to offer their lives in the struggle to achieve their own emancipation, united in action to bring about peace, justice and reconciliation, and will sacrifice still, to bless our country with progress, prosperity and lasting stability.

Consequently, it is both an experience of the particular contribution of great heroes and heroines, such as those who, when they left the confines of this university, did by their actions leave an indelible imprint on the map of human progress, and an answer to the pregnant question which the German poet and playwright, Bertolt Brecht, posed when he asked, 'Who built Thebes of the Seven Gates?'

The authentic and real experiences to which Oliver Tambo contributed so much include also a profound understanding of the meaning of the concepts of national liberation and equality among the nations, the place of these struggles in the effort to create a new world order, as well as what needs to be done to achieve these objectives.

Strangely, these matters seem to have become forgotten elements in the vocabulary of our own agenda. Is it perhaps because universally they have become too controversial to be palatable? Or is it because when we speak only of the all-important issue of human rights, we gain for ourselves the sense of warmth and universal acceptance that is born of being ensconced within a well-drilled chorus line?

Or is it because we, too, who have never known fear before, are, because of our search for the universal approval of the powerful, today afraid to speak of the genuine liberation of the peoples, lest we should be misread as meaning that we are ready to spurn the hand of support and assistance that those who have better means than we have extended to us?

Our authentic and real experience speaks of our own contribution to the effort both to achieve solidarity among and to evolve a common agenda by the peoples of our continent, so that the nations of Africa, who ineluctably share a common destiny, can unite around a common programme of action to extricate the millions of our people across the continent from the life condition which describes them as the wretched of the earth.

That same experience contains within it, and as an element essential to its integrity, the vision and episodes of a struggle of all humanity united for freedom, human dignity, peace and prosperity for all.

It tells of how, in the end, not anyone anywhere in the world stood still and watched, because they felt this: that the perpetuation of the system of apartheid in our country represented not only and merely the suffering of the people of South Africa. They could see that, as long as the apartheid system was allowed to exist as a result of their own inactivity, so long would their own humanity be denied and their dignity be violated.

The concrete actions that all humanity took to help us destroy the system of apartheid addressed also the question of what would replace that system of white minority domination.

The peoples of the world entertained the hope that out of the terrible human disaster that was the apartheid system would be born a South Africa of non-racialism, the equality of all national groups, democracy, respect for human rights, peace and human upliftment. And as they harboured that hope, they knew that if we succeeded to realise these objectives, we, who had set a negative example, might make an historic contribution to the renewal not only of our own society, but also of the world as a whole.

Those who are interested will find all we have said, and much else besides, about the authentic and real experiences of our own people and their organisations, recorded in the ANC archive for whose opening we have gathered at Fort Hare four days before we mark 21 March – Sharpeville Day – our national Human Rights Day and the day the United Nations dedicated to the elimination of racism and racial discrimination.

The Bible says: *abo banendlebe zokuva mabeve* – those who have ears to hear, let them hear!

This is a part of our country which is accustomed to issuing clarion calls, both bad and good. On its frontiers was set an agenda which defined South African history for 150 years.

Across this, the Thyume Valley, and opposite each other, are two educational institutions which made a great impact on the wider Southern

286

and Eastern African renaissance: Lovedale and Fort Hare, the one established in 1841, before the battle of Isandlhwana, and the other in 1916, after the formation of the ANC. In that sense, the one foresaw the defeat of the anti-colonial wars of resistance and the other emerged as an expression of the practical experience of that defeat.

Within the bosom of this little corner of the great territory of our country, the conditions were created within which the African people, stretching far beyond our borders, had to decide how to respond to the explosive mixture defined by the reality of defeat by the colonial forces, on the one hand, and the refusal to surrender on the part of the vanquished, on the other.

Some of the most outstanding of our own sons and daughters, who provided an answer to what would result from this riddle, came from further to the north and included John Langalibalele Dube and Pixley Isaka ka Seme.

Each of these events and many in between have a story to tell and a message to convey, all of which belong to a continuum whose discovery and authentication will continue to be an exciting intellectual journey leading to the expansion of the frontiers of knowledge.

This archive speaks to all who are interested in these important processes. But it also speaks in another language. This is the language of the reinforcement of the pride and identity of the formerly oppressed and despised, because in it will be found much which says that, after all, indeed, we were never conquered.

Within itself the archive contains another message which urges all South Africans to struggle and change.

As we move around, enveloped by the silence, the archive says to all who have ears to hear that they should not hear a still past, but must respond to the living reality that the archive is.

What was continues to be.

What is past is the heritage not only of those who seek to reflect it, but also of those who are moved to act.

The archive is a school both for the philosophers and the historians, as well as the agitators and the activists, all of whom are linked to one another by virtue of their common commitment to the full emancipation of all human beings.

Without all that is recorded in this archive, South Africa could not be what it is today and would never achieve the glory in future that is its due.

A people denied, a history suppressed, an experience spurned have at last occupied their space. From now onwards, many things can never be the same again.

From 1916 onwards, when this institution was established, many things could never be the same again when such South Africans as D.D.T. Jabavu, Z.K. Matthews, Govan Mbeki, Victor Mbobo, Oliver Tambo, Nelson Mandela, Anton Lembede and Mangosuthu Buthelezi, Seretse Khama of Botswana, Robert Mugabe of Zimbabwe, Kisosonkole of Uganda, Chipembere of Malawi, could be part of its making and development.

We are pleased and moved that the ANC archive has come home to the University of Fort Hare because this institution, which must participate and is participating in the struggle in which all Africa is engaged to give birth to the new African civilisation, understands well that our task is not only to comprehend. Having understood, we have a responsibility to act and to comprehend again, and even critically assess the value and correctness of our own actions.

The ANC archive, like the ANC itself, will be such a living reality, not dead but living, trusting that those who have ears to hear its humane message will listen and act.

I am honoured, speaking in the name of all who have brought us freedom, to proclaim the ANC Archive at the University of Fort Hare open access to all our people to whom those who have acted in the past to define a better future for our country have bequeathed the authentic and real experiences contained in the archive.

The struggle continues and victory is certain!

41

Stop the Laughter

Second Southern African International Dialogue on Smart Partnership for the Generation of Wealth, Swakopmund, Namibia, 27 July 1998

LET ME SAY SOMETHING about myself and about some other people in this hall who belong to my generation.

I am a product of the teachings and example of Abdul Gamal Nasser of Egypt, of Ben Belta of Algeria, of Habib Bourgiba of Tunisia, Mohamed V of Morocco, of Kwame Nkrumah of Ghana, of Modibo Keita of Mali, of Patrice Lumumba of Congo, of Julius Nyerere of Tanzania and Kenneth Kaunda of Zambia, of Robert Mugabe and of Joshua Nkomo of Zimbabwe, of Eduardo Mondlane of Mozambique, of Agostinho Neto of Angola, of Sam Nujoma of Namibia, of Seretse Khama and Ketumile Masire of Botswana, of Albert Luthuli, Oliver Tambo and Nelson Mandela of South Africa.

I say this because all these people taught our generation to rebel. They said to all of us, as we grew up, that we must not accept injustice and we must not accept the demeaning of our continent.

As I stand here today and speak the way I am going to speak, hopefully I will say what I will say because of loyalty to the message they communicated.

I must also say that part of what I have to do tonight is to destabilise a sense of a comfortable mutual accommodation that has attended our discussions at this interaction.

We have been speaking of a smart partnership in which everything is nice and cosy between business, government, labour, civil society, kings and queens, civil servants, police, military, big powers and small powers. All of us can enter into a mutually beneficial smart partnership. It makes you feel good. But is it real?

I am very pleased that the prime minister of Malaysia is with us. And pleased that he put this particular issue of the smart partnership on the agenda of world thinking. But I would also like to note something that is perhaps a bit strange. I know it is not strange, but it comes across as strange. Prime Minister Mahathir is a great rebel.

He challenges the orthodoxies of modern economic dialogue and says to all of us that we must understand what all of these concepts are – of globalisation, of liberalisation, of privatisation, of a borderless world, of small government.

He has been telling us that when he speaks the Ringitt suffers. I think he is basically a rebel. And in order to soften the net of rebellion he says: Let us enter into a smart partnership.

There is a town in Mississippi in the United States. It is called Dead Man's Creek. As you know, when you enter those towns in the United States, you will come across a board which says: 'Welcome to Dead Man's Creek.' Then underneath it says: 'Population: 2019.' It is a village.

There is no entertainment, no bowling alleys, no bingo, no bars. The result is that the residents of Dead Man's Creek are at home by 9 p.m. and the news on television is at 9 p.m. So they all have to watch, because there is no choice, except of course for the young men and women who might be doing some other things at 9 p.m., but generally they are watching the news.

The residents of Dead Man's Creek heard a story of President Museveni talking about an African renewal. And when they heard about it, they were greatly encouraged because it seemed to them that they would no longer have to contribute some of their personal money to famine relief in the African Republic of Kalakuta, because President Museveni said we are involved in a process of an African renewal.

Change is coming. Africa will be stable. Africa will grow. Africa will no longer have famine. And the residents of Dead Man's Creek said thank God for that.

And even the one African-American who lived in this town, Dead Man's Creek – his name was Stevie Wonder – could then say: 'I can walk proud among this community, because I no longer need to be embarrassed about the previous terrible African experiences.'

But then the local television station, the American Broadcasting Network, started reporting some of the things that were happening on our continent.

And they were reporting about Somalia, about how this modern state collapsed and reduced itself to clans.

And they saw a story about Congo Brazzaville where there was a great fight about political issues, and in the end they took to guns, and they destroyed Brazzaville and killed thousands of people.

And then they heard that a war had broken out between Ethiopia and Eritrea about a piece of land.

It was said, in this news report on the American Broadcasting Network, that a fight had broken out in the country called Guinea-Bissau because it was alleged that the Army chief of staff had stolen guns from the national armoury and exported them to the next country.

And when the president of Guinea-Bissau said: 'No, you cannot do that!' the chief of staff said: 'Let's go to war!'

And then they had a story that in a country called Togo, where elections were held recently, the counting of votes was stopped midway and international observers were locked up in the police station. They were only released when the president announced that he had won with a 58 per cent majority.

And the citizens of Dead Man's Creek laughed as you have just laughed, and said: 'But when these Africans talked about an African renewal, of an African renaissance, it must be because they have an excellent sense of humour!'

And then the following day they saw these African children with emaciated bodies, big stomachs and thin limbs carrying begging bowls, with aid agencies and humanitarian organisations attending to them. And again they laughed and said that these African politicians must be the best comedians in the world, as they had told them of an African renaissance.

And the following day they heard of a civil servant who had supervised a process by which he had made sure that all the files which said: 'The following pensioners are dead,' disappeared, so that the dead souls could come alive again so that the civil servant could collect their pensions. And they heard of the business person who wanted the contract to manage the pension system, and who bribed the civil servant on condition that he would pass these dead souls to the civil servant so that the civil servant could collect the pensions of the dead.

And the residents of Dead Man's Creek said: 'But we thought the Africans were speaking of an African renaissance.'

And then of course there was the ambassador whose head of state had made a very strong statement, asserting the independence of their country. The ambassador had been called in (you must remember that they were negotiating an aid agreement) and the master said to him: 'You must say, "Our government has carefully reconsidered this matter and we have changed our mind."'

And the residents of Dead Man's Creek said: 'These African politicians must be great comedians to have pulled this one over our eyes, and made us believe there was an African renaissance coming.'

And in the end they were told of a deputy president from South Africa who would only drink water if it was labelled Evian or Perrier. Otherwise, no, no, no, I cannot drink this water. It must be flown in from somewhere where they stick on these labels, Evian or Perrier.

The small village of Dead Man's Creek is laughing at the notion and the concept of an African renaissance, an African renewal.

I think we must stop the laughter and the only way we can stop that laughter is to be rebels again, to be rebels in the way that many of us who sit under this tent were taught to be rebels.

We have to rebel against political instability on our continent, because when something goes wrong in Somalia, the residents of Dead Man's Creek, Mississippi, United States of America, do not say something has gone wrong in Somalia. They say something has gone wrong in Africa.

And when somebody steals a presidency in Togo, they do not say somebody has stolen a presidency in Togo. They say the Africans have done it yet again. And when pictures flash across the television screens of hunger, of poverty, of devastation, of the dependence on charity, they do not say it is occurring in the Republic of Kalakuta. They say it occurs in Africa.

We are mutually dependent on one another. But I think the smart thing to do is that as Africans we must get together and say it is incorrect for anyone of us to steal a presidency – and therefore, as government, say: What is it that we can do to ensure that that does not happen?

The political parties, the religious leaders, the trade unions and all other elements of society, our intellectuals must be able to say together: We want to stop the laughter. And to do that let all of us act together to ensure that indeed this concept of power to the people becomes part of the reality of our continent.

I think it becomes necessary that as Africans, because of that interdependence, we must together understand what the challenges of the modern economy are. What is it that we must address together to ensure that our continent takes its place in the modern world economy? Do we need a common programme to develop an African telecommunications infrastructure? I say yes. Do we need a common programme to build an infrastructure that enables all of us together to address challenges of education, including distance education? Yes, I say.

Where we have centres of excellence in terms of medicine and the delivery of medical services, why don't we institute a system of telemedicine? Modern telecommunication enables that to happen, so that a village can have access to the best medical expertise on the continent without the need for ambulances and good roads over which the ambulances must travel.

What do we know of one another, in culture, in music, in theatre? Why are we great experts on American cultural products and know nothing about what the neighbouring countries are producing in theatre, in dance, in the plastic arts? Is there a way by which we can co-operate to build a culture of service in our public service, share experiences to move that public service away from the notion that the people serve the public servant so that they must come and beg and plead in order to get a form and to get the form signed?

We are at the door of a new millennium. We have been discussing with some of the television companies, the big ones around the world to say: Why don't we do a multi-part series on Africa which will start at the beginning? The series would say that this being, described as *Homo sapiens*, originates from Africa.

If you said that to many of our young people, to say *Homo sapiens* originated in Africa, they would say that they did not know that! And tell them about these great cultures of our continent. Tell them that in the fifteenth century the best doctors in Europe, the best doctors attending to the kings and queens of France, came from Timbuktu in Mali. These young Africans would not know that! What they would know is that we were enslaved, we were colonised, we were abused by African dictators and, in the end, we came to depend on the rest of the world for charitable sustenance.

But if we told this story, the story of great Zimbabwe, the story of the empire of Ghana, the story of the best in science, teaching and the arts in the African past, the creative art of the Nubian, the Benin of West Africa, the Khoisan of our region, these Africans would recover an African pride which would say to all of us: We shall no longer be subjects of derision on the part of the residents of Dead Man's Creek of Mississippi in the United States.

In the end, this is an outcome which can only come about as a result of a united offensive by the peoples of our continent.

Smart partnership is, as Prime Minister Mahathir and other like-minded people in government, in political parties, in the unions, and everywhere else say, smart partnership is the way to end the laughter at Dead Man's Creek.

The year 2000 is upon us and perhaps this is one of our most immediate challenges to demonstrate to ourselves that we can act together. It brings with it the Year 2000 problem. Hopefully, we are all of us working on this problem, because on 1 January 2000 many computers are not going to be able to work. Payments will not be made. Water systems in towns and cities will not work. Clearly, this is a complicated problem. Our minister of telecommunications said that I must say this.

I am saying this under instruction, therefore, that from 18 to 20 August 1998 there will be a Southern African Development Community (SADC) forum with five high-level delegates from each SADC country, to discuss this issue, so that we can co-operate as to what we need to do to address this particular problem.

On 19 August 1998 it will be 500 days before 1 January 2000. And perhaps we could all proclaim that day the national communication day in our countries, to raise awareness of the importance of this problem and act together to solve it.

In the end, master of ceremonies, one of the issues we must discuss, which President Museveni has been raising in a gentle way, which is untypical of him, is: How do we handle the matter of national sovereignty in a global world? How does each one of us, as individual African countries with small markets, battle to deal with this difficult situation in the world?

Can we succeed without saying we surrender some of that sovereignty to larger entities which must be democratic, with everyone equal, with no big brothers and no small brothers, and no big sisters and no small sisters? To achieve an African renewal in politics, in economics, in social life and in culture we have to act together as Africans. Of this I think that none can be in doubt.

The question that remains is: How do we do it? And what arises from that is: Are we willing to do it? But clearly, if we are not willing to do it, the citizens of Dead Man's Creek in Mississippi will continue to laugh at these Africans who talk of a vision but do not have the will to translate that vision into actuality.

42

The African Renaissance

Statement of Deputy President Thabo Mbeki, South African Broadcasting Corporation, Gallagher Estate, Midrand, August 1998

A STRUGGLE FOR POLITICAL power is dragging the Kingdom of Lesotho towards the abyss of a violent conflict.

The Democratic Republic of Congo is sliding back into a conflict of arms from which its people had hoped they had escaped for ever.

The silence of peace has died on the borders of Eritrea and Ethiopia because, in a debate about an acre or two of land, guns have usurped the place of reason.

Those who had risked death in Guinea-Bissau, as they fought as comrades to evict the Portuguese colonialists, today stand behind opposing ramparts speaking to one another in the deadly language of bazooka and mortar shells and the fearsome rhythm of the beat of machine-gun fire.

A war seemingly without mercy rages in Algeria, made more horrifying by a savagery which seeks to anoint itself with the sanctity of a religious faith.

Thus can we say that the children of Africa, from north to south, from the east to the west and at the very centre of our continent, continue to be consumed by death dealt out by those who have proclaimed a sentence of death on dialogue and reason and on the children of Africa, whose limbs are too weak to run away from the rage of the adults.

Both of these, the harbingers of death and the victims of their wrath, are as African as you and I.

For that reason, for the reason that we are the disembowelled African mothers and the decapitated African children of Rwanda, we have to say: Enough and no more.

It is because of these pitiful souls, who are the casualties of a destructive force for whose birth they are not to blame, that Africa needs her renaissance. Were they alive and assured that the blight of human-made death had passed for ever, we would have less need to call for that renaissance.

In the summer of light and warmth and life-giving rain, it is to mock the gods to ask them for light and warmth and life-giving rain. The passionate hope for the warming rays of the sun is the offspring of the chill and dark nights of the winters of our lives.

Africa has no need for the criminals who would acquire political power by slaughtering the innocents as do the butchers of the people of Richmond in KwaZulu-Natal.

Nor has she need for such as those who, because they did not accept that power is legitimate only because it serves the interests of the people, laid Somalia to waste and deprived its people of a country which gave its citizens a sense of being, as well as the being to build themselves into a people.

Neither has Africa need for the petty gangsters who would be our governors by theft of elective positions, as a result of holding fraudulent elections, or by purchasing positions of authority through bribery and corruption.

The thieves and their accomplices, the givers of the bribes and the recipients are as African as you and I. We are the corrupter and the harlot who act together to demean our continent and ourselves.

The time has come that we say enough and no more, and by acting to banish the shame remake ourselves as the midwives of the African renaissance.

An ill wind has blown me across the face of Africa. I have seen the poverty of Orlando East and the wealth of Morningside in Johannesburg. In Lusaka, I have seen the poor of Kanyama township and the prosperous residents of Kabulonga. I have seen the African slums of Surulere in Lagos and the African opulence of Victoria Island. I have seen the faces of the poor in Mbari in Harare and the quiet wealth of Borrowdale.

And I have heard the stories of how those who had access to power, or access to those who had access to power, of how they have robbed and pillaged and broken all laws and all ethical norms with great abandon to acquire wealth, all of them tied by an invisible thread which they hope will connect them to Morningside and Borrowdale and Victoria Island and Kabulonga.

Every day, you and I see those who would be citizens of Kabulonga and Borrowdale and Victoria Island and Morningside being born everywhere in our country. Their object in life is to acquire personal wealth by means both foul and fair. Their measure of success is the amount of wealth they can accumulate and the ostentation they can achieve which will convince all that they are a success because, in a visible way, they are people of means.

Thus they seek access to power or access to those who have access to power so that they can corrupt the political order for personal gain at all costs.

In this equation, the poverty of the masses of the people becomes a necessary condition for the enrichment of the few, and the corruption of political power the only possible condition for its exercise.

It is out of this pungent mixture of greed, dehumanising poverty, obscene wealth and endemic public and private corrupt practice that many of Africa's *coups d'état*, civil wars and situations of instability are born and entrenched.

The time has come that we call a halt to the seemingly socially approved deification of the acquisition of material wealth and the abuse of state power to impoverish the people and deny our continent the possibility to achieve sustainable economic development.

Africa cannot renew herself where its upper echelons are a mere parasite on the rest of society, enjoying a self-endowed mandate to use their political power and define the uses of such power such that its exercise ensures that our continent reproduces itself as the periphery of the world economy – poor, underdeveloped and incapable of development.

The African renaissance demands that we purge ourselves of the parasites and maintain a permanent vigilance against the danger of the entrenchment in African society of this rapacious stratum with its social morality according to which everything in society must be organised materially to benefit the few.

As we recall with pride the African scholar and author of the Middle Ages, Sadi of Timbuktu, who had mastered such subjects as law, logic, dialectics, grammar and rhetoric, and other African intellectuals who taught at the University of Timbuktu, we must ask the question: Where are Africa's intellectuals today?

In our world in which the generation of new knowledge and its application to change the human condition is the engine which moves human society further and further away from barbarism, do we not have need to recall Africa's hundreds of thousands of intellectuals back from their places of emigration in Western Europe and North America to rejoin those who remain still within our shores?

I dream of the day when these, the African mathematicians and computer specialists in Washington and New York, the African physicists, engineers, doctors, business managers and economists, will return from London and Manchester and Paris and Brussels to add to the African pool of brain power; to inquire into and find solutions to Africa's problems and challenges; to open the African door to the world of knowledge; to elevate Africa's place within the universe of research, the formation of new knowledge, education and information.

Africa's renewal demands that her intelligentsia must immerse itself in the titanic and all-round struggle to end poverty, ignorance, disease and backwardness, inspired by the fact that the Africans of Egypt were, in some instances, two thousand years ahead of the Europeans of Greece in the mastery of such subjects as geometry, trigonometry, algebra and chemistry.

To perpetuate their imperial domination over the peoples of Africa, the colonisers sought to enslave the African mind and to destroy the African soul. They sought to oblige us to accept that as Africans we had contributed nothing to human civilisation except as beasts of burden in much the same way as those who are opposed to the emancipation of women seek to convince them that they have a place in human society, but only as beasts of burden and bearers of children.

In the end, they wanted us to despise ourselves, convinced that if we were not subhuman we were, at least, not equal to the colonial master and mistress and were incapable of original thought and the African creativity which has endowed the world with an extraordinary treasure of masterpieces in architecture and the fine arts.

The beginning of our rebirth as a continent must be our own rediscovery of our soul, captured and made permanently available in the great works of creativity represented by the pyramids and sphinxes of Egypt, the stone buildings of Axum and the ruins of Carthage and Zimbabwe, the rock paintings of the San, the Benin bronzes and the African masks, the carvings of the Makonde and the stone sculptures of the Shona.

A people capable of such creativity could never have been less human than other human beings, and being as human as any other, such a people can and must be its own liberator from the condition which seeks to describe our continent and its people as the poverty-stricken and disease-ridden primitives in a world riding the crest of a wave of progress and human upliftment.

In that journey of self-discovery and the restoration of our own self-esteem, without which we would never become combatants for the African renaissance, we must retune our ears to the music of Zao and Franco of the Congos and the poetry of Mazisi Kunene of South Africa, and refocus our eyes to behold the paintings of Malangatane of Mozambique and the sculptures of Dumile Feni of South Africa.

The call for Africa's renewal, for an African renaissance, is a call to rebellion. We must rebel against the tyrants and the dictators, those who seek to corrupt our societies and steal the wealth that belongs to the people. We must rebel against the ordinary criminals who murder, rape and rob, and conduct war against poverty, ignorance and the backwardness of the children of Africa.

Surely, there must be politicians and business people, youth and women activists, trade unionists, religious leaders, artists and professionals from the Cape to Cairo, from Madagascar to Cape Verde, who are sufficiently enraged by Africa's condition in the world to want to join the mass crusade for Africa's renewal.

It is to these that we say, without equivocation, that to be a true African is to be a rebel in the cause of the African renaissance, whose success in the new century and millennium is one of the great historic challenges of our time.

Let the voice of the Senegalese Sheik Anta Diop be heard:

> The African who has understood us is the one who, after reading of our works, would have felt a birth in himself, of another person, impelled by an historical conscience, a true creator, a Promethean carrier of a new civilisation and perfectly aware of what the whole earth owes to his ancestral genius in all the domains of science, culture and religion.

Each group of people, armed with its rediscovered or reinforced cultural identity, has arrived at the threshold of the post-industrial era. An atavistic, but vigilant African optimism inclines us to wish that all nations would join hands in order to build a planetary civilisation instead of sinking down to barbarism.

Notes

1. Karl Marx, *Capital*, Vol. 1 (Moscow: Progress Publishers, 1965), p. 751.
2. Ibid., p. 762.
3. H.J. Simons and R.E. Simons, *Class and Colour in South Africa, 1850–1950* (Harmondsworth: Penguin Books, 1969), p. 11.
4. Marx, op. cit., pp. 752–3.
5. R.H. Tawney, *Religion and the Rise of Capitalism* (New York: Mentor Books, 1958), p. 91 ff.
6. Ibid., p. 91.
7. Ibid., p. 84.
8. Edward Roux, *Time Longer than Rope* (Madison: University of Wisconsin Press, 1966), p. 27.
9. Simons and Simons, op. cit., p. 63.
10. Ibid., p. 82.
11. Ibid., p. 84.
12. Herbert Marcuse, *Negations* (Boston: Beacon Press, 1969), p. 211.
13. Alex La Gums (Ed.), *Apartheid* (New York: International Publishers, 1971), p. 47.
14. Francis Wilson, *Labour in the South African Gold Mines* (Cambridge: Cambridge University Press, 1972).
15. Monica Wilson and Leonard Thomson (Eds), *The Oxford History of South Africa* (Oxford: Clarendon Press, 1971), p. 330.
16. Ibid., p. 167.
17. Ibid., p. 203.
18. Friedrich Engels, 'Introduction to Marx's Class Struggles in France', in *On Historical Materialism* (Moscow: Progress Publishers, 1972), pp. 264, 269.
19. Ibid., p. 270.